Understanding
Race
Relations

*Any use of a human being in which less is demanded
of him and less attributed to him than his full status
is a degradation and a waste.*

NORBERT WEINER, The Human Use of Human Beings (1950)

*Physical resources unused—lie inert. Coal left alone
for a million years is still coal. Human resources
left unutilized deteriorate.*

RUPERT VANCE, All These People (1945)

*If there is no struggle there is no progress. Those
who profess to favor freedom, and yet deprecate
agitation, are men who want crops without plowing
up the ground. They want rain without thunder and
lightning. They want the ocean without the awful
roar of its many waters.*

FREDERICK DOUGLASS, from a personal letter (1849)

Understanding Race Relations

Ina Corinne Brown

PRENTICE-HALL, INC.,
Englewood Cliffs, New Jersey

Library of Congress Cataloging in Publication Data

BROWN, INA CORINNE
Understanding Race Relations

Bibliography: p.
1. United States–Race question.   2. Race.
3. Negroes.   I. Title.
E185.61.B878   301.45'19'6073   72-2486
ISBN 0-13-936211-8
ISBN 0-13-936203-7 (pbk.)

© 1973 by PRENTICE-HALL, INC., *Englewood Cliffs, New Jersey*

Printed in the United States of America

10   9   8   7   6   5   4   3   2   1

PRENTICE-HALL INTERNATIONAL, INC., *London*
PRENTICE-HALL OF AUSTRALIA, PTY. LTD., *Sydney*
PRENTICE-HALL OF CANADA, LTD., *Toronto*
PRENTICE-HALL OF INDIA PRIVATE LIMITED, *New Delhi*
PRENTICE-HALL OF JAPAN, INC., *Tokyo*

Contents

Foreword

The term race relations as used in this book refers to the relations between peoples who think of themselves as racially different. The question will be elaborated later but at this point we can say that race, properly speaking, indicates biological distinctions, whereas the term race relations as commonly used refers to a social and cultural fact. The relations grow out of the way people think and feel about real or supposed differences.

This book is both narrower and broader than its title suggests. It is narrower in that the relations discussed are primarily those of black and white in the United States. I am not unmindful of the seriousness of the problems of other minorities, but in order to keep the book brief and sharply focused on the black-white confrontation I have purposely omitted any specific treatment of other groups. References to such groups in the United States and elsewhere are included only when they illuminate the main concern.

The book is broader than the title implies in that race relations are considered within the framework of time-space relations. Race relations

are an aspect of culture and a part of one's learned behavior. Such relations do not exist in a vacuum—they cannot be understood apart from
the social context within which they occur. Consequently account must
be taken of problems of poverty, crime, education, and economic opportunity, as well as prejudice and discrimination. Moreover, all such
problems have a history. They are set within the context of an interrelated and interdependent world. Thus at first glance the book may
seem to go far afield from its title. It is so intended. When people, black
or white, are able to see the natural history of their relationships, and
the many forces that have helped make them what they are, cherished
notions lose some of their power and may become subject to rational
considerations.

The book deals only incidentally with the details of day to day
situations, for such events are constantly changing and are documented
in every daily newspaper, in radio and television newscasts, and in a
flood of books and journals. Thus many individuals, currently in the
news, are not mentioned in these pages.

Moreover, the book is not concerned primarily with "improving"
race relations in the sense of helping whites and blacks get along more
harmoniously as an end in itself. As will be noted in more detail later,
"good" race relations in the past have usually been dependent on the
Negro's willingness to "stay in his place." Much of what has happened
since the early 1960's reflects the black man's growing unwillingness any
longer to accept subordination as the price of getting along with the
white world.

The book will not please extremists of either the far right or the
far left. It will not satisfy those who are for law and order at the price
of justice, or those who see their society as so hopelessly sick or corrupt
as to merit only destruction. It will not interest those who are seeking
quick and easy solutions. It offers no panacea and no blueprints for
action. It is, rather, a background study of the multiple factors and
complex issues that underlie our present problems. It is hoped that it will
be useful to persons who are concerned with both justice and order, and
who are willing to try to understand and deal realistically with those
problems that must be faced if we are to get on with the business of
living.

No individual, black or white, can "tell it like it is." He can only
tell it as he sees it, and his perceptions are in large measure determined
by the nature and breadth of his experiences, his training, and the
premises that underlie his judgments. I write as an anthropologist trained
in both the biological and the social sciences. Through many years of
study, research, teaching, and community experience in the United States

and elsewhere, I have had the opportunity to observe many different societies, and to know people of many races and cultures as students, colleagues, and friends. I am indebted to all of them for any insights this book may have.

In writing this book I have tried to be as objective as possible but no one who is human is without a value system. There are two biases I have not sought to dismiss. As a scientist, I am committed to a search for truth, a commitment that carries with it an obligation to report the truth as I see it, even when I may wish it were otherwise. As a person, I am committed to the belief that as human beings we have an obligation to all others of our species without regard to our minor differences of physical type, or our religious and cultural diversity. As humans we share in all the implications of the human condition, and we have a collective obligation to try to create a world in which other humans are treated as persons and not as things or objects to be exploited.

Because I have tried to present the different points of view held by Americans, there are many passages that if taken out of context could give a distorted picture of the book as a whole. I do not know of any way that an author can prevent such misuse of his material and can only ask that the reader consider the book in its totality.

The book is designed for use in two ways: as a general overview, or as an orientation to the problem and a guide for further study. Persons interested only in the general overview may read straight through without being distracted by footnotes or references. The serious student will find such notes and references at the end of the volume, arranged by chapters, with suggestions for further study. Also listed there are paperbacks and reference books dealing with aspects of the subject that because of space limitations could be treated only briefly or not at all in this book.

It would be impossible to acknowledge my debt to all the persons who in one way or another have contributed to this volume. They are all included as I borrow the words of another writer of long ago: "I thank not only him that hath digged out treasure for me but also him that hath lighted me a candle to the place."

I.C.B.

Introduction:
The Way
Things Are

1. Confrontation

In 1966 and 1967 the *Wall Street Journal* carried a series of articles on the technological achievements expected by the year 2000. The articles were later published in a book under the title *Here Comes Tomorrow.** But by 1970, still thirty years before the end of the century, so many of these predictions had become realities that a more appropriate title might have been *Tomorrow Is Already Here.* There was, however, a proviso to the predictions. A boxed insertion in each article carried the statement that these developments were "premised on the assumption that the Earth will not be incinerated in a nuclear holocaust during the next generation."

But as the world moves into the seventies the threat of a nuclear holocaust seems less immediate than the danger of social disintegration. Everywhere throughout the globe there is not only conflict between nations, but even more widespread, a breakdown of consensus within national

*All bibliographical and reference information will be found in the notes and references starting on pg. 246.

boundaries. The groups involved sometimes differ in race, but more often in nationality, religion, language, class, or ideology, and sometimes in a combination of two or more of these. Some of these factors are treated in more detail later, but it should be noted here that such problems are not peculiar to the United States. There have been student riots in Europe, and Asia; religious conflicts in Ireland; civil warfare in Nigeria, the Sudan, and Pakistan and ideological conflicts in Central Europe, Canada, Latin America, and various African and Asian countries.

In the United States it is obvious that the black-white confrontation is only one of the conflicts of ideas and values that threaten to tear the nation apart. The opposition of youth and age, the far Right and the far Left, hawks and doves, employers and employees, restive students and college administrators, factions within government and within political parties, create strains within the social fabric that sober observers call the most critical in a century.

Behind it all is a deep sense of frustration and the feeling that much of what modern man is doing is a tale told by an idiot. The fantastic fruits of today's technology are everywhere. People sit before their television sets to watch men walk on the moon and to hear the conversations between human beings separated by a quarter of a million miles. Yet they also see a hopelessly polluted environment that endangers health, if not life itself, and a population explosion that threatens to leave only standing room on the planet. They see grinding poverty and actual hunger in the midst of unparalleled luxury and affluence. They see urban blight, traffic congestion, unemployment, racial conflict and, like some nightmare running through it all, the practice of settling international disputes by brutal and suicidal wars.

Adding to the tragedy are the senseless methods of dealing with the problems. Governments continue to spend billions on military budgets leaving only a pittance for the meeting of basic human needs. Business and politics go on as usual while youths are drafted to fight in a war they do not understand and in which they do not believe. Many college students, mostly from middle-class white and relatively affluent families, seemingly see no better way to call attention to their frustrations than by shouting insults and obscenities, throwing rocks and bottles, breaking windows, rifling files, and sometimes burning buildings off and on campus. And many formerly moderate students have joined the radicals in response to the overreaction of police and national guardsmen. Increasingly people are being pushed toward the limited alternatives of anarchy or repression.

Involved in it all is a widespread crisis of confidence. There is distrust of the leadership in government, in business, in education, and in the church. One presidential commission on law and order described America as "Industrialized, technologized, and computerized; urbanized, plasticised and depersonalized; pluralistic, alienated and frustrated." Moreover, the institutions—legal, political, social, educational, and religious—to which men have looked for support and guidance, and for the preservation of both justice and order, seem to many people to be weak and vacillating, outmoded and static, if not reactionary and repressive.

In spite of this setting—or perhaps because of it—this book is an attempt to look at the problem of race relations as dispassionately as possible. There are certain basic premises that underlie the whole of the book and that are elaborated throughout the text. Whatever our differences, we are all here and the great majority of us, black and white, were born here. This is our home, and we have nowhere else to go. We were all born into a world we never made, and none of us had any choice in our race, our sex, the time or place of our birth, or the parents who bore us and brought us up. None of us is responsible for anything his ancestors did or for any events that occurred before he was born. We all share in the responsibility of doing the best we can in the world as we found it.

This book is based on the further premise that two of the most dangerous trends of our time may be the good-guy/bad-guy, either/or syndrome, and a pervasive belief in magic. The nightmare in Vietnam, which has exacerbated all other problems, is in part the result of a widespread belief that if communism is bad then all anticommunists are good, or vice versa. Many people were thus shocked when some South Vietnamese leaders turned out to be corrupt, self-seeking, and totalitarian. On the other hand, militant revolutionaries who see the United States, and indeed all western civilization, as hopelessly evil, chant the names of Ho Chi Minh and Mao Tse-Tung, Castro and Che, as if all of these men were unselfish knights in shining armor presiding over social systems that are without fault. In more narrowly racial terms the polarization is that of superior whites and subhuman blacks, or superhuman blacks and "whitey" as the embodiment of evil.

The belief in magic is equally widespread. Supposedly responsible people seek instant and simplistic solutions for complex social problems that have been centuries in the making. Many adults manifest a blind faith in the equivalents of band-aids and aspirin as cures for major social ills, and many youth seemingly believe that shouting insults and obscenities at the establishment, or chanting peace slogans, will substitute for the slow, painful drudgery involved in creating a decent social order.

2. The Coming of the Blacks

In the summer of 1963, one hundred years after the signing of the Emancipation Proclamation, 200,000 persons, black and white, marched in Washington to protest the nation's failure to implement that proclamation. *The London Daily Herald* reporting on the march observed: "Today—the clock jumped, and history changed." There have been a succession of jumps since that day and the pattern of relationships between blacks and whites has changed almost beyond recognition.

In the United States the confrontation of black and white has moved from the non-violent student sit-ins at segregated lunch counters to ghetto uprisings, followed by campus protests and the appearance of black power militants. The more militant blacks have begun presenting what they call non-negotiable demands for a variety of actions ranging from reparations for unpaid or underpaid black labor in the past, to separate black controlled colleges or separate departments, faculties, and curricula in predominantly white colleges. There are even new demands for a separate black state and threats to tear up or burn down the country if such demands are not met. These extremists proclaim that integration and the civil rights movement are dead. They wish to have nothing to do with the white world except to have whites hand over reparations for past injustices.

Obviously this extreme point of view does not represent all Negroes, and many older Negroes who have long worked for the rights of the entire race are as puzzled and as troubled as most whites are. However, the new militants are both noisy and conspicuous and they have won the allegiance of many black youth. Whites who have always tended to lump all blacks together find it easy to blame the older Negro leaders for not keeping check on those who advocate and sometimes engage in violence. It apparently does not occur to these whites that they had not been able (often they had not even tried) to restrain the violent whites who have bombed Negro homes, churches, and places of business. From popular writers and news commentators and from voluminous government reports come warnings of the polarization of black and white.

The most significant changes involve the shift in emphasis from integration to black separatism, from non-violent marches and sit-ins to militance in both rhetoric and action, and the acceptance by many blacks of the legitimacy of any means to gain the desired ends. The changing emphases are reflected in terminology for those Americans whose ancestors came from Europe and other Americans some of whose ancestors came from Africa. Persons of European ancestry are generally referred to as Caucasians, Caucasoids, or whites. In the American Southwest they are sometimes called Anglos, and those who think of themselves as Anglo-Saxons are sometimes referred to as "Wasps" (white Anglo-Saxon protestants.) Some white persons dislike being called "a white" because it implies an ideological kinship based on pigmentation. It is used in this book only for want of a better term. Those who think of themselves as blacks sometimes use the terms "Whitey" or "Honkie," and the more militant black youth may refer to any white as a fascist or racist "pig." There are even greater problems of terminology for the people of partial African ancestry. The derogatory and pejorative terms used by some whites are discussed in a later section. Negroes themselves are not agreed on the terminology they prefer and in fact they never have been, though the question has now taken on a heavier emotional significance. Following the insistence of many youth, the term black has come into widespread use, but this is a new development dating from the late 1960s. The term was widely used in the West Indies, but until recent years it would have been resented by most Negro Americans. Some older Negroes and some of those who are really biologically more white than black still wish to be called Negroes. Others who wish to stress their identity with Africa prefer the use of Afro- or African-Americans. The question was raised in Amy Vanderbilt's Etiquette column, and *Ebony* magazine polled its readers on their preferences in the matter. Predictably the *Ebony* poll showed that its readers had strong feelings on the subject, but that there was no general agreement. Miss Vanderbilt and the editors of *Ebony* agreed that people should be called whatever they wish, the problem being to know what any particular person or group prefers.

In the past the majority of people of partial African ancestry commonly used the terms Negro or colored interchangeably; less often they used African or Afro-American. Only rarely was black used as a noun though sometimes it was used as an adjective. James Weldon Johnson wrote *Black Manhattan, The Autobiography of an Ex-Colored Man,* and *Negro Americans, What Now?* W.E.B. DuBois wrote *Black Reconstruction* and *The Souls of Black Folk,* but he also wrote numerous books in which Negro appeared in the title, and he was long associated with the National Association for the Advancement of Colored People. There was an African Methodist Church and a Colored Methodist Church, which later changed the "Colored" to "Christian." The terms "soul brother" and "soul sister" are now widely used within the Negro group.

Some blacks reject the term Negro as being a European designation associated with slavery though this is not entirely accurate. There is of course no general "African" word for Africans any more than there was a general term for all of the aboriginal inhabitants of the Western Hemisphere. Each African and American-Indian people had its own language and they referred to themselves and their neighbors in tribal or national terms. In many cases their name for a neighboring group was a derogatory one while they called themselves by a term that could be translated as "men," or "the people." Flattering one's own and downgrading other people was no European invention.

Some of the early Arabic records refer to Africa below the Sahara as "the Land of the Blacks" and the French frequently used "les Noirs," but the word Negro used by the Spanish and Portuguese is presumably derived from the Latin *niger*, meaning black. During the slave trade various terms were used—Africans, blacks, Negroes, Moors, Blackamoors, and frequently tribal terms as Ibos or Shantees (Ashanti). When slaves obtained their freedom they usually referred to themselves as "free persons of color."

The Portuguese slave traders frequently used the term "blacks," but even in an early period this referred not so much to color as to condition. A black was an African who was a "heathen," who spoke an African language, and who dressed and acted like an African. When he became a Christian, spoke Portuguese, and wore European dress he became "white." Some of these physically black but culturally "white" Africans were very insistent on not being identified with their pagan countrymen.

Along with the rejection of the term Negro has come the rejection of many of the patterns that are associated with white. Until this switch in emphasis in the 1960s there were strong class distinctions within the Negro group: dark skin and frizzy hair were distinct handicaps. Periodicals and newspapers serving the Negro community were filled with advertisements of preparations to be used in straightening the hair and lightening the skin. "Good" hair that did not have to be straightened was prized. Although such periodicals still carry these ads they are now more likely to refer to "relaxing" the hair and "brightening" the skin. However, among many young people the "Afro" hair style and some variety of African dress has become the fashion. "Natural" is perhaps a more accurate word for the hair style, as African peoples have traditionally dressed their hair in a variety of ways; it seldom was left in its natural state.

As will be noted later, the use of the term black and the rejection of hair styles appropriate only for hair that is naturally straight, or only slightly curly, play an important role in the struggle for identity. In this book the various terms for Americans of partial African ancestry are used interchangeably, the choice often depending on the context. It could hardly be otherwise with terms about which the people most concerned are not in agreement.

It should be emphasized that there are numerous other things about which Negroes are not in agreement. Even the preference for the designation black, Afro-American, or Negro is to some degree indicative of different emphases and points of view. But regardless of these differences in specific goals and methods, there is unquestionably a new mood that must be taken into account if we are to have any real understanding of race relations today.

3. Race and Racism

In the late 1960s it became common to attribute all the problems of Negroes to white racism and to describe the United States as the world's most racist society. The words racism and racist have been used in so many different ways that they have ceased to be useful as a means of communication. Beyond the explanation given here, the terms will be used in this book only in referring to other people's use of them, because the use of value-laden terms that mean different things to different people tends to obscure rather than to illuminate the real problems involved.

Basically, racism refers to the assumption that behavior is determined by race. The term is usually used in a pejorative sense, although it can mean simply the belief that biologically determined mental and moral characteristics are "packaged" with the observable and measurable physical ones by which races are usually designated. Even the term "scientific racism" has been used to describe what may properly be called a racial interpretation of history, that is, the belief that peoples of different races will have different histories and cultures because of their race. Later chapters in this book document the fact that there is no scientific validity for either the notion of racial inferiority or the racial interpretation of history. Anthropologists who study both race and culture are generally agreed that culture affects race more than race affects culture.

As the term is commonly used, racism implies prejudice and discrimination. Whitney M. Young in his *Beyond Racism: Building an Open Society*, defines racism as "the assumption of superiority and the arrogance that goes with it," and he points out that the average white American simply cannot fully understand what racism is. He defines three basic categories: overt and blatant expression of prejudice on the part of whites, ranging from racial slurs, to refusal to sit next to a Negro on a bus, to joining lynching parties; a more refined form that involves all kinds of subtle discriminations and assumptions about Negroes; and an even more subtle, and in many ways more condescending, form which he calls "putting up with outrageous behavior" from a black man simply because he is black. This third form of behavior carries the implied assumption that the blacks have to be humored and pacified as one would humor a child or some one who is not wholly responsible.

Although many aspects of these behaviors are more fully treated in other sections of this book, three things should be made clear at this point. One is the distinction between institutional structures and personal behavior and the relation between the two; another, as Whitney Young suggests, is the variation in both the degree and the form of expression of individual prejudice; and the third is the fact that "racism" is only one form of a larger and more inclusive pattern of ethnocentrism that may be based on any one of a number of factors, many of which are non-racial in character.

There is no question that racial bias and discrimination are built into most American institutions. The United States thus can be called a "racist" society in that it is racially divided and its whole structural organization is such as to promote racial distinctions. The way our cities are set up and the whole pattern of segregation that long had the sanction of law as well as custom, have all combined to separate whites and blacks and to keep them ignorant of one another, but especially to keep whites ignorant of blacks. These patterns are an outgrowth of slavery and their development is more fully discussed elsewhere. The important point here is that once such patterns become established they tend to persist. Handed down from one generation to another as a part of the individual's learned behavior, they tend to mold the members of the society. Both the white and the black people living today were born into a social situation, not of their own making, which has helped to mold their thinking, their attitudes, and their behavior in general. It takes a special kind of effort to break away from the pattern in which one has grown up. A recognition of this fact and an effort of both whites and Negroes to face it and do something about it will be far more effective than trying to make all white Americans feel guilty about being a part of a racist society.

The individual "racist" is thus in large measure a product of institutional racism, but to assume that all members of a "racist" society are alike is a distortion of reality. All ethical distinctions are blurred when we lump together as equally guilty the Ku Klux Klan members or other individuals who join in the bombing of Negro churches, homes, and businesses—those who lynch and murder blacks—and those who have been honest and fair in their dealings with Negroes and who, often at considerable cost to themselves, have taken stands on the side of justice and equal rights for all. To say, as some blacks have said, that the whites who have helped Negroes did so from paternalistic motives or to keep the Negroes quiet, is to assign a singleness of motive that not only does injustice to many such individuals but also fails to take realities into account. Undoubtedly most people, white and Negro, act from mixed motives that do not always rise to the level of awareness, and all of us are given to rationalization. Probably no white person—or black either—is wholly free from prejudice, but they are definitely not all guilty of it to the same degree. As one preacher remarked to his congregation, "The Bible says we have all sinned and come short of the glory of God, but some have come a lot shorter than others."

There are also personal and class distinctions in the forms in which prejudice is expressed. Lower-class people are more likely to give physical expression to their feelings. The lynchings, murders, and bombings are never the direct work of more responsible members of most communities, but these violent expressions usually occur in communities in which there is a permissive atmosphere. Some of the responsibility for the more overt and physically brutal injustices must be laid at the door of the "better" white people who engaged in a variety of discriminatory practices and who sometimes openly defied federal law and Supreme Court rulings, thus giving sanction and support, however unintentional, to forms of overt physical violence which they might then publicly deplore.

Finally, it is important that what is called racism be seen as a part of the larger problem of ethnocentrism, of dominance and subordination, of power and powerlessness, and of the exploitation of the weak by the strong. Unquestionably color prejudice is deeply embedded in the modern world and is a major factor in the frustration and deprivation of millions of the darker peoples everywhere. In spite of diminished control, the people in power throughout the world today are predominantly white and therefore the greater responsibility rests upon them. But as will be made clear in later sections of this book, the white-black prejudice so pronounced in the world today is not "natural," nor is it a result of black inferiority. It is rather a special development that grew out of the historical relations of Europe and Africa.

It in no way minimizes the evils of race prejudice, or the responsibility of white Americans, to point out that more often than not exploiters and exploited have been of the same race and that African peoples were often involved in bitter intertribal wars long before Europeans had any influence in Africa South of the Sahara. Black men, being human, throughout history have exploited other blacks, just as white men have exploited other whites. Tyrants and exploiters come in all colors. In other words, American racism is a variety of man's inhumanity to man that falls along racial lines primarily as a result of historical accident.

We do not make progress by substituting one error for another or one half truth for another. No person can read the remainder of this book without being made fully aware of the damage done to Negroes and to the society as a whole by prejudice and discrimination of white against black. Moreover, it is made clear throughout this book that institutional arrangements as well as personal attitudes must be drastically revised. But if these injustices are to be remedied the problem must be seen in its broader context. The real evils are the exploitation of the powerless by the powerful and the relegation of human beings to less than fully human status on the basis of their membership in a particular group, whether that grouping be based on race, language, nationality, religion, or class.

4. What Are "Good" Race Relations?

Many blacks are as disenchanted with the idea of "improving race relations" as they are with the emphasis on law and order at the expense of justice. "Good" race relations have usually meant racial harmony achieved within the framework of the subordination of the minority group. Not only may good relations be defined differently by the different parties to the relationship, but even if both groups agree that the relationship is good it may represent a short term accommodation at the expense of a more important long term goal. A brief look at the past will make this distinction clear.

During the slavery period, except for the free Negroes, the relations of black and white were not so much relations between races as between bond and free. White people generally thought such relations were good when the master was generous and kindly and the slaves industrious, obedient, and supposedly contented. But in a broader light one must see that only a degraded human being makes a contented slave. The slave attained fully human stature only when he came to the realization that he was a person, not a thing; and at that point the owning of his body by another person became intolerable. White persons have no difficulty in understanding this as far as their fellow whites are concerned. "Give me liberty or give me death" is seen as noble and right for their own kind. Yet they could hold to the belief that the "best" black men were those who were docile and content under the bondage of their persons.

After freedom "good" race relations, particularly in the South, was dependent on the willingness of black people to accept a role of subordination and to "stay in their place." Black people are now saying that a man today can no more maintain his manhood in such socially defined and mandatory subordination than he could under slavery in an earlier day. Really good race relations from the Negroes' point of view can come about only when there is true equality in the sense of white and black being equally accepted as human beings and equally entitled to the rights and duties that are supposedly accorded all citizens. Many blacks therefore are no longer interested in racial harmony as such. Some of them are saying they could not care less about either being "understood" by whites or getting along with them. Many of the vociferous "demands" that have so alarmed some whites are simply demands that blacks be able to enjoy the same freedom and responsibilities that whites have long taken for granted.

One of the often puzzling aspects of the race relations drama is the fact that improvement in the social and economic conditions of Negroes frequently is accompanied—temporarily at least—by a worsening of relations. As the Negroes get better education, better jobs, and greater freedom, the relations worsen because there is increased competition for jobs and status but also because the old familiar relationship of dominance and subordination gives way to patterns that are unfamiliar and untried and that white people see as a threat to the established order. There is nothing unusual about these facts. It is a commonplace of history that rebellions most often occur not among the most downtrodden but among those who have glimpsed a better day.

In a sense the race relations problem can be summed up as a division of values and goals growing out of the fact that whites and Negroes view their relationship from different positions in the social structure. The white people on the whole have set up for themselves a set of values and goals that are quite different from those they deem appropriate for Negroes.

This division is, in large measure, a heritage of slavery. The virtues of the master are the vices of the slave, and this pattern still governs the thinking of a large portion of the white people in America. Courage, ambition, independence, pride, and a degree of daring or aggressiveness are the virtues of a master class, whereas patience, obedience, docility, loyalty, industry, and faithfulness are the qualities that make a good slave or servant. The "good" Negro in the eyes of many white people is the "old time" Negro who exhibits, at least to the white world, the slave virtues. The Negro who dares exhibit the virtues reserved for the master class is "getting out of his place." The ambition and will-to-succeed pattern which is socially approved for the white person is not only frowned upon but prohibited to Negroes in communities in which many of them live. The Negro thus lives in a society in which the values of the dominant group are constantly before him, and yet the society itself penalizes him when he strives toward the goals it sets.

There are certain minimum essentials in a democratic society: a recognition of the value of the individual, such freedom of the individual as is consistent with the freedom of others, the right of the individual to be judged on the basis of his personal worth, equality before the law, equality of opportunity for education and for occupational choice, and the full admission of all citizens to all privileges and obligations of citizenship. Furthermore, if judgment on individual merit is to be fair, each person must have the opportunity for the fullest development of which he is capable.

It is on this last point that some Negroes have based their demands for "reparations" and favored treatment in education and employment. The subject is more fully discussed in later chapters but it should be noted here that simply removing existing obstacles to equality will not put people on an equal basis. Deprivations are cumulative not only in the life of the individual but from one generation to another. Therefore the assumption that "treating everybody alike," or choosing the best qualified person for the job, constitutes "fairness" overlooks important factors.

It should be noted also that in the considerations just stated, opportunity does not mean that all persons are of equal ability or that everybody is entitled to the same specific opportunities. We know that, apart from race, human beings vary in their capabilities, in their motivation, and in their ability to make use of certain opportunities. To say that everybody has a right to go to college regardless of his capability to do college work, or that everybody is entitled to a white-collar job or to promotion, regardless of his ability, energy, or ambition, is to distort the picture as much as one does in denying such opportunities on the basis of race or color.

Thus equality of opportunity would not mean a classless society in which everyone is treated alike regardless of his personal qualities; rather it would imply freedom to rise to whatever levels one is capable of. By removing all obstacles to individual achievement and by rewarding both excellence and social responsibility, the society could guarantee the maximum use of its human potential. For the first time in human history, mankind is capable of making a truly human life possible for all human beings, but the accomplishment of such a goal is a long-range and complicated undertaking that will call for a drastic reordering of priorities. These problems are given further attention in later sections.

This book is based on the assumption that all our problems are interrelated and anything that contributes to the solution of one of them helps them all. But the assumption also involves the belief that no one of them can be treated in isolation. Thus while the central concern of the book is with the specific black-white confrontation in the United States, the problem is viewed in historical perspective, and within the broader context of the relations of human beings who see life from different points of view.

2

Race, Culture, and Human Relations

1. The Varieties of Human Groups

What we commonly call race relations can be understood only in the larger context of human relations, particularly that aspect of human relations that has to do with the attitudes and behaviors of people as they are identified with groups. And since all such attitudes and behaviors are learned, any relations between groups must be seen as aspects of culture.

Perhaps the simplest way to describe a group is as an aggregate of individuals who under some circumstances and for some purposes think or speak of themselves as "we" in relation to other aggregates of people who are thought of as "they." Because children are for a long period dependent on other people for survival and because no human being can live entirely to himself, we all grow up and continue throughout life as members of groups. An individual can be, and usually is, a member of many different groups, and of course there are groups within larger groups, and there may be overlapping between groups. It is the relatively permanent and cohesive groups which directly influence human behavior that concern us here.

The most common of these is the family, which is found in some recognizable form in every human society known to us. It is the primary group in which the members most often and most persistently think of themselves as "we." In Western countries today the family is thought of primarily as husband, wife, and children, but there are many one-parent families and many adults who have no meaningful family connections. In some other parts of the world, and formerly in the West, the family was thought of as encompassing a much larger kin group with reciprocal rights and obligations.

In many traditional societies there are clans made up of families or other related groups, and these clans may have an overall relationship in what is often loosely defined as a tribe. Larger and more formal political units in which kinship is not the major factor we recognize as states or nations. It will be useful, however, if we think of all these units, whatever their composition, as groups or as societies which are simply large, relatively permanent groups with some special characteristics of their own.

Within many societies there are subgroups that may have little in common with one another except for the fact that they are all under the same political control. Their differences may be linguistic, cultural, sectional, racial, tribal, ideological or nationalistic or there may be any combination of these. Sometimes such groups live together in relative harmony with a common loyalty to the state or nation, but in the modern world there are many examples of civil wars or other conflicts growing out of such differences.

Such diverse groups within nations have sometimes resulted from the conquest of weaker groups by stronger, or as the result of immigration, or as the result of the missionary efforts of Christians, Muslims, or Buddhists. Sometimes diverse groups have been united under the control of a colonial power and the boundaries then set up were carried over when independence was gained.

In India, Southeast Asia, and Africa there are united under single governments many subgroups that may feel themselves quite different. Such subgroups may speak languages more unlike than Hindi and English, and there may be cultural, religious, political, ideological or sectional patterns that set the people apart. Sometimes there are deeply felt hostilities between groups that have resulted in civil wars and the division of countries. The separation of India and Pakistan, the civil war in Nigeria, conflicts in the Sudan and in various parts of Southeast Asia all have grown out of such differences.

A whole new set of group differences developed during the period of exploration and conquest when Europeans spread out over the globe, not only taking over the lands of native peoples but often bringing in other groups as laborers or as immigrants. Sometimes the Europeans did not actually settle the country but nonetheless maintained economic and political control until recent times, as the British in India and Africa, the Dutch in Indonesia, the Belgians in the Congo, the French in Africa and in Vietnam, and the United States in the Philippines. In other areas they settled and became the dominant, if not always the majority group, as the Dutch and British in South Africa, the Portuguese in Brazil, the Spaniards in most of the rest of Latin America and the British and French along with other immigrant groups in what is now the United States and Canada. The problems in the United States and Latin America were made more difficult by the bringing in of African slaves, thus creating a new element in the population with which relationships were complicated by differences in physical type and culture, and also by the heritage of slavery.

Many contemporary group problems are ideological and political. At the time when the Western imperialist nations were relinquishing their control over their colonial possessions, Communist Russia and China were establishing new forms of imperial control over such countries as Latvia, Esthonia, Lithuania, Hungary, Czechoslovakia, Poland, East Germany, and Tibet. Special kinds of relationships have arisen out of particular situations such as that of the Jews in Nazi Germany and the Arab-Israeli conflict. Even within relatively homogeneous societies of the same race, language, and religion, there may be sharp class differences though the lines are often loosely drawn and there is usually some degree of interclass mobility.

This necessarily sketchy survey of the varieties of group differences points up several facts of significance for the understanding of race relations patterns in the United States. Group differences are practically universal; group hostility and the exploitation of the weak by the strong is by no means limited either to the Western nations or to peoples of the white race, and some of the bitterest hostilities and the most cruel exploitation have occurred between peoples of the same race. Furthermore, compared to the racial, linguistic, cultural, and religious differences among groups elsewhere, the race relations problems of the United States appear to be relatively simple. To be sure there are questions of race and history, but linguistic and religious differences are generally absent, cultural differences are either absent or minimal, and ideological differences are not of the first order.

2. The Nature of Group Attitudes

Group attitudes and hence group conflicts do not arise when people treat other people as individuals and regulate their conduct on the basis of individual characteristics and behavior. However, when all the persons of group *A* lump together all the persons of group *B* and treat them as if they were all alike, regardless of whether or not the assumption of likeness is valid, group consciousness is developed, the persons of one's own group become "we" and the others are what Kipling called "only a sort of they."

Actually there are a limited number of basic ways in which one group may respond to another that appears to be strange or different. One may be indifferent or interested; the response may be hostile, friendly, or neutral, and group feelings may vary in degree or intensity with the particular circumstances. But whatever form they take, in-group feelings seem to be universal and grow out of the fact that human beings can live only as members of groups, with whom they develop a feeling of identity or belonging and from which they acquire a value system, ideas, ideals, and practices.

It is possible to have a strong sense of group solidarity without regarding other groups as inferior. However, the practice of looking down on people who are different apparently is almost as old and as universal as man. This pattern has been defined as ethnocentrism or the view of things in which one's own group is made the center of everything and all other groups are scaled or rated with reference to it. The view if not the name was familiar to the Greeks in the fifth century B.C. "The Persians," wrote Herodotus, "look upon themselves as very greatly superior in all respects to the rest of mankind." This attitude was not peculiar to the Persians for in another connection Herodotus remarks: "If one were to offer men to choose out of all the customs in the world such as seemed to them best, they would examine the whole number, and end by preferring their own; so convinced are they that their own usages far surpass those of all others."

The Chinese once considered their country the center of the universe, and we are familiar with modern nations who have had a masterrace complex; but Europeans and Chinese had no monopoly on the idea that "we are the people." It is an anthropological commonplace that many peoples of the simpler cultures regarded themselves as superior to their neighbors and indeed to the rest of mankind. Frequently they had names for themselves that meant "men," "human beings," or "the people."

This practice of looking down on other groups seems to grow out out of the fact that the habits and customs with which one grows up come to seem not only right but natural, and the ways of other people queer, inferior, and even unnatural. There are, of course, exceptions. When people in simple societies come in contact with peoples of obviously superior power and material achievement they sometimes accept the more powerful group's estimate of their relative worth.

In stratified societies there may be strong class feeling, its form depending on the particular nature of the relationships. During the period of slavery and in the decades following, poor whites and free Negroes often felt extreme hostility toward one another. Both were insecure and resented competition. Upper and lower classes often arrived at an accommodation that involved an accepted relationship of dominance and subordination. If the slaves, the servants, or the tenants on a great estate accepted their humble status and the master's conception of their relative positions, the subordinate group was often included, at least in a limited fashion, with the master's in-group. This was true only when the members of the less privileged group identified themselves with the interests of the master's group and did not compete for status.

Several things regarding group attitudes should be made clear. There is no simple, universal origin of class or race prejudice. There are certain tendencies that grow out of the nature of the human organism and the nature of society—that is, the dependence of the human infant and the necessity of living in groups with which one establishes a feeling of identity. But the attitudes between any given groups develop in specific situations and the explanation of any relationship and the corresponding attitudes must be sought in the particular situation. Whether groups are hostile or friendly, feel themselves superior or inferior, are cooperative or competitive, will depend on the history of their relationships with one another, and possibly on the preconceptions they had of one another before actual contact took place.

It is also important to note that while attitudes may persist in a given group after the circumstances that gave rise to them have changed, it is also true that attitudes can, and sometimes do, change. The enemies in one war have at times become the allies in the next one, and groups formerly despised may come into favor, or the reverse.

3. Race and Group Relations

On the surface it might appear that the term race relations has a simple, self-evident definition, that is, the relations between peoples of different races. However, such a definition does not take into account the actual realities with which we deal. Although race relations are a form of group relations, races as such are not necessarily groups. People of a given race, biologically defined, constitute a group only when they define themselves as such or are so defined by others. There can be "race relations" when there is no actual race difference and there can be race differences without relations that could properly be called racial. These seeming contradictions grow out of the fact that, strictly speaking, races are biological constructs—that is, they are populations that can be identified by their having in common certain combinations of physical characteristics or, in the newer terminology, populations having a common origin and sharing a common gene pool. Race in this biological or anthropological sense is the subject of subsequent chapters. Our concern here is with groups who think of themselves as races and are so regarded by other people. While such groups are often distinctive enough to consider physical appearance part of their group identity, such differences may be ignored when present, or assumed to be present when they do not actually exist. However when groups believe such differences exist, their relations take on the characteristics of race relations.

Races as such should not be defined by any aspect of behavior that is learned or acquired. There is no Latin race, no Irish, Jewish, Aryan, French, or German race, and there never was an Anglo-Saxon race. These terms refer to peoples who were distinguished by their language, religion, culture, or linguistic patterns, and these characteristics do not coincide with inherited physical characteristics or a common gene pool. However, when we use race as an adjective in the sense of race prejudice, race attitudes, or race relations, we are dealing not with biological realities but with the perceptions of people and the way they think, feel, and act toward believed-in difference. What determines their behavior is not a biological reality, but their perception of real or assumed differences.

The term race relations is thus a social construct that refers to groups that have been described as socially-supposed races. Two points are important here. First, physical differences enter into relations only when such differences are recognized and believed to be important. Second, when people feel strongly about differences of any kind they are apt to believe that the differences are physical or biological even when they are obviously cultural, linguistic, or religious, that is, learned and not inborn. It is the differences perceived as, or believed to be, physical that make for race relations.

To put this in another way, the attitude toward a group may be called racial when there is an ascribed status that is assigned to all members of the group regardless of their individual characteristics or attainments, and when the characteristics by which the group is identified are assumed to be due to the physical facts of race and hence unalterable. The attitudes are likely to be stronger and more easily perpetuated when the members of each group are readily identifiable and when no person can thus escape his group membership by altering his speech, economic status, or general behavior. Thus the "high visibility" of the Negro is an important factor in Negro-white relations.

Where for whatever reasons feelings are strong, group differences, whatever their nature, may be defined as racial and firmly believed to be such. In the United States race has been defined legally and socially. While the majority of persons defined as Negroes do give some evidence of their African ancestry, even those who are indistinguishable from whites are considered to be Negroes if it is known that they have even one Negro ancestor. Nobody knows how many of these biologically white but legal Negroes have "passed" and thereafter were accepted as white. Consequently many supposedly "pure" whites have such persons among their ancestors.

In a stratified society, people of the aristocratic and privileged classes may not only have an in-group feeling of superiority toward the less privileged classes but may also attribute the difference in status to differences in biological heritage. This may be done even when there is no observable physical difference in the two groups. There was once a popular belief that the "poor whites" of the South were the descendants of the white indentured servants of the colonial period and that the low status of ancestors and descendants could be accounted for by their inferior biological heritage. Many people in England once believed the "lower classes" to be biologically distinct from upper-class Englishmen.

As will be elaborated later, this attributing of class, religious, social, linguistic, or economic difference to inborn physical qualities serves an important function in justifying discriminatory practices. As Robert Redfield pointed out, in so doing you push the problems out of the social category for which man is responsible into the biological category where God can be held responsible. A comforting doctrine for the privileged was found in the lines of a British hymn written more than a century ago:

> The rich man in his castle,
> The poor man at his gate,
> God made them, high or lowly,
> And ordered their estate.

It is significant, however, that these lines did not refer to white and black but to the upper and lower classes of England.

4. Race Relations as an Aspect of Culture

It will be easier to understand our race relations patterns if they are seen as a part of our learned behavior, that is, as cultural patterns. A culture can be defined simply as the sum and organization of a given people's ways of thinking, feeling, and acting. Culture in this sense is not a matter of what we usually call refinement. Both Beethoven and the Beatles are now a part of Western culture, but which one you prefer is a matter of individual taste.

Culture is best understood in terms of its function, or what it does.

It is in this sense an adaptive mechanism, or a body of ready-made solutions to life's everyday problems. All human groups face essentially the same problems. They must all find ways to utilize their environment so as to obtain food, clothing, and shelter. They must all establish certain patterns of relationships between men and women, old and young, kin and nonkin. They must have some arrangements whereby children are cared for and trained in the ways of the society. They must have some way of dividing up the work, and rules about the rights and duties of the various members. As far as we know, all societies consider certain ways of behaving right and other ways wrong. All have some system of beliefs and practice that can be called religion, ways of rewarding and punishing people, and ways of encouraging people to act according to the common good as their particular society defines it. Although these human problems are basically alike, they differ in specific ways and there are various ways in which the problems can be met. Any culture, therefore, is in some ways like all other cultures and in some ways peculiar. It always represents a given people's body of solutions at a given time in their history.

In a heterogeneous and highly mobile society such as the United States there are not only numerous sub-cultural groups, but within each of these groups there will be many alternative ways of behaving. Of course, certain overall patterns characterize not only the United States but all Western societies, as contrasted with certain patterns common in the traditional societies of Asia or Africa. Whatever the patterns are in any culture, they are interrelated and are passed on, with modifications to be sure, from one generation to the next as a part of the social heritage. Continued group life is possible only when it is in some degree predictable. That is, we must have some idea of what is expected of us and what we may expect of other people. Our culture makes it possible for us to act sufficiently alike to meet the practical problems of getting food, clothing, and shelter. It provides us with a system of values and a body of common meanings without which we would likely act at cross purposes. Culture then limits as well as channels our behavior.

A child is always born without cultural patterns, and he normally will acquire the patterns of any culture into which he is born, or to which he might be taken immediately after birth. From the moment of birth he begins to learn his culture. The way in which the birth takes place, the way in which the infant is handled, the routines by which he sleeps or is fed, are only a few of the thousands of ways in which the culture "teaches" him. Children learn by precept and example, by formal and informal teaching, and, perhaps most of all, by observation and imitation. The child learns the routines of the society in part by just being there as an observer and a participant in the ongoing activities of daily life.

Child-rearing practices have been described as a way of making history, for the child not only learns the habits of eating, sleeping, dressing, and the other routines of daily life; he also learns speech patterns and acquires values, goals, ambitions, hopes, and fears that are related to the family and community patterns to which he is exposed. In the course of his enculturation the child tends to be molded into the kind of person his society considers desirable. In a very simple society there may be a general idealized pattern toward which all males are pushed and another deemed suitable for females. In stratified societies, and those with sub-cultural groups, there may be different patterns regarded as desirable for members of different classes or groups.

It is easy to assume that people we disapprove of behave the way they do because they are consciously mean, selfish, greedy, or prejudiced. In reality, individuals seldom think of themselves in such terms and may be genuinely astonished to discover that they are so perceived by others. Much of the behavior currently defined as "racist" is not the result of conscious decision or even of conscious thought. It is a part of the taken-for-granted behavior learned in childhood along with other culture patterns and never consciously examined. While each human being comes into the world as a unique individual, none starts out with preconditioned attitudes, prejudices, or specific ways of behavior. But he does arrive in an already structured world so that long before he is able to speak or to understand the spoken word, he is being socialized or enculturated, that is, conditioned to fit into the world about him. He is already learning his culture. There are in the United States, as in most large nations, a variety of regional or sectional, class, or family patterns, that will in large measure determine the particular way in which any given individual views the world.

In an earlier day many people continued throughout their lives to accept without question the patterns of their culture as not only right but natural. Even subordinate groups often accepted their disadvantaged lot as inevitable, if not right. People who are not exposed to alternatives do not find it easy to envisage an unfamiliar pattern and may even resist such patterns that are clearly to their advantage. When woman suffrage was an issue in the United States the biggest obstacle to its acceptance was the resistance of many women themselves. However, if people are exposed to alternatives, old patterns in time tend to break up. Slavery was no longer possible after large numbers of slaves became aware that being black did not automatically condemn one to servitude.

Today with rapid communication and increased mobility, with the findings of science and the events of history generally made known, people everywhere are becoming aware of the alternatives to old ways. They have access to facts of history and interpretations of science that were previously unknown or unavailable to them. There have thus been opened up to them new conceptions of themselves and of other people. Much of the turmoil of the world today can be traced to the fact that modern communications and mobility have made people everywhere aware of cultural alternatives. All of these things are of the greatest significance in our changing patterns of race relations.

5. Our Maps of Reality

One of the oft repeated phrases of the 1960s was the admonition to "tell it like it is." But facts are not simple, unambiguous, and uncomplicated. They are always interpreted by the viewer. In his book *Evolution in Action* Julian Huxley reminds us that our actions are always related to what he calls our maps of reality. Our perceptions, he says, are not snap shot pictures of reality projected into our minds but quite elaborate mental constructions derived from the kinds of experiences we have had. The Chinese put the same idea into a proverb when they said that two thirds of what a man sees exists behind his eyes and not in front of them.

Even in a world of mass communication and great mobility, our experiences and hence our perceptions vary, and we thus get quite different maps of reality. North Americans see things differently from Chinese, Russians, Africans, or Latin Americans who, of course, also see things differently from one another. Within any one country or even within a community, people will perceive things differently because of their individual experiences and also because of the different positions from which reality is viewed. Old and young, parent and child, teacher and pupil, employer and employee, urbanite and rural dweller, northerner and southerner, rich and poor, or black and white, all represent diverse sets of experiences and different positions. And even within any of these categories, perceptions will vary because no two people ever have the same genetic make-up or exactly the same experiences.

Many people in the United States today divide everybody into black and white on the assumption that one's racial identity is the primary, if not the sole factor, in one's way of thinking, feeling, and acting. Color consciousness is, of course, a major factor in the perceptions of people in many areas of the world. This is particularly true when segregation practices have been a constant reminder of racial differences. But many other factors enter into our perceptions. White people vary in their attitudes toward Negroes in terms of such things as age, education, economic position, and occupation; Negroes themselves vary in their attitudes toward whites and toward other Negroes. Militant young blacks are often as much at odds with conservative, middle-class Negroes as they are with the white world. And even middle-class Negroes are far from thinking alike, as became evident in one city of the upper South when two Negroes were elected to the city council. Both men were well educated, middle-class lawyers, but except for questions that directly affected the Negro community, they almost consistently voted on opposite sides of any issue. It is significant commentary on the perceptions of white people that most of them were surprised that the two Negroes did not vote the same way. Nobody was surprised that the white members of the council rarely voted as a unit.

Actually apart from individual genetic differences, two other things are involved in our maps of reality. On the one hand is the continuing body of experiences that help determine our general points of view and basic attitudes, and on the other hand is the particular position from which we view a given situation at a given time. Our differences today are in large measure a part of our social heritage, and they are related to the kinds of families we had, the social and economic position of our parents, the churches and schools we attended, the section of the country we lived in, and our own education and economic standing. These all enter into our status positions. In a stratified or otherwise complex society we may have different statuses with reference to different groups. Although such positions cannot be precisely defined, they are basically what we mean when we talk about the middle class, the affluent, or the poor. *However*, in a society that has racially defined groups, individuals or families may have a racially determined status and at the same time occupy one of the numerous status or class positions within the racial group with which they are identified. Such individuals' maps of reality will be affected both by the racial identification and by the class position within the racial group. Thus a middle-class Negro will have some things in common with middle-class whites but will likely share some of the disadvantages, and thus some of the perceptions, of less privileged Negroes.

Our temporary positions or roles also affect our perceptions, as exemplified in the generation gap. Old and young are likely to see things from different points of view; but youth is not a permanent state, and as the young grow up, especially if they become parents, their points of view tend to change. Moreover we may alter our points of view with changing situations. The school teacher who goes to summer school, and thus finds herself in front of rather than behind the teacher's desk, may discover she reacts as a student rather than as a teacher. The man who works regularly as an employee may take the role of employer when he hires a yard man or a carpenter to work on his house. Thus both our more or less permanent statuses and our changing roles enter into our perceptions at any given time.

It is unlikely that we shall all ever see things alike, and not many of us are capable of comprehending the whole. The youth of today have a point in their emphasis both on telling it like it is and on the importance of dialogue—if the latter really is interpreted as a two way exchange. A part of our problem of understanding lies not only in our failure to listen to the other person but also in our failure even to be aware that there are many ways of perceiving the same situations. Furthermore, it is important to understand not only how a group perceives others but also how it perceives itself. For the way a group perceives itself may have little in common with the way it is perceived by others.

The physical layout of our cities that separates the rich and the poor, and the segregation practices that have isolated blacks from whites, have left many of the comfortable and privileged totally unaware of how the underprivileged live and of the frustrations and restrictions that are the daily lot of black people. Even before the days when the militant youth were screaming epithets and obscenities at policemen the perception of what a policeman was—or was supposed to be—had distinct racial and class overtones. The privileged white child in the suburbs was taught that the policeman was someone who protects you. The child in the ghetto was likely to see the policeman as someone who would put you in jail. There is equal divergence over the meaning of the terms law and order. To the privileged the important thing is to avoid tension and conflict. To the underprivileged, and especially to the black underprivileged, the important point is to get justice, and disorder may be seen as a weapon in the fight for rights that have been denied them.

There is one further fact of importance in our differing maps of reality. If we are to understand our different perceptions of circumstances and events, we must look behind words and overt acts to the premises that underlie them. A Chinese proverb has it that the beginning of wisdom is to call things by their right names. But this is only half the problem because we may disagree as to what the right names are. What is really essential is that we know how each one defines a situation so that communication about it is possible.

If a white man starts from the premise that Negroes are racially inferior, his belief that it is for the social good that schools be segregated becomes understandable. If a Negro starts from the premise that all whites are trying to reduce the proportion of black people, then his opposition to birth control clinics in Negro neighborhoods becomes understandable. To understand the premises of the other person does not require that one agree, but awareness of both our own and the other person's premises is essential to any rational discussion. The real points at issue are the premises on which the behavior rests.

Many of the "non-negotiable" demands of student groups, the "Black Manifesto" with its demand for "reparations," as well as the positions of the various groups considered reactionary or far rightest, are generally accepted or rejected on the overt behavior level. The map of reality that supports this behavior is often ignored. Anthropologists long ago learned that if they were to understand the behavior of people in other cultures—behavior often bizarre or incomprehensible by western standards—they must first understand the premises on which the behavior rests. If the premises are granted, the behavior usually makes sense. Therefore any change or modification of behavior is usually brought about not by attacking the overt behavior directly but through a reconsideration of the premises on which it rests.

Race relations are thus essentially the relations between two groups who have different maps of reality, including different premises. A preliminary to any understanding of the problems involved requires that we reexamine our own premises and preconceived ideas and understand the role that differences in perception play in the behaviors we designate as race relations. One important factor in all of this lies in our beliefs about the meaning of race and the significance of color. These beliefs and the premises on which they rest are considered in the following chapters.

3

Race and Race Differences

1. Race and Public Policy

Many people who think segregation of the races in the United States is right and proper base their contention on the supposed inferiority of Negroes. They argue that Negroes as a group are inferior to white people; that desegregation will result in bringing schools and other institutions down to the level of the inferior group; and further, that close association will lead to intermarriage and race mixture, resulting in both biological and cultural deterioration.

It is important that we be clear at two points. How people shall be treated is a moral, ethical, and legal question. On the level of personal relationships the question is settled by one's own conscience and values; but on the level of civil rights, equality of opportunity, and access to public services the question is settled by law. Individuals are required to abide by law though they are free to use any available legal means to effect changes in a law they believe to be wrong or unjust. And, of course, where existing laws are not enforced, persons who are denied their legal rights are free to use any lawful means to obtain redress.

Negroes were made citizens of the United States more than a century ago, and as citizens they presumably had conferred upon them all the rights and duties granted to, or required of, other citizens. No one with a knowledge of the facts could seriously contend that Negroes actually have been allowed to exercise such rights or to perform such duties. The supposed racial inferiority of Negroes has been used as a justification for differential treatment. Therefore, it is important that the scientific facts about biological differences be made clear. Ideas do have consequences, and rational behavior calls for sound premises. This chapter attempts to put into the simplest terms possible the relevant facts about race and race differences as scientists now understand them. There are no final answers, and all the specialist can hope to do is to arrive at increasingly close approximations to truth. The opinions of scholars change as new evidence and new methods of analyzing old evidence become available, and progress in one field often depends on progress in other fields. Men could reach the moon only after centuries of accumulated and ever revised knowledge of various related fields.

There is perhaps one other point that should be made clear. Competence in one scientific field does not automatically make one competent in other fields. The fact that one is trained as a scientist should have taught one to be doubly careful about making generalizations outside his own particular area of competence, and the majority of scientists do exercise such care. However, there is now and then some person competent in his own field who fails to recognize this cardinal rule. This failure is particularly unfortunate when uninformed judgments are made in the field of human behavior which has a twofold base, genetic or biological, and social or cultural. The two can never be fully separated, and it takes knowledge and experience in both the biological and the social sciences to properly interpret the sources of human behavior. Moreover, valid interpretations cannot be made on the basis of knowledge or experience that is limited to any one race, culture, or geographic area.

2. What is a Race?

Many people take it for granted that a race is a definable entity with specific boundaries. In old-time geography books man was neatly divided into five races: white, yellow, brown, black, and red. These were illustrated by pictures of a dignified blond European with a classic profile, a Chinese coolie, a skinny little Malay, a heavy featured, frizzly haired and very black African Negro, and an American Indian of the noble savage type adorned with a feathered headdress. It was all very neat, simple, and orderly, and the fact that most of the world's peoples did not look like any one of these "typical" examples was not of too much concern. It was generally accepted that along with the physical characteristics went certain mental and moral traits that were believed to be racial.

Scientists, too, once more or less accepted these ideas, but they ran into difficulties as soon as they tried to define the entities and set up the boundaries. The difficulties lay not only in the limitations of their knowledge but also in the nature of the material with which they had to deal. Until recent years very little was known about the genetic factors involved. Classification was thus made on the basis of observable and measurable characteristics, the phenotype, which does not necessarily reflect the genetic constitution or genotype, except as it is manifested phenotypically. Several different combinations of genes may produce the same phenotype, and as of now we cannot always infer the genotype from the phenotypical manifestation. Two children in the same family may be alike phenotypically in that both have brown eyes, but one child may have two "brown eye" genes while the second child may carry a recessive "blue eye" gene that is masked by the gene for brown.*

The definition of race that became generally accepted was a population having in common a certain combination of physical characteristics that set them off from other populations having other combinations of such characteristics. The definition was far from satisfactory, but in the light of the knowledge then available it was perhaps the best that could be done. Anthropologists had their hands full trying to keep people from including in the definition of race all sorts of learned behavior. In spite of these long continued efforts, one must still repeat endlessly that religion, language, culture, and nationality are things you learn or are born into, not born with, and that Aryan, Jewish, French, German, Anglo-Saxon, and Latin are linguistic, national, religious, or cultural—but not racial—terms.

Anthropologists tried various ways of making classifications by hair form, skin color, facial features, head form, height, skeletal type, and through the use of various indices. The number of races arrived at depended on how and where the divisions were made, but with any procedure there were problems for which there were no answers. For exam-

---

*This statement, of course, is an oversimplification of a very complicated process. Such terms as these and "Negro genes," "white genes," etc. are used for convenience. They are put in quotation marks to remind the reader that they are short-cut oversimplifications.

ple, all the dark skinned people would include African Negroes, the Australian and Tasmanian aborigines, the Melanesians of the Pacific, and many of the peoples of India and Ceylon. But these peoples were not at all alike in physical features, hair form, or body hair. Moreover, they were "types" rather than interbreeding populations that could be presumed to have had a common origin.

There came to be rather generally accepted a sort of compromise that put most of the peoples of the world into certain broad categories, usually designated as stocks, or divisions, and sometimes as primary races. These categories were usually labeled Caucasoid, Mongoloid, and Negroid, with Australoid sometimes being a fourth division. Within each of these divisions there were many variations and obviously there were many people who did not fit anywhere. Some of these people, such as the Polynesians, were assumed to be mixtures of two or more of the basic stocks.

There were also various subdivisions. The Negroids were generally divided into African and Oceanic Negroids or Melanesians. There was no agreement as to what was to be done about the Bushmen and Hottentots or the pygmy Negroids found in both Africa and Oceania. There were also problems in subdividing the African peoples who showed considerable variation in physical type.

There were fewer problems about the Mongoloids who were generally put into three main subdivisions, sometimes called Old World or Classic Mongoloids for those in China, Japan, Korea and Southeast Asia, Oceanic Mongoloids or Malaysians, and New World Mongoloids consisting of American Indians and the Eskimos.

The Caucasoids were variously grouped, the commonest being a division into Nordic, Alpine, Mediterranean, and Hindu. It was obvious, however, that there really was no entity that could be called either a Nordic or an Alpine "race," and there were equally serious problems about the others.

There was even less agreement about the Australoids, the Polynesians, and various other minor groups that did not seem to fit anywhere in particular.

Certainly the several billions of people in the world are not all alike physically and one can arrive at a sort of common sense classification that does not do too much violence to reality. The terms Mongoloid, Negroid, and Caucasoid do correspond at least to some degree with observed differences and can serve as convenient tags to indicate roughly the differences that characterize most Asians and their descendants or relatives elsewhere, the Africans South of the Sahara, and the Europeans. The peoples of North Africa, Southwest Asia, and India are generally included with the Europeans as Caucasoids, although there are clearly problems of classification, particularly with reference to the peoples of India.

It should be clear, however, that there is simply no way in which all the peoples of the world can be classified into neat, orderly, and precise racial categories. A race in any defensible definition of the term is not an aggregate of human beings who are all alike. With the possible exception of some very small and isolated populations, there is no such thing as a "pure" race and moreover, there never was. It should be emphasized that all such classifications are typological or phenotypical, based on observable and measurable physical characteristics that may or may not correspond to genetic likeness or common origin.

Anthropologists and scientists of related interests are still trying to arrive at an understanding of man's origin and development. They are not agreed on all the details, but there is general consensus that all men belong to a single species and that the varieties of men have developed as geographic populations. The species is thus a closed system with internal intergradations, while races, however we define them, are open systems that can and do freely interbreed. The size and distribution of a particular "race" would then vary by definition, so there is no necessary agreement as to how many races there are or precisely how they are to be defined.

In fact, some physical anthropologists would like to discard both the term and the concept of race. They stress the fact that all living peoples are of one species, and instead of emphasizing differences, they prefer to arrange all human varieties on one continuum. Other anthropologists who agree that the term race is associated with many misconceptions and emotional connotations still feel that it is better to continue to use the word in the way it is used to describe the varieties within non-human species.

In any case, in the light of present genetic knowledge it now seems more useful to define races as breeding populations on the basis of gene frequencies. Races so defined may differ in few or many genes and in degrees of frequency of any particular genes. Moreover the mapping of gene frequencies is only in its beginning and any divisions made must be considered tentative.

Because races, however defined, overlap, they create a continuum that can be broken at any number of places. How many groupings there are, whether called races or any other term, will depend on the points at which one makes the separations. These points, in turn, might depend on the particular problem one wishes to study. And within any category, however established, there would be wide individual variations and perhaps subgroupings. Therefore, however we describe a race or a population, it most certainly will not be a description of each individual within that race or population.

Moreover, races or populations are not static or permanent entities. The specific gene frequencies may well change from one generation to the next. Even when there is no mixture with other populations, mutation, genetic drift, and natural selection may still operate to change the frequencies of particular genes. And since races are open systems, populations may blend into one another at their geographical margins or when in or out migration occurs. The difference between one population and another may consist in a greater or lesser difference in few or many gene frequencies. If there are genes which affect the outward appearance of people, the populations may appear to be different; but if populations vary only in the frequency of genes such as those for blood groups, they may appear to be the same.

The emphasis upon breeding populations rather than typology does not mean that genetic differences are not important in human behavior. It does mean that such differences are primarily individual and do not depend on the "race" to which one is supposed to belong. That is, the differences we designate as racial are not absolute differences between all the members of the two populations but merely the difference in the frequencies of certain genes found within each population.

Although there is as yet no ideal classification of races, the existing ones, though tentative, do serve as cataloguing devices. They are not mere inventions. They are neither more nor less objectively real than races of other species though they are more difficult to study. But while the differences are real, the number of races we choose to recognize is a matter of convenience and the names given to racial divisions are arbitrary. Therefore the number of races will depend on the purpose of the classification.

In summary, the anthropologist can say that in the light of our present knowledge races are best defined as interbreeding populations that differ from other populations in certain gene frequencies. As of now, nobody can say with authority how many races there are or what they are, because any choice depends on the factors being considered and, to that extent, the choice will be to some degree arbitrary.

Moreover, the particular choice made is of no great significance except in terms of the problems being studied. Man is a single species and the differences found between populations are minor compared with the basic likenesses. Migration and mixture of peoples have been going on at a greater or lesser rate throughout human history and the genes we share as a species far outnumber those that have any known racial connotation. Furthermore, our individual differences far exceed the differences among the populations we label races. As far as human behavior is concerned, perhaps the most important thing that can be said about races and race differences is that they should not be taken too seriously.

3. How Races Came to Be

Practically all scientists are agreed that all living men belong to the same species. There is less agreement as to the time, place, and specific processes by which the earliest forms that can be labeled *Homo sapiens* arose, or the places and times of the variations which we generally designate as races.

It was once rather generally thought that man first developed into modern form and then more or less invented culture. But the fossil finds and investigations of recent years indicate that man's biological and cultural development proceeded together and were interrelated, that is, the physical and genetic endowment of the human species now living evolved as a result of, and hand in hand with, the development of culture. Washburn says that tools, hunting, fire, complex social life, speech, and the brain developed together to produce ancient man, and much that we think of as human followed rather than preceded the use of tools. These cultural activities had a biological feedback so that man became not just the producer of culture but in a biological sense, its product.

Some physical anthropologists hold to the theory that the ancestors of modern races differentiated before man reached the sapiens level, and the forms ancestral to modern races developed not only in different places but at different times. Most specialists, however, think that the evidence points rather to a single species' origin with later differentiation and recombinations. In any case, with increased control over environment and movement into different areas, the development into different varieties was more or less assured. A subdivision of a species into isolated populations, plus time to allow for a sufficient number of generations, is all that is needed for race formation.

In the light of modern genetic knowledge there is rather general agreement that the formation of races can be traced to mutation, isolation and genetic drift, in-or-out migration with consequent mixture, and natural or social selection. Racial differentation is the end result of natural selection on the raw materials provided by random mutations in a genetically isolated population. It is probable that all these mechanisms were in operation at once with the relative importance of each depending partly on population size and partly on accident. The primary factor in the end must be selection which always acts in combination with other factors.

The term selection means that organisms possessing certain characteristics survive in relatively larger numbers and leave relatively more offspring than do other organisms of the same kind having different characteristics. The idea is simple but the actual process is complicated, and there are many factors that may determine the relative contribution to the next generation made by different sets of individuals.

Much attention has been given to the question of natural selection as adaptation to the physical environment, that is, whether the color of the skin, the shape of the nose, the kind of hair, or body size and build are to be accounted for by their survival value in different environments. It is considered likely that some or most physical characters have some selective advantage, but this cannot be assumed to be true. Washburn says that the word selection covers the result of many biological and social factors such as economics, child care, social controls, mating practices, religion, and language. These and many other things add up to both differential fertility and differential mortality. It is in this way that not only the natural environment but cultural factors enter into the formation of races.

Mutations arise in any population. As they represent genetic alteration, they are the basic raw materials of genetic variation. It is only through mutations that new genes are introduced into the human gene pool, though genes new to a specific population may be introduced through admixture. The rate of mutation is affected by radiation which is now a culturally introduced as well as a natural factor.

Variation may occur within small isolated populations through genetic drift. If the group thus isolated is small some genes might simply not be represented in the members making up the group. Or, since each parent transmits only half of his chromosomes to any offspring some genes might not be transmitted. Even in populations not so small, the chance fluctuation in gene frequencies with succeeding generations may often result in genes being lost. In times past there were various events that could have resulted in reducing the numbers of a population, thus allowing genetic drift a good chance to operate. Again, population size is related to both natural and cultural factors.

From man's earliest beginnings there have been movements of peoples that have resulted in the mixture of populations and the alteration of gene frequencies. As men spread over the earth, populations became established in geographic areas, yet there was never complete isolation. There was always mixture on the geographical margins and intergradations within the species. Thus races became established but always with sufficient gene flow to prevent speciation.

Until the period of exploration and conquest when the sailing ship and the compass allowed long sea voyages, the mixture of different populations occurred mainly on their borders or through land migrations that were relatively slow. Much of the earlier movements of people are still unknown to us. We do know that Negroes had filtered through the corridors of the Nile for thousands of years and had been carried by Arab traders across the Sahara to North Africa and Mediterranean Europe as early as the tenth century.

Beginning in 1441 Prince Henry's expeditions down the west coast of Africa brought captives into Portugal. With the opening of the New World, Europeans not only moved into the Western hemisphere displacing, absorbing, or coexisting with the native Indian tribes, but also transplanting millions of Africans. The Negroid peoples today are thus found not only in their African homelands but as mixed Negro-white populations in South Africa, the Caribbean, and in North and South America. They occur in varying proportions and are variously defined, the definitions depending in part not only on the degree of mixture with white and Indian but also on the social structure and the accompanying usages.

As we have seen, populations, whether or not they are defined as races, are not necessarily static entities that remain unchanged over long periods of time. Some racial groups like the Negritoes, the Bushmen, the Ainu, and perhaps the Basques, once apparently occupied a much larger territory and were much more numerous than at present. Other peoples such as the American Negroes are sometimes referred to as races in the making.

But whatever variations have occurred in man, and however they have come to be, he has remained a single species with a single corporate genotype, a single gene pool. All men share biologically so many common features and all are fundamentally so similar because an advantageous genetic change anywhere in the species was, and still is, able to diffuse from its place of origin to become a part of man's genetic paternity.

4. Are Race Differences Significant?

With few, if any, exceptions the scientists who know most about the question are in general agreement that there is no way to "prove" that "races" are either equal or unequal in genetic endowment. They are emphatic in their insistence that we have no conclusive evidence that any major racial group is inferior to any other group. And given the fact of our species likeness and the amount of individual variation within races it is reasonable to assume that within any large population the whole range of human abilities will be found. Individuals of genius have arisen from all sorts of racial origins.

To put this in terms of the present concern, there is no basis for supposing that there is any correlation between the physical characteristics by which races may be designated and innate capacity or intelligence. If there is no basis for such an assumption, then the races so defined could not be ranked in terms of inferiority and superiority.

Most of the criteria used in the conventional racial categories have to do with physical characteristics that are of little or no consequence in human behavior except as they are made so by the way people feel about them. Color of skin is primarily a matter of the degree to which various pigments are present, and the same thing can be said for the color of the hair and eyes. Almost all other such known differences are quantitative, being in effect a bit more or less of this or that measurement or index. If we use the newer concept of population, we again find no basis for any correlation between the known gene frequencies and the intelligence or innate capacity of the people involved.

There are of course some biological and physiological differences among different populations, such as apparent predispositions to certain illnesses and the incidence of the sickle cell trait and the Rh factors. But these are a matter of gene frequencies, and they cannot be used to predict the characteristics of any individual. The fact that possibly ten percent of American Negroes have the sickle cell gene does not in any way affect the genetic constitution of the ninety percent who do not have it, any more than the fact that a fairly high percent of certain European populations have the Rh negative gene affects the condition of those who do not.

If a people have lived in geographic isolation in which they developed certain inherited physical traits it may be argued that they must have developed certain innate mental characteristics also. This may have been possible, but all that we know about the mechanism of inheritance suggests that whether one has fair or dark skin tells us nothing at all about what "mental" qualities he may have. Some genes vary independently, and individuals identical in respect to one chromosome are frequently found to differ profoundly in respect to the arrangement of genes in some other chromosomes. Although genes do seem to operate in what someone has called an orchestra rather than as soloists, as far as we now know only a few of man's genes can be called "racial" in the sense that they have to do with those physical characteristics by which races are designated.

The arguments on the significance of the IQ and the myths for which there is no factual evidence are treated in later sections. Here we shall look at some of the other factors that have led anthropologists to an almost complete unanimity on the question of racial inferiority and superiority. Anthropologists, who more than any other group have lived with peoples in various parts of the world, do not see any large population as innately inferior in capacity. Even the peoples with the simplest technologies are usually found to be quite competent in dealing with the environment in which they find themselves.

As was indicated in an earlier section, races, however we define the term, are not clear-cut fixed entities or closed systems made up of people who are identical or even very much alike in many ways. So to what races do we refer when we speak of racial inferiority or superiority? A great many black people both in Africa and in America show an unusual sense of rhythm and what we might call general musical ability. Shall we then say that musical ability and dark skin are inherited together? Many people seem to think so, but there are Negroes who are not musical, and there are dark skinned peoples in other areas of the world who show no evidence of such ability. And of course there are many musically gifted fair skinned people. This does not mean that musical talent may not be inherited. It does mean that we may not assume that given the genes that produce a dark skin, one may also expect to find the genes responsible for musical gifts.

Even if reliable measures to test individual or racial differences were available, who is to decide what is superior and inferior? Someone has to decide how to balance literary ability against artistic, scientific bent against philosophy. Even if it could be demonstrated that some populations have greater aptitude along certain lines than others, it is extremely unlikely that any single "race" would excel in all ways. We know in fact that it does not.

Moreover we must ask, "superior under what circumstances?" What may be a disadvantageous trait in one environment at one time can prove advantageous in another place and time. The sickle cell trait appears to be adaptively useful in certain malarial areas, and it seems probable that certain other physical characteristics may be useful in the tropics and others in colder climates. It is possible that races developing under different conditions may also develop special aptitudes. But the fact that a population is favored or gifted in one way while another population has other advantages and other gifts is in no way a measure of general inferiority or superiority. Again, we do not even know that such special aptitudes do exist in populations. Moreover, race differences are most probably related to environment of a remote past, largely superseded by the environments created by civilization to which all races may be equally adapted or unadapted.

If any such racial "gifts" do exist they are a matter of gene frequencies and do not apply to all individuals in the population. The "white" race seems to be in the technological lead for the moment, but even in the technologically advanced societies there are many white persons who are ignorant or inept when it comes to technology. These inept ones include not only many of the uneducated but also many persons with Ph.D.'s and Phi Beta Kappa keys who know next to nothing about the higher levels of physics, chemistry, or mathematics. The most that some of us can do is to push the right buttons—and then only when they are clearly labeled.

Many people who are ignorant of other cultures and of culture history point to what they consider the superior achievements of "white" civilization and insist that other races, particularly the Negroid peoples, have never produced any civilization worthy of the name. But people of different races have been in the cultural lead at different times. If the judgment had been made before relatively recent times (as man's history goes) the peoples of Northern and Western Europe including the British Isles would have been counted among the backward peoples. All civilization rests on certain basic discoveries and inventions, not one of which can be credited to Europeans. Our major domesticated plants and animals, the use of metals, the wheel, the plow, writing, the alphabet, coinage, the calendar, our numbering system, paper, printing, gunpowder, the compass, and all the major religions were discovered, invented, or created by other peoples. The Chinese and the Koreans had printing four hundred years before Gutenberg. Inventions are both cumulative and transferable, and the Europeans were the fortunate heirs of the inventive genius of various other peoples.

These early civilizations to which we owe so much go back to the beginnings of agriculture in Southwest Asia some eight or ten thousand years ago. Other centers of development were in Egypt, in the Indus Valley region of what is now Pakistan, in China, and somewhat later in Middle and South America. In his *Back of History* Williams Howells reminds us that empires had risen and fallen in Mesopotamia several times over while Western Europe clung to tribal life and went uncivilized for many centuries more. In fact for a long period of man's history, most Europeans were "just natives." "White" civilization thus rests on the collective shoulders of most of mankind.

Moreover, if race were a primary factor in culture we should expect a more uniform cultural level among peoples of the same race. American Indians were basically of the same race, yet their cultures varied from that of simple hunters and gatherers to the highly sophisticated Maya, Aztec, and Inca peoples. In Africa we find the same variations from simple villages of cattle keepers or gardeners to the powerful kingdoms of ancient Ghana, Melli, Hausa, Ashanti, Benin, and Dahomey. And when Greece and Rome were at their heights, many other European areas were primarily sources of slaves for their more sophisticated neighbors to the south and east.

In an article in the *American Anthropologist* in 1963 S. L. Washburn draws the following conclusions: The conditions that lead to the formation of races no longer exist and what may have been a useful characteristic in a given environment in times past may have no relevance at all today. No race has evolved to fit the selective pressures of the modern world. Man and his capacity for culture have evolved together. All existing men are adapted to learn any language, to perform a fabulous variety of tasks, to cooperate, to enjoy art, to produce religion, philosophy, and science. The members of every living racial group have learned a vast variety of languages and ways of life, and we now have a species whose populations can learn to live in an amazing variety of complex ways.

5. The Battle of the IQ

Since the IQ tests were widely used in World War I they have been cited as evidence of the racial inferiority of Negroes. The question took on added emotional tone with the 1954 Supreme Court ruling requiring desegregation in public schools. Most recently the whole question of nature versus nurture has been revived with implications that "the poor" as well as Negroes—of whom a higher proportion than among whites are poor—are of lower intelligence than the rest of the population, and are therefore incapable of profiting by the kinds of educational services appropriate to children of higher intelligence.

There are two separate problems here that are almost invariably confused. One has to do with the relative roles of nature and nurture, or heredity and environment, in the individual's behavior. The other shifts the problem from individual differences to a comparison of groups variously defined as classes, castes, races, or populations. The two questions should be kept separate for purposes of analysis though they are obviously interrelated in practical terms.

The nature-nurture controversy is an old one and has to do with the relative importance of the individual's genetic makeup on the one hand and the kind of experiences he has had on the other. In an earlier day some psychologists held to the extreme behaviorist view that individuals are really born equal and that given the maximum suitable environment almost any kind of person could be produced. Not only could doctors, lawyers, merchants, and chiefs be made to order, but also musicians, artists, scientists, and philosophers.

In more recent years some behavioral scientists and others have approximated this view in holding that all normal members of our species are more or less biologically identical in capacity. At the other extreme were persons who insisted that heredity was of primary importance with the individual's social environment playing a decidedly secondary role.

As in so many other issues, the choice does not lie between one or the other of these extremes. It is hard to see how any one can question that both are important or that there are individual variations in each. Anthropologists who are trained in both the biological and the social sciences, and who have had experience with peoples of many different races and cultures, are generally quite clear that any individual at any moment of his life is what he is because of the continuous interaction of an everchanging organism in an everchanging setting.

Theodosius Dobzhansky points out that man's paramount adaptive trait is his educability which is a universal property of all nonpathological individuals. In all cultures, primitive or advanced, the vital ability is, and always was, to be able to learn whatever is necessary to become a competent member of the group in which he finds himself. But this environmental plasticity is not incompatible with genetic diversity, and genetic differences do have behavioral consequences. Dobzhansky also says that the heredity is particulate since it is the sum total of the genes inherited, but the development is unitary since it represents a single non-recurrent process of an individual which is brought about by all the genes that the organism has. Some traits such as blood groups are almost wholly genetic; others such as the specific language one speaks are almost wholly environmental, though the capacity for language is genetically based. There are various traits that are affected in various degrees by one or the other. But one cannot generalize about the totality. There is no organism without genes and none without environment: Life itself is a constant interaction between the two.

Many people apparently think of "intelligence" as a character inherited as a unit. Actually, of course, one does not inherit characters at all but a complex combination of genes and chromosomes which under given circumstances produce an organism with given potentialities and possibilities. Again Dobzhansky points out that what biological heredity does is to determine the response of the developing organism to the environment in which the development takes place. Thus the observed degree of heritability for a given character difference may be valid only for time, place, and the material studied. The heritability is not a constant which can be established once for all.

Since the total of the actual genetic material is carried in the particular sperm and ovum that unite to form the organism, the outer limits of the individual's potential would seem to be laid down at the moment of conception. Except for so-called identical twins, this is a new deal of the cards for each individual. He cannot get any gene not carried by one or the other parent but since he gets only one of each pair of chromosomes from each parent, and since an almost infinite number of combinations is possible, each individual is a unique organism different in many ways from either parent and from any other child born to the same parents. Thus no two individuals ever begin life as equals, and there is no such thing as identity whether children are of the same race or even born of the same parents. Moreover, from the moment of conception the interplay of heredity and environment begins. Thus no two organisms not even the identical twins" actually ever start life on the basis of complete equality.

Regardless of the genetic makeup of the individual, the uterine environment is important to the realization of the potentials of the developing organism. This fact was tragically illustrated in the malformed infants whose mothers had taken Thalidomide. At the moment of conception the new organism may have the potential for a fully formed normal body and mind but the use of certain drugs by the mother, diseases such as German measles, or Rh incompatability, may have such deleterious effects that by the time of birth certain of the organism's original potentialities have already been modified or terminated. There is also increasing evidence that malnutrition of the pregnant woman may affect the realization of both the physical and mental potentialities of the developing organism.

This interplay of heredity and environment continues throughout the individual's life, though the evidence suggests that the earliest years may be the most important. Good nutrition and a secure, yet stimulating, environment cannot change the outer boundaries of the original potential set by the genetic structure, but they can make a difference as to the degree to which specific potentials are realized. Obviously no individual can ever achieve his full potential, if for no other reason than that the choice of one path of development may result in the blocking off or closure of other paths. Dobzhansky further points out that the interaction of genes with the environment continues to determine the development of a given person from conception to birth, to maturity, to senescence and to death. The development of the whole continues as a process throughout life.

Education is a form of management of the environment and all human genotypes respond to some extent to this management. They do not respond uniformly and different genotypes may profit by different forms of management. The phenotype obviously cannot be inherited; it can only develop as life goes on. All the traits, characters, or features of the phenotype are, of necessity, determined by the genotype and by the sequences of environments with which it interacts. Thus intelligence cannot be considered as a unit or as the result of either heredity or environment. Rather the observed variations have both genetic and environmental components that cannot be fully separated, and the effect of each will vary in one or another trait.

Although we can use conventional IQ tests to predict the individual's ability to perform in certain ways under certain conditions, we are on entirely different ground when we attempt to use them to compare groups. In the first place, there is no such thing as "equalizing" the environment. Aside from the fact that different genotypes respond differently to the same situation, no two individuals, even in the same family, ever have the same environment. An older child with a younger sibling, a sister with a brother, have different factors in their environments. Even twin sisters if one is pretty and the other homely have a very important difference in this fact alone. When we get outside the family and particularly into different social classes or different races, the environments may be totally noncomparable.

As has already been indicated, a particular phenotype must always be judged in a particular environment. In the United States Negro children have been subject not only to the cumulative cultural deprivation of their families but generally speaking have had poorer schools and more limited opportunity. In addition there are the questions of self-image, incentive, motivation, and cultural expectation, all of which are factors of the greatest significance.

It is true, of course, that in the tests made, Negroes have consistently showed up with lower scores on the average than those made by whites. Because numerous tests have shown essentially the same results some people have concluded that innate racial differences must be involved. But consistency in the results of the tests can be equally interpreted as consistency in the social and psychological deprivations that have affected Negroes at all economic levels.

The best known of these tests were made on more than a million recruits in World War I. In 1923, Dr. C. C. Brigham, then professor of psychology at Princeton University, published a report of his analysis of these tests in which he concluded that they showed whites were superior to Negroes, persons of North European ancestry were superior to those from Central Europe, and the Central Europeans superior to South Europeans. Later and more detailed analysis showed some interesting results. It was discovered that urban subjects, white or Negro, did better than rural subjects; northerners made better scores than southerners; and Negroes in some northern states averaged higher scores than whites in some southern states. Although Brigham's 1923 analysis was widely publicized few people seem to have heard of an article he published in the *Psychological Review* seven years later. In this article Brigham says "that study with its entire superstructure of racial differences collapses completely—comparative studies of various national and racial groups may not be made with existing tests." He then adds with refreshing candor, "one of the most pretentious of the comparative racial tests—the writer's own—was without foundation."

A curious footnote to these analyses is found in the fact that while many people continue to press for the further testing of white and Negro differences, there does not seem to be any comparable interest in trying to find out whether urban whites are really more intelligent than rural whites or white northerners more intelligent than white southerners.

These studies, of course, bring up the whole question of whether there are any really culture-free tests. Although no anthropologist with experience in other cultures is likely to agree, such claims are still made. In a letter to the editor published in the *Wall Street Journal* of July 7, 1969, a representative of a test reporting service cited as an example of culture-free tests one in which geometrical figures or drawings of the naked human foot or hand were used. Out of five or six such items the student was to identify one as being different from the others and to mark it as his answer. The successful use of such tests with Mainland Chinese and the Taiwanese was cited as evidence of their being "culture free."

Such tests actually are far from culture free. The naked human foot and hand are indeed familiar in all cultures, but pictures are not and neither are the marking of answers or the idea of taking tests. Looking at pictures is a learned response. In our culture if the baby holds his picture book upside down someone turns it around for him—that is, if he has a picture book, as some slum children do not. The Chinese have a picture culture so it is not surprising if they do well on a picture test. Would nomadic Arabs whose religion forbids pictures do as well?

Klineberg lists some of the other environmental and cultural factors that enter into test results. Among these are previous schooling, socio-economic level, degree of familiarity with the language used, experience with the kind of problems that enter into the tests, experience with tests in general, motivation or desire to do well, rapport with the investigator, speed or tempo of activity, physical well-being, self-image, and so on. Some of these factors affect one group, others another. Many of them are applicable not only to persons of other cultures but to social and economic classes and sub-cultural groups within our own culture. Many of them are particularly applicable to children whose position is racially defined, who have a negative self-image, and who are assumed to be inferior.

It is, of course, quite conceivable that there are differences in the frequencies of the genes that affect "intelligence" in different populations though we now have no way of measuring such frequencies. However, as was pointed out earlier, "intelligence" is not a unit character and the individual is not affected by two discrete units one of which can be labeled heredity and the other environment. Rather the individual is always at any moment a product of a continuing interaction between the two, and the relative importance of each will differ with the character under consideration. There is no evidence that the genes that affect whatever it is that we call intelligence are in any way correlated with the physical features that are ordinarily associated with what we call race, or with the gene frequencies that are now used to distinguish populations. Even the genes for the pigment of skin, hair, and eyes are not always inherited as a unit.

There is, however, an even greater fallacy in the judging of individuals by group tests. There is always overlapping between groups. Moreover, as Dobzhansky reminded us, each genotype functions in a particular environment that may or may not be one in which the highest potential of that genotype can be achieved. To provide educational or any other opportunity on the basis of one's membership in a particular social or racial category is both unfair to the individual and socially wasteful. Negroes in the United States are a socially defined group that includes all persons known to have had Negro ancestors, even though they may be more white than Negro. Moreover, even African Negroes were by no means uniform. To make one's opportunity dependent on one's degree of pigmentation is nonrational; to make it dependent on a legal or social definition of race is even less defensible.

6. Why Don't They Find Out?

Periodically there is a demand that we should "find out once for all" whether there are racial differences in intelligence. Usually, these demands have come from the uninformed, some of whom have accused anthropologists of being afraid of what they might find. Occasionally some scientist from another field has insisted that such an investigation be made. It appears that usually these are persons who lack an understanding of modern genetics, who are ignorant of culture history, or who are without experience in other cultures.

The anthropologist's lack of interest in such studies—a lack commonly shared by many if not most geneticists and psychologists—can best be accounted for in the words of the old saying, "You can't get there from here." To try to prove any one race inferior or superior to another is like trying to prove that yellow apples are better than red ones or vice versa. It depends on whether you are interested in calories, in particular vitamins, texture, taste, keeping, eating, or baking qualities. It also depends on the taster's preferences and on the particular place where the apples were grown.

Anthropologists reject the demand for proof because they know that what they would find would be worthless as evidence. To get results that have any validity, one must have a defensible research design, not one based on faulty premises. Responsible scientists feel they should not waste time and research funds in enterprises from which no valid conclusions can be drawn. There are too many things we need to know and could learn about human behavior to waste time on trying to prove that one group is on the average superior or inferior to some other group. No matter what the results we would still have no clue to individual potential.

The belief that there are significant innate "racial" differences in man is rooted in an outmoded and indefensible concept of race. If it were true that "races" were clear-cut and fixed entities in which all members of a race so defined were alike in all respects, and if "intelligence" were an all-or-nothing proposition that was inherited as a unit in the same package with facial features, pigment, and hair form, then the question of inferior and superior races might make sense. But these beliefs bear no relation to what we now know about human heredity and the formation of races.

That there may be variations in the frequencies of genes that in certain combinations and under certain circumstances might lead to the development in a given population of a high proportion of persons having some one kind of special aptitude is possible. At present we have no way of knowing whether this is true, and if it were true it would be a far cry from the theory that there are general levels of superiority and inferiority that can be correlated with the specific physical characteristics by which races are generally defined.

Much of this chapter has been devoted to the reasons why practically all anthropologists and many, if not most, geneticists and psychologists reject the notion of racial inferiority. In summary, the reasons are as follows:

1. There is no way in which the populations of the world can be divided into neat, orderly, "races."
2. Races, however defined, are not fixed entities with precise boundaries. Typologically defined races based on phenotypical likenesses do not correspond to genetic reality.
3. In the light of modern genetics, races can best be defined as interbreeding populations sharing a common gene pool. But since there are no fixed boundaries between such groups, the number and characteristics of the populations defined as races will depend on the purpose of the investigator and the points on the continuum at which the divisions are made.
4. All living peoples belong to the same species, and our species likenesses are much greater than any differences that can be labeled racial.
5. However races are defined, individual differences within races are greater than the differences between races. The individuals constituting any race, however defined, will vary to some degree in every conceivable way.

6. There is no known correlation between the characteristics by which races are defined and intelligence however it may be defined.

7. There is no characteristic that can be labeled intelligence that is inherited as a unit. One only inherits particular genes which in particular combinations and under particular circumstances develop in a certain way.

8. The developing organism has a specific and ever-changing environment from the moment of conception to death. The individual at any moment of his life is the result of this continuous interaction between the hereditary material and its environment. There is no life process without both.

9. Excepting the so-called identical twins, no two genotypes are ever identical and no two persons ever have exactly the same environments. Even in similar environments what is favorable for one genotype may be unfavorable for another.

10. As of now there is no way by which the human genotype can be fully separated from the environment with which it interacts to produce the phenotype.

11. Contrary to popular ideas there are no "culture free" tests and none that can measure the original genetic endowment apart from the environment in which the organism has developed.

12. Negroes in the United States have never had full equality of opportunity with whites. Although some Negroes have had some opportunities denied some whites, all Negroes have been subject to certain stresses and strains growing out of their racial identification. Such stresses are known to affect individual development and performance.

13. The great masses of Negroes have been subjected to acute deprivation, and the proportion of those in poverty is high. We now know that malnutrition of the mother affects her unborn child and that severe deprivation during a child's earliest years can affect its development irretrievably.

14. While on the average Negroes show lower scores on intelligence tests than do whites, all such tests reflect cultural as well as genetic factors. In the World War I army tests, white urban subjects averaged higher on the tests than rural subjects. Northerners outperformed southerners, and Negroes in some northern states showed higher test scores than whites in some southern states.

15. In all groups tested there is overlapping between groups and variations within groups. Thus groupings made on the basis of race will put some high and some low IQs in each group.

16. Group averages are not useful in predicting the behavior of individuals. The fact that the members of one group show an average performance above those of another group will tell us nothing about any particular individual in either group.

17. Basing opportunity on group identification rather than individual performance is socially wasteful. However we define the term, "races" do not think, or imagine, or create. They do not work, vote, go to school,

engage in riots, commit crimes, sing songs or write books. They do not have a mentality or a gift or an IQ. Only individuals function in a society, and it is the individual's performance that counts.

18. To the question, "Why don't they find out?" a statement made in *Current Anthropology* in June 1962 by Stanley M. Garn is still a valid answer: If we now knew what intelligence is (which we do not), if we could measure it precisely (which we cannot), and if our measurements were unrelated to the previous experiences of our subjects (which they are not), we could talk about race and intelligence. At the present time we cannot.

4

The Mythology of Race

1. Myths of Blood

An understanding of the nature and function of myth is important to an understanding of race relations. Some of the most powerful and persistent myths have to do with real or assumed biological differences, and the validating of social practices by an appeal to such differences is both old and widespread. Many of these myths have to do with blood. Most of us are familiar with the fairly widespread rites of "blood brotherhood" whereby ritual kinship or tribal membership is established by means of an exchange of blood.

Although it is now common knowledge that the mechanism of inheritance involves genes and chromosomes, the notion that blood is the carrier of heredity persists. Many people still believe that a child inherits not only the blood of its parents but through them the blood of the ancestors on both sides. We now know, of course, that while the genes that determine blood types are inherited, no blood passes from parent to child. Each organism makes its own blood and none of the blood of the ancestors "flows in one's veins."

The lack of any relation of blood to heredity should be evident from the fact that the life of an infant born to an Rh positive father and an Rh negative mother is sometimes saved through replacing its total blood supply by transfusion. Such replacement in no way affects the child's characteristics, and it will pass on to its descendants genes and chromosomes inherited from its parents. It will not in any way be affected by the characteristics of the donor whose blood replaced its own.

However, our patterns of thought and speech help to keep alive various misconceptions. People still use such expressions as "royal blood" or "blue blood," and we speak of blood lines, blood ties, or blood kin. We distinguish relatives as being by blood or marriage, and we use such expressions as "blood is thicker than water," and "blood will tell." Even anthropologists in the not too distant past sometimes used such terms though they certainly knew that blood has nothing to do with inheritance.

It is only a step from the idea of blood as the means of heredity to the idea that people of different races have different blood. With reference to Negro-white crossings many people seem to have the idea that it is something like mixing ink with milk. We hear the terms "full blood" or "half-blood," usually with reference to Negroes or Indians, and the term "mixed-blood" is commonly used to refer to Negro-white or Indian-white ancestry. Many people also speak of Jewish blood and even of English, French, German, Anglo-Saxon, or Italian blood. Nobody seems to refer to American blood. However, our common racial attitudes are revealed in the frequent references to Negro or white blood.

Blood myths were used by the Nazis to justify the destruction of millions of Jews. The Nazi race program was based on the beliefs that races could be rated according to their superior and inferior qualities, that the so-called Aryan race was the highest in the scale, and that Aryan or Nordic Germans were the finest manifestation of the Aryan spirit. Non-Aryans were useful only to the extent that they served Aryans, and any measures were justified that kept "Aryan blood" free from contamination by mixture with non-Aryans.

There is, of course, no such thing as an Aryan race much less Aryan blood. German Jews were for the most part indistinguishable from other Germans—so much so that they were required to wear badges in order that they might easily be identified. A myth regarding the "prepotency of Jewish blood" was used to support the thesis that one drop of "Jewish blood" made one a Jew. It was through such distorted doctrines that the Nazis destroyed or forced into exile some of Germany's most brilliant citizens. The recent scientific achievements of the United States would scarcely have been possible if American doors had not been opened to the scientists who thus escaped the fate decreed by the Nazi blood myths.

Although less virulent than the Nazi racial myths, the myths regarding Negro and white blood are still widely believed in the United States. During World War II the belief in blood as the means of inheritance was still so widespread that the Red Cross felt compelled to segregate the blood of whites and Negroes in blood banks. Some of the less enlightened public officials even proclaimed that the mixing of white and Negro blood in blood banks would result in the "mongrelizing" of the nation and the possibility of white persons having black babies. Strangely enough these persons seemingly saw no danger in an injection of serum derived from the blood of monkeys, horses, or other animals.

There is no known racial difference in normal human blood. There are variations in the frequencies with which the various blood group factors, the Rh factors, and the sickle cell factors occur, but these are all matters of genes that are differently distributed in different populations. With minor exceptions all the various blood groups are found in all large populations though with different frequencies. It is important that the blood of donor and receiver be matched in transfusions, but it is quite possible that the life of a white man could be saved by a transfusion from a Negro while he could be killed by a transfusion from his own brother. A white man having a transfusion from a Negro would be no more likely to acquire Negro characteristics or to pass on such characteristics to his offspring than he would risk losing his masculine qualities by a transfusion from a female donor.

Blood myths also show up in numerous state laws (since declared unconstitutional) regulating interracial marriages. Although such laws were usually worded so as to forbid the marriage of whites with specified peoples (presumed to be races) such as Mongoloids, Malays, Negroes, Indians and even "Cherokees," they sometimes specified the amount of "Negro blood" that made one a Negro. There were references to one-fourth, one-eighth, or one-sixteenth Negro blood, but generally anyone known to have had a Negro ancestor was simply labeled a Negro. This pattern has curious ramifications in that it implies a certain potency that one might assume the "master races" would claim for themselves.

2. Myths of Race Differences

Myths regarding the supposed racial characteristics of Negroes have served as a validation or justification for segregation and for inferior schools and other patterns by which Negroes were "kept in their place." If darker peoples are inferior, particularly if God made them that way, then white supremacy gets into the same general category as the divine right of kings.

One of the oldest and most untenable myths about racial inferiority holds that African Negroes are more primitive and ape-like than other races. As it has been several million years since the separation of the human and ape stocks, it is hardly conceivable that one human group should be "closer to the apes" than another. Curiously enough, some people who accept this myth reject the fact of evolution. In any case the persons who hold to this view seem to have indulged in selective observation. A trip to the zoo and a mirror would reveal that apes have thin lips, straight hair, and a great deal of body hair, all of which are Caucasoid rather than Negroid characteristics.

Some people attach a great deal of significance to the supposition that Negroes have smaller and less complex brains than whites and are therefore incapable of high intellectual development. However, brain size and weight are related to body size and weight. The brains of women generally are smaller than those of men but so is their body size. Moreover, within the normal human range there is no known correlation between brain size and intelligence. The people who point to the fact that in some series the average of the Negro brains was slightly less than the average of the white overlook the fact that Chinese, Eskimos, some African Negro groups and Neanderthal man all show average brain size larger than the European averages. Moreover, the common fallacy occurs here of equating averages with individual measurements. None of the averages tells us anything at all about the size of the brain of any particular Negro, Chinese, Eskimo, Neanderthal, or European individual.

As to the complexity of the brain, there is increasing evidence that nutrition and other environmental factors both in the prenatal state and in early childhood are important in brain development. In any case there is great individual variation and, however we may define the term race, there is no way by which the race of a particular person can be told by an examination of the brain. W. E. LeGros Clark, a professor of human anatomy at Oxford, stated, that in spite of statements which have been made to the contrary there is no microscopic or macroscopic difference by which it is possible for the anatomist to distinguish the brain in single individuals of different races. What this adds up to is that the size and quality of one's brain is an individual rather than a racial matter.

It was once firmly believed by many people that the sutures in the Negro skull closed early and thereafter no further development of the brain was possible. It was stated that Negro children could learn very well until they were about twelve years old but thereafter the closure of the sutures prevented further mental growth. This was a convenient myth that was used to justify the failure to provide education for Negro youth, and, of course, the absence of educational opportunity served to reinforce the myth. With the increasing number of Negroes receiving college educations and earning graduate degrees, this particular myth became too absurd to believe. The extensive studies made by Dr. T. Wingate Todd showed conclusively that there was one modal type of human suture closure of the cranium that was common to both whites and Negroes.

Another persistent myth holds that African Negroes and other peoples from the less technologically developed areas are "child races" and that they must therefore go through a long developmental process before they can "catch up" with more advanced peoples. This construct confuses race with culture, and genetic equipment with learned behavior. It is true that it would be difficult to teach an African Negro in an isolated village to think, feel, and act like an American, black or white, but it would probably be equally, if not more, difficult to teach the average American to think, feel, and act like the African villager. In either case, there is no evidence that anything other than culture is involved.

Closely related to this myth is the one that Negroes are naturally servile, that they are lazy, childlike, and irresponsible and thus must be "looked after" for their own good. But in their African homeland some Negroes were masters and others were slaves though, of course, most of them were neither. And the kingdoms of Ashanti, Dahomey, and Benin were not built by people who were servile, lazy, childlike, or irresponsible. The facts more fully documented elsewhere in this book show that the slavery and plantation system and the subsequent sharecropper and segregation patterns were cultural arrangements that placed a premium on servility, docility, dependence, and unquestioning obedience. Such patterns were learned as the price of survival, and the myth that they were "natural" served as support for the arrangement.

In recent years increasing numbers of African Negroes, born into technologically simple cultures but given educational opportunity, have shown themselves quite capable of earning advanced degrees in British, European, and American universities. The causes of cultural development along specific lines are complex and obscure, but there is no evidence that race plays any significant role in the matter. The people who blame "cultural backwardness" on race overlook the fact, documented elsewhere in this book, that at various periods in history different peoples have been the culturally advanced ones. If man's cultural progress were a matter of race, we should expect the present day Egyptians to be more "advanced" than Europeans or their American descendants because the Egyptians had a highly developed civilization when Europeans were no more than wandering savages of whom the then civilized world had never heard. The individual's genetic endowment can no more be inferred from the culture into which he was born than it can be inferred from such physical characteristics as the color of his skin, his facial features, or hair form.

3. Myths of Race Mixture

A whole series of myths have grown up about the consequences of race mixture. There is no evidence that any serious biological evils result from race mixture as such. The problems that do arise grow out of the way people think, feel, and act about it. That is, the problems are social, not biological in character. They are, however, rationalized as biological. Common notions regarding race mixture are that the offspring of such unions are emotionally unstable, that the children of mixed unions inherit the worst of both parental stocks, that the more "primitive" type determines the character of the offspring, and that race mixture results in "disharmonic crossings." There are also beliefs that race crossings are "unnatural," and that if a population becomes racially mixed both biological and cultural deterioration is sure to follow. There is also a persistent belief in a black baby myth.

The notion that people of mixed racial ancestry are emotionally unstable as a consequence of such mixture confuses biological and cultural factors. When people of mixed racial ancestry are unstable as, like any other people, they sometimes are, sufficient explanation can usually be found in the individual's particular makeup and experiences, as with persons of any race, or in the fact that the children of mixed unions frequently find themselves culturally rejected by one or both parental groups. The two racial groups involved are often of different cultures or different classes, and the cultural or class conflict is a more realistic explanation than the mixture of incompatible "blood."

The myths that children of racially different parents inherit the worst of both parental stocks or that the more "primitive" type determines the character of the offspring, have no supporting evidence whatever. The child receives one of each pair of chromosomes from each parent and, as far as we now know, the particular chromosomes received are in each case a matter of random selection. To suppose that deleterious genes show a particular affinity for one another in race crossing is to move into the realm of fantasy. All races are mixed and such mixture has gone on since the beginning of our species. Moreover, many outstanding individuals from Alexander Pushkin to Ralph Bunche have been of definitely mixed racial ancestry. Strangely enough many people who believe that people of mixed ancestry inherit the worst of both stocks also attribute the success of such persons to their "white blood."

The idea that the more "primitive" type determines the character of the offspring is reminiscent of the Nazi mythology about the "prepotency" of the Jews. Such notions have no basis in fact. No race has any monopoly on the so-called primitive characteristics and while certain "racial" genes are dominant over their partners from another race— the genes for dark skin and eyes seem to be at least partially dominant over the genes for fair skin and blue eyes—neither is more "primitive" than the other. The idea that "one drop of Negro blood" makes one a Negro is absurd on the face of it.

The idea that racial mixture may result in physical "disharmonies" is based on such inadequate evidence and is in itself so inconsequential that it is difficult to see how it could ever have been taken seriously. Equal or greater disharmonies are found in persons of the same race. In any case, if such disharmonies did exist, the consequences would be minor compared to the serious effects that often follow in the union of an Rh negative woman with an Rh positive man of the same race.

A curious combination of contradictions is involved in the myth that "God made us different" and therefore race mixture is wrong. "If He had wanted us to mix, He would have made us all alike." This belief is often held by people who profess to a literal belief in mankind's common descent from Adam and Eve. To get around this problem there is the myth of "the curse of Canaan," in which somehow it is only Ham's descendants who are to become black and be the hewers of wood and drawers of water. The Bible actually says nothing about anyone's being turned black.

Closely related to these myths are two other contradictory ones. One myth holds that races have an instinctive aversion to one another. Of course, if this were true there would be no need of segregation laws to keep the races separate. The other myth holds that race mixture must be prevented because it is "unnatural"—the other animals each seek their kind; the blue birds and the black birds don't mix. These beliefs take no account of the fact that the animals who "seek their own kind" are of the same species and in general could not mix with the animals of a different species. (There are some minor exceptions.) Blue birds and black birds are of different species. By all the criteria on which such judgments are made, human beings are of the same species with intergradations between races or subspecies, and unless restrained by taboos or other cultural arrangements they freely interbreed whenever they come into prolonged contact.

It was once believed that the descendants of racially mixed people suffered biological deterioration and after a few generations became sterile. The evidence against this notion is overwhelming. In fact, some geneticists have suggested that among humans, as among some plants and animals, mixture may result in what is known as heterosis or hybrid vigor, that is, the mixed offspring may be larger, stronger, or more vigorous than either parent. There are numerous studies of the mixture of Europeans with African Negroes, Hottentots, Polynesians, and other peoples. These mixtures have resulted in physically vigorous, mentally competent, and emotionally stable offspring.

The notion that racially mixed populations suffer cultural deterioration as the result of such mixture shows a lack of knowledge of the periods of flowering and decline of civilizations. Many peoples reached their height following the stimulation of contact with other peoples in which the mixture was probably coincidental rather than causal. In 2000 B.C. the people in what is today England were living in an isolated primitive state while the peoples of Egypt and Southwest Asia who had long been in contact with various other peoples had already achieved high levels of civilization. Two British scientists, Julian Huxley and A. C. Haddon in their book *We Europeans* call attention to the fact that in situations where the mixing of races appears to have caused cultural deterioration it can usually be traced to the fact that the peoples of the different races were also from different cultures. It was the alien culture, not the alien genes, that caused the strain. Whether culture contact causes cultural disorganization or renewed creativity seems to depend on the peoples involved and the specific conditions of their coming together.

4. The Black Baby Myth

Although the negative reaction to race mixture appears to be a learned emotional response, there are many generally accepted beliefs that support and supposedly validate such responses. One of the most persistent of these supporting myths is that of an apparently white couple to whom a black baby is born. The myth has many variations but its essential structure is that the couple appear to be white and are so accepted by the community until the child is born. Then it is revealed that one of the parents had somewhere in his or her family line a Negro ancestor. In some versions the couple knew of the "Negro blood," but usually it is supposed to come as a surprise to one or both of them. It is of the essence of the story that both parents look white.

A personal follow-up of such stories has revealed no case in which such an event actually occurred. There is no verifiable case found in the literature; and it is, of course, contrary to all that we know about human heredity. The genes for dark skin color are at least partially dominant over the genes for fair skin. Therefore if either parent had the genes for dark skin that individual would appear dark and could not "look white." There is no way by which such genes could be hidden away "in the blood" or elsewhere to emerge in later generations.

Of course if both parents had Negro ancestors they might have a child that looked somewhat more Negroid than either parent, but no child could receive more "Negro" genes than the combined such genes of the two parents. Someone has said that in the light of what we know of genetics if an apparently white couple has a black baby one of three things has happened: babies were mixed at the hospital; there was a biological miracle; or somebody broke the Seventh Commandment.

It is significant that while it is easy to find persons who "know" of such cases it usually turns out that the knowledge is second or third hand. In the three cases in which the sources could be traced either the child in question was examined or it was described by responsible individuals who had seen both the child and its mother.

In one instance the reported black baby was born to an educated middle class white couple who, for various reasons, were unpopular in the small town to which they had recently moved. Concerning this particular baby there were wildly elaborated impossibilities including a story that the baby's blood had been "tested" and proved to be Negro. There is, of course, now no way in which a person's racial affiliation can be "proved" by blood tests.* An investigation showed that the child did not actually look Negroid. Its hair was straight, fine, and so light as to appear almost as white as albino hair. Its scalp and skin were dark though by no means black and appeared even darker than they were because of the contrast with the hair. The child's appearance indicated not Negroidness but some pathological condition and it did not live long.

The second child, who appeared to be a mulatto, was born to a blue-eyed blond woman whose husband and other children were also blue-eyed and blond. Both parents insisted that the mulatto child was theirs and that he did not look any different from the other children. An investigation by a trained social worker revealed a generally unstable family and a pattern of promiscuous relationships on the part of the woman that reportedly included Negro soldiers in a nearby army camp. As the baby was born at home there could not have been a hospital mixup. In the light of the other circumstances the most logical explanation appeared to be a broken commandment rather than a biological miracle.

The third case also involved a blond, blue-eyed woman who was living apart from her husband. As she wished to place the child for adoption, the agency responsible requested that the infant be examined by an anthropologist. The child was dark and distinctly Negroid in appearance. The mother, however, insisted that the father was her "boy friend"

---

*The so-called paternity tests can show whether a given man could or could not be the father of a given child. They cannot prove that any specific man is the father and they tell us nothing about the race of any of the persons involved. Even the sickle cell trait is not limited to persons of African ancestry.

and that he was a redheaded Irishman. The mother was told that given her own blond coloring the child's father must have been at least as dark as the child. After social workers had several long, patient, and non-judgmental sessions with the mother she finally "remembered" that she once allowed a Negro porter to spend the night with her and that the timing of his visit was such that he could have fathered her child.

Although an apparently white couple cannot produce a black child, two mulatto parents may have children that are anything from a very dark Negroid type to children that are completely white. A true mulatto is an individual with one white and one Negro parent. If a blue-eyed, blond white is mated to a "pure" Negro, the children would all be true mulattoes with one of each pair of chromosomes "white" and one "Negro." Such children would have dark eyes and fairly dark skin but each would of necessity carry the genes for blue eyes and fair skin. If such a mulatto mated with another mulatto who also had one blue-eyed parent, the offspring of these two mulattoes could be anything from blue-eyed blonds with no "Negro" genes to dark "pure" Negroes. That is, one child could conceivably get all the "white" genes from each parent while another child might get all the "Negro" genes from each parent. Other children might have any combination in between. While it is unlikely that such an all-or-nothing distribution should occur, it is theoretically possible, especially since only a limited number of the human genes appear to be "racial" in the sense of affecting one's appearance. Moreover, as Bentley Glass points out in his *Genes and the Man*, the blond, blue-eyed offspring of the mulatto parents would be genetically white and could not themselves pass on to their children the "Negro" genes they did not possess.

Many people overlook the fact that while a child gets half of each parent's chromosomes he does not necessarily get one fourth from each grandparent. In fact, in each pair of genes the child receives, only two of his four grandparents can be represented. Theoretically a child might not inherit a single chromosome from a particular grandparent. It is obvious that we do not have to go back too many generations until we have more ancestors than chromosomes, a fact that may be disconcerting to persons who like to trace their ancestry to some notable who lived in the distant past.

In racial terms the same procedure applies. To say that a person is one-fourth or one-eighth Negro because one grandparent or great grandparent was a Negro is highly inaccurate. In spite of the "averages," one does not automatically get a specific number of chromosomes from any given ancestor beyond the parental generation. If a child has one true mulatto and one white parent (which would mean one Negro and three white grandparents), he cannot be more Negroid than the mulatto parent since at least half his chromosomes must come from the white parent. Another child of the same parents might have no "Negro" genes at all. Thus genetically, the supposed "one-fourth Negro" can be anything from half Negro to "pure" white, depending on which genes were transmitted by the mulatto parent.

It should be remembered that more than one pair of genes are responsible for skin color and that white persons may be blond or brunette so that the genes for skin color contributed by a white ancestor may vary considerably. Furthermore, there are now practically no "pure" Negroes in the United States. An unknown number of white persons also have "Negro" genes of which they are not aware. Nobody knows how many persons who are of mixed ancestry "pass" each year and become absorbed into the white population. A person light enough to pass successfully is in no danger of being betrayed by having a Negroid child unless he mates with a person having observable Negro characteristics. Nobody can transmit genes he does not have.

There are two other factors of significance in race mixture. The genes that determine the physical characteristics that are generally labeled Negro are not necessarily inherited as a unit. Persons of mixed ancestry may have dark skin with narrow noses and thin lips or they may have light skin with Negroid hair and features. Moreover, very few of the human genes are "racial" in the sense that they have any observable effect on those characteristics by which people are commonly identified as white or Negro. Only a fraction of our genes are involved directly in hair form or color, eye or skin color, and the facial features. Anatomists could point to other differences but there is always much overlapping.

What all this adds up to is that all human beings belong to the same species with various intergradations within the species. Even though each individual is a unique organism, all humans are basically alike and our inborn individual differences far outnumber the differences between groups that we label races.

5. The Function of Myths

A myth, in the anthropological use of the term, is a story, incident, or belief that serves not so much to explain as to support or validate accepted patterns of behavior. Although rumors seem to be myths in the making, the validations offered by myths lie in events, circumstances, or experiences of the past from which generalizations regarding desirable or undesirable conduct can be made. Myths are thus supportive of things as they are, or as we would like them to be. They are related to, and generally support, the social structure or particular social usages that are important to the structure. Although not verifiable factually, myths may embody an element of truth, and they may have some social usefulness in maintaining patterns that are important to the stability and cohesion of the society. But they may also exert a powerful influence in the perpetuation of error. Once a part of the body of beliefs, myths may be unquestioned and unchallenged and may stand in the way of much needed change. It is significant that both rumors and myths tend to flourish in times of change when the established order seems to be threatened.

Myths are common to most of the peoples of the earth. The commonest validations are that the ancestors did it that way, the gods or spirits so ordered it, or that a given way of behaving is "natural," that is, it is in the nature of things and therefore is not to be questioned and is ignored at one's peril. Throughout the world, rules against incest, forbidden marriages, and rituals enjoined are embodied in myth. For example, the Australian aborigines tell of the Dawn Beings who went about making water holes, establishing totem centers, and setting examples for their descendants to follow. Sometimes the myths are positive in that the example is the way one should behave. Other myths are negative and serve as warnings as they depict the consequences of antisocial behavior. In any case they serve to show how things were, or how they ought to be.

As this chapter has indicated, modern peoples are not immune from the power of myths. We grow up with them as a part of our social heritage, and it generally does not occur to us to question them. Even persons with scientific training may accept uncritically many folk beliefs that they have not had particular reason to examine.

Americans frequently validate their behavior by myths that supposedly reveal God's will. Such a myth showed up with reference to the establishment of daylight saving time. Many rural people felt that setting clocks back would be inconvenient especially since it would interfere with established rhythms of feeding and milking. Their protest, however, often took the form that this was a presumptuous interference with "God's time." Such persons seemed unaware of the fact that clocks are a man made device and that sun behavior could more properly be said to represent "God's time."

Supporting myths of biological inferiority are not peculiar to societies in which people are of different races, nor are they the exclusive property of white people. A Malay creation myth accounts for racial differences among men by the Creator's inexperience. He made the first man of clay and baked him in an oven but took him out too soon. The pale face and stringy hair of the man was unattractive as are this man's white descendants. With his second effort the Creator left the man in too long, and he came out with the burnt skin and frizzled hair of the Negroes. On the third try the result was just right—a beautiful golden-brown man who became the ancestor of the Malays.

It is obvious that American myths about race support the biracial structure and its associated patterns of dominance and subordination. The ape-like physical features, the smaller brain, the body smell put Negroes in a different category from whites. The myth of the early closure of the sutures could justify the failure to provide education. The image of the Negro as childish and irresponsible could justify paternalism. And since race mixture would disturb these cultural arrangements, the myths regarding the consequences of such mixture have served as warnings of what will happen if the barriers of segregation are removed.

Such myths tell us a great deal about the culture of the people who believe them. Americans are a people with a Judeo-Christian, democratic heritage of which they are proud. They cherish the doctrine that all men are created equal, that a man is to be judged by what he is, and that any boy may be president. If they have been brought up in the so-called Bible Belt, they may have been taught that God is no respecter of persons and that we are all children of God. They may have been taught that all Christians are "one in Christ Jesus." Above all, they are a people who "want to do right" and who think that "doing the will of God" is the way to do right.

And yet they have been brought up in a society in which there were bond as well as free and in which the most serious discriminations have long been practiced. There seems to be a sort of human necessity for coming to terms with such contradictions. All societies have such contradictions in some form and they find various ways of reconciling or removing them. The easiest way out of what Myrdal called "An American Dilemma" was to relegate Negroes to an inferior status, not only to believe they were different and "didn't count," but to lay the responsibility for this difference on the Creator.

Myths of the Negro's inferiority provided support for the maintenance of slavery and for the continued pattern of dominance and subordination. If Negroes were not fully men, or at least if they were inferior men, the ordinary rules would not apply. In fact, a virtue could be made of applying a different set of values and standards to Negroes. If they were an inferior race they could not profit by the opportunities open to other people, and their participation on a basis of equality would result in biological as well as social deterioration of the country as a whole. And since all of these differences were assumed to be biologically determined and not the result of social practices, God and not man was responsible. In fact this is the way he planned it and thus to maintain the pattern is to do his will. By this device one may discriminate against the Negro, even exclude him from the church on Sunday morning, and yet stay in God's good graces because, after all, it was God who made us different.

It should be remembered that myths are not conscious or deliberate fabrications. They are rather psychological necessities arrived at unconsciously. In one of his essays James Baldwin remarks that "the nigger is a white invention, and white people invented him out of terrible necessities of their own." As Dr. Kenneth Clark points out in his *Dark Ghetto*, insensitivity is a protective device. People *have* to believe that the predicament of the masses of Negroes reflects their inherent inferiority; that the poor are to blame for the squalor and disorder of the slums; that the victims of social injustice are somehow subhuman persons who cause and perpetuate their own difficulties. People have to believe these things or else give up their belief in a just and merciful God and their image of themselves as decent, humane persons who want to do right. The myths support and validate the beliefs. Once accepted, such myths become a part of the folklore entrenched in the body of beliefs handed down from one generation to another. In literate societies they become recorded in popular—and sometimes in supposedly scientific—literature.

5

The Black
Image

1. The Myth of the Negro Past

In the late 1960s there were started for Negro youngsters a number of summer programs that were sometimes referred to as "liberation schools." One of the avowed aims of these schools was to teach black children the black man's history. In some communities the charge was made that the children were being taught to "hate Whitey," and the schools were either closed or denied the public funds by which they had been supported. However, educators, whether white or black, generally agreed that it was of the utmost importance that both Negro and white children learn of the black man's African background and of his role in American history. They emphasized the importance of historical accuracy and the fact that Negroes would be done a grave injustice if one distortion was simply replaced by another. They insisted that both the black and the white child are entitled to the truth about the Negro but that a sentimental glorification of the Negro's past is as wrong, and, in the long run, as socially harmful, as the prejudiced denigration of that past which has so long prevailed.

There could be no question of the need for corrective measures. A favorable public image is considered so important that business firms, agencies, and organizations of various kinds as well as many individuals employ public relations staffs to see that the desired image is projected. The Negro peoples as a whole have long suffered from a distorted and almost wholly negative public image. The individual self-image, which is both a cause and a reflection of the public image, has had a disastrous effect on the ambition, self-confidence, and performance of countless black children.

There are actually two factors here that need to be understood. One is the assumption that the Negroes have no past worthy of the name; that Africa was a land of primitive savages who lived in jungles "in a state of nature"; and that throughout history the Negroes were the culturally backward peoples. The facts regarding the history of the Negro people in Africa and in the United States are the subject of a subsequent chapter.

The second factor is the subject of this chapter and has to do with the way in which this negative black image was developed and perpetuated. Essentially the image is based on the assumption that not only were the Negroes culturally backward but that prejudice against darker peoples has been found everywhere throughout history and is therefore innate as well as a natural response to the racial inferiority of the Negroes. It is further assumed that the African Negroes were naturally servile and that, as a consequence of their inferiority and servility, they have everywhere been slaves.

None of these assumptions is borne out by the facts. The Negroes' handicapped position as well as the distorted image are the result of a long series of circumstances. At various periods of the world's history, different peoples have been in the cultural vanguard, and at other periods these same people have lagged behind while formerly backward peoples have moved into places of leadership. There have been periods when in some places whites ruled over blacks, and other times and places when blacks ruled over whites. Furthermore, the singling out of Negroes as objects of prejudice is a relatively recent phenomenon having its origin in specific circumstances. Contrary to popular notions, it did not characterize the ancient world; it was not a factor in the relations of black and white in the Middle Ages; and in the early period of contact of European and West African rulers their relationship was one of basic equality. Slavery became associated with race, and color with inferiority, only after the slave trade to the West was well under way. The evidence for these generalizations appears at various places throughout this book.

However it seems in order here to give a brief summary of the way in which these erroneous ideas were developed and how they have been perpetuated.

2. Slavery, Race, and Color

Slavery was widespread in the ancient world and, as was noted in an earlier chapter, ethnocentrism or the we-are-the-people syndrome, was almost universal. These patterns, however, were not racial or at most were only incidentally so. Masters and slaves, conquerors and conquered, dominators and dominated, exploiters and exploited were almost always of the same race. Usually they were neighboring peoples, often members of the same society or political unit. The masses of slave laborers in Egypt, Greece, and Rome were of the same race as their masters. Throughout Negro Africa both masters and slaves were black, and in the Western hemisphere among the Maya, Aztec, and Inca, both masters and slaves were Indians. To be sure, the conquerors or the exploiters often rationalized or justified their behavior on the basis of the supposed biological inferiority of their victims, even when the imputed racial differences were perceived rather than actual.

In many areas of the world the lot of the domestic slave was little worse than that of the poor in general, and in some cases the slave was better cared for in that he was an economic asset to his owner. With little in the way of machinery or other mechanical agents, human energy was the major source of power available. Thus all the earlier civilizations of which we have any record were built in some measure on the backs of the poor, whether they were slaves, forced laborers, or merely so poor, powerless, or inept that they were forced to drudge for a pittance in order to live at all.

Moreover, until well into the Middle Ages, and in some cases later, slavery was so dependent on the wheel of fortune that it literally could happen to almost anybody. In some areas it was not uncommon for people to gamble their own freedom or, in times of famine or stress, to sell themselves or members of their families. While the lot of many slaves, as well as the poor in general, was about as wretched as could be imagined, favored slaves might gain their freedom and rise to high positions. Because they were not distinguishable by race, those who gained their freedom bore no physical evidence of their former status and it could in time be forgotten.

The best documented of the older records are those of Egypt. The Egyptians made captives or vassals of the various neighboring peoples they conquered. They spoke scornfully of the Negroes to the South of them and at one point erected a barrier which they forbade the Negroes to pass. This barrier is often cited as proof of the Egyptians' prejudice against the blacks. But the Egyptians erected a similar barrier against the Bedouin, and they spoke with equal scorn of the "troglodytes," the Asiatic sand dwellers, and the blue-eyed Libyans. The Egyptian artists pictured their miserable war captives being brought home and, apparently for color effect or contrast, the artist sometimes painted a black Negro, a mulatto, a hook-nosed Hittite, a bearded Hebrew, and a fair Libyan chained together. The evidence suggests that the whole complex of dress, weapons, the way of wearing the hair or beard, were quite as important as color or other physical features in distinguishing the various peoples with whom the Egyptians had contact. Apparently they made no distinction in their neighbors except in terms of their strength or weakness as enemies, or their usefulness as allies or tributaries.

After the Greek cities were established in Egypt, the Greeks had frequent contact with Negroes who seemed to have aroused interest and curiosity rather than prejudice. Greek artists sometimes fashioned the heads of Negroes on cups and vases and occasionally placed a Greek or an Asian head on one side and a Negro head on the other. The slave population of Greece was enormous, but Negro slaves were always a minority. The majority of Greek slaves were white and were obtained from Italy, Armenia, Arabia, Palestine, Asia Minor, and the valley of the Lower Danube. The Greeks looked down on all non-Greeks as barbarians, but as most slaves were of the same race as their masters there was no occasion to associate race or color with the slave status or with inferiority. One opponent of Athenian democracy complained that it was impossible to distinguish slaves and aliens from citizens because all dressed alike and lived in the same way.

In Rome as in Greece, the great majority of the slaves were white and for the most part indistinguishable from their masters in physical appearance. The Roman slaves came from Greece, North Africa, Spain, Asia Minor, Syria, Thrace, Gaul, Britain, and the Danubian lands. Among them were Jews, Egyptians, and Arabians captured by pirates. Less frequent were the black slaves variously called Ethiopians, Nubians, or blacks. Although Roman slaves found it relatively easy to gain their freedom and to rise in the social scale, the Roman citizens felt superior to all the peoples they conquered and enslaved. The Greek slaves in Rome were often better educated than their masters, but they were deemed "the worst of the lot," degenerate and decadent. They were sometimes described as cowardly, loquacious, and inept. The Syrians were said to be patient as donkeys and fit only to be slaves. The Gauls and Spaniards were called "wild, barbaric peoples," and there were references to the "illiterate Britanni." There is no evidence here that the black slaves, always very much in the minority, were put into a different category.

With the spread of Christianity and the rise of Islam, slavery in the Mediterranean world came to be based on religion. The church began its career as a powerful institution with Constantine. As time went on it was more and more conceived of as an instrument of world order, the glory of God demanding that the whole world be brought under its sway. Pagans, infidels, and heathen came to be regarded as enemies of the faith, hence wars against them were "just wars," and the prisoners of such wars could rightly be enslaved. The Muslims represented powerful rivals and their occupation of the holy places gave the Christians a new impetus for war against the infidel. Intolerance increased with successive Crusades. From the seventh to the early sixteenth century the Mediterranean was the scene of constant piratical activity in which Muslims enslaved Christians, Christians enslaved Muslims, and both enslaved pagans. Whereas most of the pagan slaves in Greece and Rome came from Europe or Southwest Asia, the Muslims early began bringing pagan slaves out of Africa. This religious justification of slavery continued until the slave trade to the West was well under way, and in fact was continued by the Muslims into the present era.

There are numerous accounts of the sons of Christian parents captured and brought up in Moorish households and the reverse. A whole contingent of the Moorish army that sacked Timbuktu at the end of the sixteenth century was made up of such captives from Spain. The first leader of the expedition was a blue-eyed eunuch of Granada who had been captured as a child and brought up as a Muslim in the royal palace in Morocco. At no time throughout this period was slavery associated with race. Outside Africa itself there were far more white slaves than black, and masters seemed to have the same unflattering opinion of the slaves whatever their race or color.

We are told that slavery in Africa was of the domestic variety with the slaves commonly treated very much as members of the household. This was probably true of Africa as well as of other areas with respect to household slaves, but the brutality of treatment and the loss of life when people were enslaved and taken out of their home territories are beyond the comprehension of most people today. Many people are aware of the brutal slave trade to the West and the high death rate on the infamous middle passage in which slaves were packed spoon fashion into the hold of the slave ships. It is no excuse of the European slavers to point out that this was only one particularly hideous aspect of an inhuman system that had been in existence a long time.

Until the European slavers appeared on the West coast of Africa late in the fifteenth century, the great bulk of the Negroes carried out of their homelands went to the Muslim countries of North Africa, Egypt, and Turkey. The march across the Sahara was deadly, and only the young and strong could survive it. Attractive young women were wanted as slaves and concubines, and travellers from Bornu to Tripoli reported that the route was strewn with thousands of skeletons of girls and young women who died en route. An equally brutal aspect of the trade was in eunuchs, wanted in important Muslim households. The brightest and most personable young men were castrated in such a crude fashion that reportedly not more than a tenth survived the operation. Eunuchs were shipped to the countries of the North and East, but they were as freely used in the Sudan as in any other Muslim country. Some rulers in the Sudan and elsewhere had several hundred eunuchs in their harems, and the practice continued into the present century.

What is important for our understanding is the fact that throughout at least a thousand years the slave trade was not racial in character. The weaker pagan peoples of Europe and Southwest Asia were as much at the mercy of the Greek and Roman conquerors as the weaker peoples of Africa were at the mercy of their more powerful black neighbors. Slaves had been carried out of Africa from the earliest times, but when the Arab and Berber Muslims spread throughout the Sudan in the ninth century and later, the traffic across the Sahara increased. However, this African trade was not white against black or Arab against Negro, but Muslim against pagan, and the powerful against the weak. Most of the black rulers of the Sudan became Muslims at least in name. A few did not accept the Muslim faith, but all of them raided the more primitive tribes for slaves. E. W. Bovill in the *Golden Trade of the Moors* records that in addition to the slaves wanted for export, there was a heavy demand in the Sudan itself where many of the chiefs owned thousands of slaves. Consequently, raiding the pagan tribes in the hills and forests became a major occupation throughout the whole of the Western Sudan. Only the young were taken. The rest were slaughtered or left to die. The Arab writer Edrisi describes the great slave mart at Kumbi in Ghana that supplied slaves for the Arab market in the North and East. This pattern of raiding the more primitive tribes was in existence as early as the ninth century and was a common practice of the Sudanese from the Atlantic to the Red Sea until relatively recent times.

There was a separate trade from East Africa to Asia which will be referred to later. It never reached the proportions of the trade to the West but did take on a particularly ugly form as carried out by an Arab-Swahili combine in the 1840s and the decades following.

Given all these circumstances—which are more than amply documented in the books listed in the bibliography for this chapter—the notion that all slaves were Negroes and all Negroes were slaves is obviously erroneous and absurd. Moreover, there was no occasion to associate

inferiority with either race or color. To be sure, most people were ethnocentric and were likely to look down on any one who was different, and
people of sophisticated cultures could be quite contemptuous of people
whose ways were considered crude. But this was not primarily a matter
of whites feeling superior to blacks, or of Europeans or Arabs feeling
superior to Negroes. As will be noted in more detail later some of the
Negroes in parts of Africa were at times culturally more sophisticated
than their European counterparts.

Moreover, in spite of the brutal slave trade carried on by the Muslim
Arabs and Berbers against the pagan blacks, we should not underestimate
the contributions made to the life of Africa by these same people. Their
role in the continent will be detailed at more length in the following
chapter, but to keep the record straight a brief statement is in order here.
Both East and West Africa were long involved in a two-way traffic with
the Muslim world. Islam won the loyalty of many of the rulers of both
East and West. The Muslims brought not only a unifying religion, but a
language that functioned much as Latin did in Europe, writing, the
scholarly traditions of the Hellenistic civilizations, and influences from
as far away as India and China.

As Basil Davidson points out, these additions could be absorbed
and used without destroying the general fabric of traditional society.
The overall impact was one of reinforcement and renewal, not of destruction. The Muslim states of the Sudan, like those of East Africa, were
genuinely Negro and were laid firmly on African foundations. An important element in the picture was the fact that there was no bar to any
kind of race mixture. The Muslims, whether Arab, Berber, or Negro,
ruthlessly raided the pagan tribes for slaves, but the non-Muslim Negro
rulers were equally brutal in their exploitation of the more primitive
tribes. For example, the black Mossi rulers never became Muslims but
they were noted for their skill in the operation by which black eunuchs
were made for the Muslim trade.

Furthermore, all of these activities must be seen in the light of the
moral and ethical climate of the period. These were indeed "crude and
cruel times when human life was cheap" and ambitious rulers grabbed
and kept whatever they could. All of the great empires, whether Asian,
European, African, or American Indian were built on bloodshed and
conquest, and the exploitation of the weak by the strong was taken for
granted. Brutal and long-continued as the Arab-Muslim slave record
was, its effect on the African peoples was far less devastating than the
briefer but more systematic and far-reaching slavery operations and later
exploitation by the Christian West.

There is one other point that should be made clear. Although the
African rulers were always partners in the slave trade and any black that

was marched across the Sahara or put aboard a slave ship was sold to the slaver by some other black, this really was seldom a case of Africans "selling their own people." To be sure, Africans were not exempt from common human frailties, and an African chief or king did sometimes sell some of his own people who were guilty of crimes or were political rivals who needed to be gotten out of the way. And doubtless there were people who sometimes sold an unpleasant or recalcitrant relative. Europeans who were not supposed to sell their fellow Christians sometimes did so and could be excommunicated when they did. But the general rule was that you sold strangers, outsiders, enemies, heathens, heretics, or infidels, but not your "own people."

Non-Africans generally miss the point that in this period of history —and indeed the idea still prevails in many places—Africans felt no unity either as Africans or as blacks. Throughout most of Africa a man's feeling of identity was with his own clan, or tribe, or nation, or even his own extended family, not with Africans or blacks in general. This was in part a religious unity. Each African group had not only its own language but also its own gods and spirits. Thus the African chiefs and kings who sold slaves did not think of themselves as selling their "own people." They were selling other people who happened to be black and to live in Africa, just as Europeans thought of themselves as buying people who happened to be black and to live in Africa. Neither buyers nor sellers thought of these captives as being in the same category as themselves. Unless we understand both this limited loyalty and the general conception of slavery as being the normal lot of some people—both concepts being usual for the times and circumstances—we shall totally misjudge not only the Europeans and the Arabs, but also the blacks who sold what, to us, in the light of a later day, appear to be "their own people."

3. The Notion of Racial Inferiority

As we have seen the notion of racial inferiority was not common in the ancient world, and until well after the slave trade to the West was established, religious rather than racial difference was used as a justification for enslaving various peoples. Even in the early colonial period in this country, this religious philosophy played a part. In Massachusetts in 1646 one Captain Smith kidnapped some Negroes on the Coast of Africa. He was required to send them back, apparently because he had stolen them instead of buying some taken in "just warres." Moreover the "act of chaceing the negors upon the Sabbath day" seems to have been considered almost as bad as "ye haynus and crying sinn of man stealing." As Basil Davidson puts it, the notion of black inferiority was born aboard a slave ship. It was in fact a gradual development that came to full flower in the West when the old religious justification would no longer suffice. In Britain and Europe it came into full force only after the slave trade was ended and a justification was needed for the colonial exploitation of Africa. The strength of the prejudice varied from one country to another, and, even within the different sections of the United States, the intensity was correlated with the social structure in particular areas.

In general, the farther Europeans were removed from direct contact with Africa, the greater their ignorance and prejudice. The South Europeans were closest to Africa, and though they had been kept from direct contact with the interior of the continent by the Muslim domination of the Mediterranean and the trade routes of the Sahara, they did have contacts with North Africa, Egypt, and the rest of the Muslim world. They were therefore less provincial than the North Europeans. They were themselves among the darker Caucasoids, and Negroes had been in the Iberian Peninsula as both slaves and free men since at least the eleventh century, and probably much earlier. Slavery was a familiar pattern to them and was non-racial in character. During the long period of Moorish domination of the Peninsula the Moors, who were in general darker than the rest of the population, were not only the master group but were superior in education and cultural attainments. There was therefore among the Spanish, and particularly among the Portuguese, no association of color with inferiority.

Thus when the Portuguese began their slaving operations in the middle of the fifteenth century their operations were based on the belief that all heathen lands were legitimate areas of conquest. A papal bull of Nicholas V authorized the Portuguese "to attack, subject, and reduce to perpetual slavery the Saracens, pagans, and other enemies of Christ." There was, however, one proviso—the captives must be converted to Christianity. It must be remembered that there was at this time a firm belief in a literal hell, and it was considered a blessing to live this life in bondage if this were a means of saving one from an eternity of hell fire.

The Portuguese were consistent in their acceptance of the converted pagans. The literature of the period abounds in references to the "black Portingalls" who were accepted as white as soon as they became Christians. The term Negro came to be considered equivalent to pagan. There were no barriers to race mixture in or out of marriage and mulattoes frequently rose to high positions. According to Sir Hugh Wyndham they were decorated with the Order of Christ; they commanded Portuguese ships; and they became interpreters and advisors to native chiefs and resident Europeans.

The North Europeans, especially the British, were far from Africa and were generally provincial in that they had had little contact with non-Europeans. Slavery had long since given way to serfdom, and although there were wide class differences, there were no significant differences in race. They did come, as did most of the Africans they encountered, from a highly stratified society in which there were rich and poor, powerful and powerless, upper and lower classes, ruler and ruled. They were not so much color-prejudiced as simply inexperienced and ignorant. Their first approaches to the slave trade were tentative and ambivalent. When Richard Jobson visited the Gambia River in 1620 he was offered slaves by the local rulers. To their surprise Jobson assured them that the British did not buy or sell one another or any "that had our owne shapes." Jobson seemed unaware of the raids of the British privateer John Hawkins who was already selling black captives to the Spaniards in the New World. And he may not have known that the year before twenty blacks of their "owne shapes" had been bought by his fellow countrymen at Jamestown.

When the British did get into the trade they took over some of the Portuguese patterns, including the religious justification, but the Church of England lacked the missionary zeal which the Pope enjoined on Catholics. There was some talk now and then of the glory of converting the heathen, but for the most part little was done toward that end. The notion of racial inferiority not only developed gradually among the English-speaking peoples, but its strength varied with geographic, historical, social, and economic factors. It actually came into play in England much later than in America as a consequence of the nature of the contact and the size of the slave population.

There were never many Negroes in Britain, either enslaved or free, and in 1772 slavery was made illegal there. However it was another thirty-five years before British citizens ceased trading in slaves. English kings, various nobles, and other people made fortunes on the slave trade. James Oglethorpe, the founder of Georgia, did not at first admit slaves to that colony, but he was a director of the Royal African Company which long held the monopoly of the British slave trade. Although the British were more color conscious than the Portuguese, their distinctions were based to a large extent on class differences that only gradually, and much later, became racial. The Royal African Company had as its business partners the African chiefs and kings on whom it depended for a steady supply of slaves. These African rulers did not in any way feel inferior to the British. They were jealous of their own status and prerogatives, and they were treated with the respect due their positions.

The slave trading companies frequently brought the sons and nephews of their African partners to England or the Continent for education or a sort of grand tour. One writer says that there were generally from fifty to seventy-five of these young men in Liverpool besides those who went to London or Bristol. These visitors were well-received and sometimes presented at court. In the minutes of one of the trading companies is an order for expenses for "two black gentlemen" to include board, lodging, clothing, incidentals, and "shewing them the town." The presence of these African youths and the alliances with native kings were a help rather than a hindrance to the trade in slaves, for the native rulers were essential as partners in the business. Some blacks were young gentlemen that English ladies made pets of and others were "perishable commodities" to be thought of in terms of profit and loss.

With minor exceptions the North American colonists knew the Negroes only as slaves or freed men. Although the earliest ones known in the colonies were probably in much the same category as white indentured servants, as the trade developed all slaves were Negroes and most Negroes were slaves. The early justifications of enslaving the heathen in order to convert them and of enslaving only those captives taken in "just wars" lost their force as slaves became Christians and as children were born to slave parents in this country. Furthermore, the plea that they were better off as slaves than they had been in their own country did not seem to warrant the keeping of succeeding generations in bondage. At the same time vast industrial and economic changes were making the slave system increasingly profitable. It was at this point that there came into full play a philosophy of justification that has lasted down to the present day.

This philosophy justified slavery and the slave trade on the basis of the supposed inferiority of all Negro peoples. They were, after all, not only different in appearance but of alien language and culture. Whatever skills they had had in their homelands did not necessarily fit into their new lives. And the Americans knew nothing of the African rulers or the blacks that the English referred to as "the better sort." The Negroes thus came to be regarded as sons of Ham, cursed from the earliest days, and destined to be hewers of wood and drawers of water. With the Negro thus effectively and permanently assigned to his place, life might go on comfortably in the old patterns, and there was no need to concern oneself with the "Dark Continent" out of which the black man came. With no interest in or knowledge of the African background of the slaves, and with all slaves Negroes and almost all known Negroes either slaves or their descendants, the notion of the racial inferiority and natural servility of the Negro became firmly established. This attitude was reinforced by the generally accepted ethnocentric approach to other cultures and later by a missionary philosophy that identified the Christian message with Western civilization.

Because Africa was off the line of march of Western civilization and its history little known, the notion that the Negro peoples had no history and no culture came to be accepted as a fact and as further proof of the Negro's innate inferiority. Except for a sort of paternalistic interest in Liberia, the American people have had no stake in Africa. Until very recent years even the Negroes in America were for the most part indifferent to, and even ashamed of, the continent from which most of their ancestors came.

Ironically, the ending of the slave trade was a factor in the development of the notion of black inferiority in Britain and on the continent. Just as the Americans needed a justification for holding succeeding generations in bondage, the various European powers needed a justification for taking over the continent of Africa. As long as the slave trade continued the African rulers were business partners and were so treated. The cessation of the trade caused serious economic and social disruption in the areas in which it had become the major economic resource, and it changed the pattern of relationships between the Europeans and Africans.

There was another important factor that entered into European attitudes in general though we shall deal here only with the way in which the English-speaking peoples were affected. As we shall see in more detail later, Europe was backward for thousands of years while the peoples of Southwest Asia, Egypt, India, and China developed complex civilizations. During the Middle Ages there were no serious cultural gaps between the Sudanic and East African states and those of Northern and Western Europe. When there was such a gap it was often in favor of the African. Basil Davidson points out that Ghana in the Sudan was a great empire and was so described by an Arab writer in 1067 which was just one year after a Norman army invaded a then little-known island called England.

At the beginning of the colonial period (which can be roughly put in the middle of the last century), the cultural gap was actually wide and deep and this time in favor of the Europeans. As Davidson points out, the Europe that invaded Africa was an entirely different Europe from that of medieval times while Africa was still in a prescientific and preindustrial age. A combination of geographic, historical, economic, social, and other factors, led to the expansion of Europe and its economic and technological growth just at the time when other, and sometimes related, factors were causing a slowdown and ultimate reversal of African developments. Thus somewhere along the way the balance shifted, giving Europe the advantage that the African states had once held.

The Europeans seemingly forgot what little they had once known regarding their own and Africa's past. They came to believe that Africa had always been backward and inferior. The fact of physical difference was the easiest and most obvious explanation. As we have noted earlier, ethnocentrism seems to be an almost universal habit, and when people are of different physical type, such differences tend to reinforce and perpetuate ethnocentric attitudes. Moreover, as we will note later, the very nature of the European contact and their obvious technological advantage tended to accentuate and perpetuate the differences.

4. Reading History Backwards

The notion that Negroes were racially inferior and that Africa was a cultureless blank grew out of ignorance, ethnocentrism, and the need of a justification for enslaving the Negroes and later for the colonial exploitation of Africa. Once established these ideas produced a sort of cultural and historical blindness that led to a distortion of history and interpretations based on preconceived notions rather than available evidence. This sort of retrospective judgment has been aptly labeled reading history backwards, that is, projecting into the past ideas, attitudes, and patterns of life that actually were developed in later times and under other conditions.

Reading history backwards took several forms. The idea that Africans were inferior and had no culture worthy of the name became so firmly fixed that even when there was ample evidence to the contrary, such evidence was either ignored or explained away. Although the material on the Negro-Arabic civilizations of the Middle Ages was not readily accessible, there was abundant evidence of highly developed kingdoms on the west coast and of the fact that the Europeans, including the British, had once dealt with them as equals. Many of the early narratives regarding Africa were available to literate persons and the minutes of the Royal African Company as well as such periodicals as the *Gentleman's Magazine* of the day carried accounts of these relationships. All of this evidence came to be ignored. When such things as the Benin bronzes or the ruins of Zimbabwe could no longer be ignored they were attributed to foreigners or to foreign influence.

A second form of reading history backwards involved the assumptions that the blacks had always been regarded as inferior and that there had always been prejudice against them. There are repeated statements that the Egyptians regarded their Negro neighbors with contempt. But the evidence, cited elsewhere, clearly indicates that the Egyptians showed the same kind of contemptuous attitude toward all the peoples they conquered or enslaved. There is nothing in the record to indicate that they singled out the Negroes as being different.

We find the same assumptions regarding the relations of other peoples with the Negroes. There is the oft-repeated statement that "of course" the Greeks and Romans despised their black slaves. This "of course" reveals a retrospective judgment. The Greeks and Romans generally had nothing good to say of their slaves of any race, but there seems to be no evidence that they made any distinction on the basis of color. W. W. Buckland in his *Roman Law of Slavery* says that slavery did not imply any difference of race or language. Any citizen might conceivably become a slave; almost any slave might become a citizen.

Even the early Arab travellers to the Sudan are reported (by European writers) to have "looked down" on the Negroes. But an examination of what these Arabs actually said seems to indicate that this was enthnocentrism, not prejudice against color as such. They found the customs of the country strange and the architecture and some of the amenities less sophisticated than in the older Muslim areas. They, as well as the more advanced Negroes, did clearly look down on the more primitive tribes. But most of the Arab travellers were ultimately impressed with the Sudan and the rulers of its kingdoms and empires as well as by its black scholars.

There were also times and places in which it was the blacks who regarded the whites as inferior. Ibn Battuta who traveled in the Sudan in the middle of the fourteenth century spoke of the contempt in which some of the blacks held white people. Richard Jobson, an English gentleman who visited the Gambia River in 1620 and 1621, describes the "perfectly black" Mandingoes as being the "Lords and Commanders" of the country and the "Tawney Fulbies" who "live in great subjection to the Mandingoes under which they seem to groane."

Jobson also described the black Marabouts, Muslim religious leaders whom he referred to as "Mary-buckes," who showed "a poore opinion concerning us and our profession." He was much impressed with "the great bookes, all manuscripts of their Religion," many of them "being very great and of a large volume." (Job ben Solomon, a young man who was kidnapped by two Mandingoes and sold to an American slaver was the son of a Marabout. Job reportedly could write the Koran from memory. His slavery is briefly recounted in a later chapter.)

Perhaps the commonest form of this sort of retrospective judgment lay in the assumption that any evil, cruel, or uncouth behavior of blacks was a racial characteristic. One of the most glaring examples of this form occurs in Stanley Lane-Poole's account of the Mamluk or slave dynasty in Egypt when white Circassian or Turkish Caliphs often alternated with blacks in ruling the country. Lane-Poole was a distinguished British scholar and he gives an apparently unbiased account of the facts. The debauchery, cruelty, and corruption of the white caliphs is reported as fully as the corresponding behavior of the black ones. In fact, one gets the impression from his account that the whites may have been worse than the blacks. He tells of one black Caliph who had a love of learning and who surrounded himself with poets and critics with whom he engaged in discussions of history and literature. But when the Turks got the upper hand they used their power in despoiling the palace, emptying the treasury, and destroying the Caliph's priceless library of more than 100,000 volumes.

The incredible part of this otherwise scholarly account is the author's interpretation of the behavior of the Caliphs. He offers no explanation of the white Caliphs' actions, or else explains them in personal terms or relates them to the disorganized state of the country. The conduct of the black rulers, however, is attributed to their "blood." They committed every atrocity "that black blood suggests." Their debauchery was such "as black blood could devise." The Caliph, "like all blacks" delighted in music. His lavish table was attributed to "the blacks jolly sensuality," and he was said to have showed the unbridled love of luxury and ease that "marks the black in office." Several of the white Caliphs were guilty of equal or greater debauchery and cruelty. One of them was reported to have had "an inordinate love of wealth and luxury," but the author does not attribute this characteristic to his "white blood" or the fact that he had red hair and blue eyes.

To be sure, as we have noted, after the opening up of the Western Hemisphere, the African nations fell behind as Europe moved forward. It is thus not difficult to see why the average British or American person, ignorant of culture history and limited in his understanding of cultural difference, saw the Africans as racially inferior peoples. But it is more difficult to understand, or excuse, the British and American scholars who accepted and helped to perpetuate these ideas.

These scholars surely knew that throughout recorded history peoples who were in the vanguard at one period often fell behind while previously backward peoples moved into the forefront. They knew that Europeans, especially Northern and Western Europeans, were living at primitive levels when empires existed in Egypt and Southwest Asia, and that India and China were for long periods technologically more advanced than Europeans. They knew that the British and Germanic tribes were still barbarians and the source of slaves when Greece and Rome flourished. And they surely knew that the Moors in Spain had carried on the Hellenistic tradition and preserved a cultural continuity with the East that might otherwise have been lost for all time. And these scholars had at their disposal the history of the British relations with the West African peoples, and various kinds of documentary evidence that gave a much fairer picture than the one generally projected.

Yet the great contributions of the Arabs were generally ignored and the Africans apart from Egypt were written off as inferior peoples with no history of their own. It became convenient to attribute the decline of Egypt, Greece, and Rome to race mixture with inferior peoples, but these scholars seemingly saw no necessity for finding a racial explanation for the thousands of years when their own ancestors were barbarians. Even if the Africans had always been as backward as they were made out to be, there was no getting around the fact that the Europeans, especially those of the North and West, were the rankest sort of newcomers on the stage of world history. Their cultural advance had taken place in the space of a few hundred years following thousands of years of backwardness. And when the advance did come it was built on the foundations laid by numerous other peoples.

It is difficult to account for the downgrading of everything African on the part of so many scholars who had every reason to know better. There were, of course, always some exceptions, but from the middle 1800s until well into the present century, men otherwise distinguished for their scholarship showed an ignorance and bias that is hard to believe. Davidson cites as only one example a Professor of Colonial History at Oxford who in the early 1900s described life in Africa before the Colonial period as "blank, uninteresting, brutal barbarism." Lane-Poole's *History of Egypt in the Middle Ages*, cited earlier, was published in 1901 but the statements quoted were unchanged in later editions.

By the 1920s there was ample anthropological evidence to support the long-neglected historical records, and some British historians and other scholars were writing in a different vein. However, many of the older ideas have persisted among some British and American scholars, to the present.

5. Perpetuating the Myth of Inferiority

While the history of the Negro in Africa was largely ignored, the role of the Negro in America has been generally distorted. The myth of the Negro's inferiority served as a justification for slavery and for the continued segregation and subordination of the Negro population. These facts combined with general ignorance of both Africa and the Negro's life in America mean that the black man has had an extremely bad press. Ignorance, indifference, inertia, and prejudice on the part of writers, editors, and publishers of school texts, encyclopedias, and other materials long served to maintain and to perpetuate the stereotypes. Part of the responsibility must rest with parents, teachers, school boards, and the public in general who accepted, and sometimes demanded, publications that portrayed a middle-class white world in which neither the blacks nor the poor, white or black, had any significant part.

Such distortions are, of course, not the peculiar property of middle-class white Americans. The same sort of distortion occurs in the accounts of the relations of national groups. The descriptions of wars between nations as recorded in their respective school textbooks would hardly be recognized as referring to the same events. The heroes of one side are the villains of the other, and race often has nothing to do with it except as physical differences furnish a visible and convenient label.

But the fact that ignorance, unawareness, prejudice, and ethnocentrism are common throughout the world, and are only sometimes racial, does not in any way lessen the deadly impact on the people who are its victims. Until well into the 1960s most of the materials used in American schools from kindergartens through college were written from the point of view of the middle-class white. In most of the materials the Indians were as discriminated against as the Negroes. The fact that Europeans were the intruders on the North American continent and the early settlers could hardly have existed without the help of the Indians, was generally ignored. In most of the descriptions of the settling of the country, the Indians are treated as if they were merely obstacles—along with the weather, the terrain, and the wild animals—to the white man's western expansion.

The Negro along with the white poor, was more likely to be simply ignored. If the Negroes were mentioned at all in the history books or school readers they were usually shown as cotton-picking, possum-hunting, watermelon-eating, or banjo-playing, "darkies." Sometimes there was pictured a faithful black mammy or a story-telling Uncle Remus, but the more likely image was that of a lazy, irresponsible, or happy-go-lucky individual who could not have survived without the care of the white man. The white colonists who revolted against what they considered British tyranny were revolutionary heroes whose descendants proudly banded together as sons and daughters of the Revolution. Black slaves who revolted against the bondage of their bodies were reported not as heroes but as criminals.

The young black militants who set out to put Denmark Vesey and Nat Turner in the class with revolutionary heroes were, in their own eyes at least, merely trying to counteract the distortion of history and the double standard in judging the actions of black and white. They felt they had every reason to "hate Whitey" and to "liberate" black children from the negative image of the black man that the white world had fostered. When the wheat is separated from the chaff, one can deplore the teaching of hate but recognize that there was no lack of provocation.

Because there is so much prejudice on the one hand and sentimentality on the other, and so much ignorance in general, a brief statement of what scholars do know about the black man's past is in order and will be the subject of the following chapter. These will be summary statements, and problems of space will prevent their full documentation, but reliable sources are given in the Bibliography, and the author's own research in this area is documented in earlier volumes also listed in the Notes and References and in the Bibliography.

6

The
Black Man
in History

1. The Peoples of Africa

Africa, as far as we now know, is the original home of the Negroes. It is, of course, a continent, not a country. It is more than three times the size of the continental United States, and extends from north to south for more than five thousand miles. It is varied in topography and soil, and its climate ranges from the mild Mediterranean type of the northern and southern tips to the tropical lands on either side of the equator where, as one Arab traveller expressed it, the sun is wondrous hot. It has ice-capped mountains, two major desert areas, tropical rain forests, and grass lands. Contrary to popular notions only about five percent of the continent can be called jungle.

There is no basic agreement about the races of Africa. Most authorities agree, however, that the peoples of Egypt and North Africa belong in the same general category as other Mediterranean peoples. Pygmy Negroids are found in Central Africa, and in the Southwest there are Bushmen and Hottentots who differ in some significant ways from other African peoples. Except for the white settlers and Indians of South and East Africa, who obviously had their origins elsewhere, the rest of the continent is, for the most part, occupied by dark skinned peoples who in varying degrees conform to the general Negroid type. There are many variations in height, hair form, facial features, and color. There has been continuous movement in Africa, particularly up and down the Nile corridor and across the Sahara, and obviously much mixture has taken place.

A language is almost as difficult to define as a race, and the number of languages in Africa would depend on where one draws the line between different speech communities. It is generally agreed that the number of distinct languages will be somewhere between eight hundred and a thousand. Joseph Greenberg, an American authority on the languages of Africa, groups them into four major families; the one covering the largest geographical area he calls the Niger-Congo, one subfamily of which comprises the various Bantu languages. It should be noted that even within the Niger-Congo family the languages may vary as little as Spanish and Portuguese or as much as French, Russian, and Hindi. These linguistic differences obviously create serious problems of administration and education. Within a single political unit, such as the Congo, there may be as many as two hundred separate speech communities. Contrary to popular notions, African languages are neither simple nor "primitive."

There are wide differences in African social patterns, including the whole round of customs and beliefs, material culture, and political organization. There are, of course, general likenesses among many Negro African institutions, but in particular instances they may vary greatly. If we look at Africa in the past—and in many cases the description would still hold—there were some people who lived by hunting, fishing, and simple hoe cultivation; others kept cattle and had developed elaborate social and religious rituals in which cattle played a major role. Some groups lived in simple villages ruled over by petty chiefs, while others had developed powerful kingdoms some of which could properly be called empires. There were in some places towns and cities of considerable size, craft guilds and markets, with complex division of labor.

Most books on the religions of the world have lumped all the native Africans—along with numerous other peoples—under the blanket term of "animists," which is a general catchall designation that serves as a coverup for ignorance about them. African religions are neither simple nor all alike, though most of them do have some basic characteristics in common. Everywhere there is a belief in a High God or Creator, and almost everywhere a belief in ancestral as well as nature spirits. In many of the societies there are hierarchies of lesser gods. In every case the religion is closely tied in with the social system. Today there are considerable numbers of Africans who are Christians, and Islam has spread over wide areas.

Like the religions of Africa, the arts are far from being the "crude imaginings of primitive men." Basil Davidson calls them the embodiment and statement of old and intricate speculations and traditions about the nature of the world and man's possible place in the world. The various art forms he calls "the literature, the holy books, the poetry of African beliefs." Today the art forms of Africa are recognized and appreciated as significant contributions.

In sum, the African continent, including what is usually referred to as Negro Africa, has a continuous and worthy cultural history that has too long been obscured. It is far from being a museum of barbarism whose populations have remained stagnant through some natural failing or inferiority. Africa is now seen to possess a history which demands as serious an approach as the history of any other continent.

2. The Negro in the Ancient World

Both American whites and American Negroes like to claim the Egyptian "cradleland of civilization" as their own heritage. Neither claim has more than psychological value. The Egyptians were biologically ancestral to neither, and cultural developments are not correlated with race. Nobody deserves either credit or blame for a past in which he had no part. However, many white people seem to feel that anything done by anybody with a white skin, however distant in the past, should be counted as evidence of white superiority. These are often the same people who assume that black men have a record only of savagery and slavery. Some little known facts may help set the record straight.

Although the early Egyptians were basically Caucasoid and were both physically and culturally related to the peoples of Southwest Asia, they had deep African roots and associations. Moreover, if we use the common American legal and social definition of a Negro as anyone who shows any evidence of even partial Negro ancestry, many Egyptians would have to be defined as Negroes. As far back as our evidence goes, the Egyptians were mixing with all the surrounding peoples which in due time included the Negroes to the south of them. H. R. Hall, writing in the *Cambridge Ancient History*, refers to two of Egypt's greatest rulers of the Twelfth Dynasty, distinguished by character and energy, as showing a Negro strain which he attributes to the fierce Sudanese invaders from the South. Such mixture had gone on for many generations before Egypt reached her maximum cultural development, a fact that may be disconcerting to people who cherish the belief that race mixture always results in cultural deterioration.

The Egyptians secured slaves and captives from all the conquered and dependent peoples around them. Some of these people were already slaves in their homelands and were taken along with cattle and a variety of products as war booty or in trade. Others were sent as tributes to the Pharaoh. Sometimes chief's children were included and these might be educated in the royal household as hostages and later put in charge of their home territories. At various times these captives were Libyans, Israelites, Phoenecians, Hittites, Cretans, and the people of Kush or Punt, as well as from various Negro tribes farther to the South.

These early Egyptians boasted of, and probably exaggerated their exploits. In Breasted's *Ancient Records of Egypt* we find numerous accounts of "smiting the Troglodytes," or the sand dwellers. One picture shows a Bedouin of the Sinai region on his knees, held by his hair. The inscription reads "Smiter of Barbarians." By the Third Dynasty Snefru was "hacking up the land of the Negro, bringing 7,000 living prisoners and over 200,000 large and small cattle." These cattle would seem to indicate that even at this early date the Negroes were anything but wandering savages.

As early as the Sixth Dynasty Pepi I was using both Libyan and Negro mercenaries in a war against the Bedouin. From this period on, active commerce was engaged in with the Negroid tribes to the South. From 1500 to about 800 B.C. the greater part of Nubia was composed of two great tribute paying provinces, Wawat and Kush. These Nubians were anything but docile, and as soon as the Pharaoh turned to the North to deal with the Bedouin, Wawat would come to life again and have to be "hacked up" or overthrown. In due time the Negroes were in Egypt not merely as slaves and captives but as hired warriors and also as settlers.

While the Hyksos (c. 1750–1575 B.C.) were still ruling Egypt nominally, a reportedly black king established himself in the Delta. He called himself "King of the South and the North" and had his name written in a cartouche as *Nehsi Ra*, "the Black of Ra." At a somewhat later period a Nubian prince or chieftain married an Egyptian lady and established himself at Napata where he ruled Egypt for several years. He was succeeded by his son Piankhi who later became "Lord of all Egypt." Piankhi was succeeded by his brother who married Piankhi's daughter and became the founder of the twenty-fifth or Ethiopian Dynasty.

The Egyptians seemed to have had much the same attitude toward all their neighbors. The inscriptions are full of references to their "vile" or "wretched" peoples, often shown kneeling at the Pharaoh's feet. The epithets seem to have been impartially bestowed on the Hittites, the Libyans, and the Syrians as well as the Negro chieftains. However, the French scholar, Champollion, interprets a painting found in one of the ancient tombs as indicating the races of man as the Egyptians saw them. Nearest the god is a reddish individual clothed in white robes, the inscription indicating the race of man, that is the Egyptian himself. The second man is unmistakably a Negro, the Egyptians' nearest neighbor. The third person is a bronzed man with a thick black beard and a many colored garment, the Asiatic. The fourth man is described as having a white skin and blue eyes. He is dressed in a rough animal skin and tattooed on different parts of his body, what Champollion calls a *"veritable sauvage."* To the civilized Egyptian the blond man from the North was a savage.

Like other Mediterranean peoples, the Greeks seem to have derived their first notions of the Negro peoples from the Egyptians, though it is not outside the realm of possibility that some contact may have been made through Crete. Vague references in the Iliad and the Odyssey refer to the "blameless Ethiopians," burnt or black faced men, who dwelt beyond Egypt to the South on the borders of Ocean Stream. They are mentioned in connection with the gods, who were supposed to repair to the banks of the Ocean to feast on the sacrifices offered there. The Greeks seem to have used the term Ethiopia, meaning "land of burnt faces," for any area occupied by dark skinned peoples, including the Negroes. E. A. Wallis Budge in his *History of Ethiopia, Nubia, and Abyssinia* says he became convinced that the Ethiopians described by Herodotus and others were not Abyssinians but the natives of upper Nubia and the Island of Meröe and the Negroes and Negroid peoples who inhabited the hot moist land which extended from southern Abyssinia to the Equator.

Herodotus writing in the fifth century B.C. gives a vivid description of the various peoples who served in the armies of Xerxes. He says the eastern and western Ethiopians differ in nothing save their hair, the eastern ones having straight hair and the others being "more wooly haired than any other people in the world." Elsewhere, he refers to Ethiopia as the last inhabited land in the direction of the setting sun, where gold is obtained in great plenty, huge elephants abound, and men are taller, handsomer, and longer lived than anywhere else.

The black slaves in Greece and Rome were too few in number to have been of any great significance. They seem to have been regarded with interest and curiosity because of their physical difference but, as noted in the preceding chapter, the evidence does not suggest that they were considered different from the great masses of white slaves and captives who far outnumbered them.

Moreover, it should be noted that the Northern and Western Europeans, including the Britons, played no part in the ancient civilized world except as slaves to the Greeks or Romans. Throughout this entire period they would have been classed as barbarians. On the other hand, Egypt's Negro neighbors played an increasingly significant role. They were at first slaves and captives in Egypt as were Egypt's other neighbors. Later they were employed as soldiers in the Egyptian armies where Budge says these "Black Battalions" were noted for their bravery and prowess. As time went on they became an integral part of the Egyptian population at all levels with more than one Pharaoh showing in his features his partial Negro ancestry.

It is now known that the Negro and Negroid peoples in this general area developed distinctive cultures of their own which, as Basil Davidson points out, appeared insignificant to later historians only because they were compared to Egypt and erroneously assumed to be merely attenuated and degenerated appendages to Egyptian culture. On the contrary, the Negroes of Meröe, a center of Kushite civilization, developed one of the greatest iron-founding centers of the ancient world. Meröe, says Davidson, became very much a civilization in its own right, and it exhibited a great depth and range of culture.

We know little about the rest of Africa during this period, but in early Christian centuries there were kingdoms and even empires that could not have sprung full-blown from cultural wastelands. The archaeological record is still very sketchy and incomplete, but the available evidence all points to a continuous cultural development throughout the continent.

3. Black and White in the Middle Ages

The highest development of social and political organization among the Negroes grew up in the region known as the Sudan between the Sahara Desert and the tropical rainbelt to the South. Until recent times these people were little known to the Western world, and even today many people do not even know of their existence. Almost the only records about the Sudanese people were written in Arabic and many of these were lost or destroyed. Only a few of those that did survive are available in English or French translations. Because the Sudanese kingdoms were influenced by the Arab and Berber Muslims, and the written language of the area was Arabic, many people assume that these civilizations were not really Negro. This is like saying that English civilization is not really English because the people borrowed both the Christian religion and the alphabet from others, and they got printing, paper, and the compass from non-English sources.

With the rise of the Muslim world in the seventh century, there began a new flowering of culture based on the Greek tradition and en-

riched through contact with India and China. In the early eighth century the Arabs and their North African allies—the people usually referred
to as the Moors—displaced the Visigoth rulers in Spain. They brought
Eastern architecture, science, mathematics, medical and commercial
knowledge to the West. Some of the finest libraries of the world were to
be found at the Universities of Cordova and Granada, and when the
Moors were later pushed into Africa they developed libraries at Fez and
Morocco. Professor Melvin Knight in his *Economic History of Europe*
says that when Christian Europe was scraping off priceless classics to get
parchment for recording childish chronicles in bad Latin, the Moors
were manufacturing paper and writing scholarly commentaries on the
works of Aristotle and other Greek writers.

The Arab and Berber Muslims seem to have reached the Sudan
sometime in the ninth and tenth centuries. While the Negroid peoples
of the Sudan were then non-literate—as were most of the peoples of Europe at the time—powerful Negro states were already in existence. All of
these came under Muslim influence in one way or another, and the Muslim religion became widespread, though by no means universal. Many
of the common people and some of the rulers maintained their traditional
religious beliefs. Arabic became the language of the intellectual circles
and the schools, and the entire region developed a close and continuing
contact with the Muslim world. We have noted earlier the darker side
of the slave-trading activity of the region, but this was only one aspect
of life in the Sudan, as it was in most other areas of the world at that time.

Various important kingdoms and empires flourished in the area.
Some of these were developed under the stimulus of the Muslims and
could be called Negro-Arabic in character. Others grew up before or outside of the Muslim influence. Among the oldest, longest and most noted
of these were the Empires of Ghana, Mali, and Songhay. All of these,
while affected and sometimes ruled by non-Negro or Negroid kings, were
certainly black empires and basically Negro in any but the most limited
use of the term. There were various other less noted but important
groups, among them the Mossi States, which represented a civilization
which was uniquely Negro. The Mossi rulers never accepted Islam.

One of the earliest and most important empires was that of Ghana
from which the modern state of Ghana takes its name. North African
and other Arabic writers mention Ghana as early as the ninth century,
but its origin was probably much earlier, possibly in the fourth or fifth
century. It had a continuous existence, though with many vicissitudes,
well into the thirteenth century. According to tradition the early ruling
dynasty was white, but before the Arab invasion the white dynasty had
been replaced by a black Mandingo one under which it reached the peak
of its power in the ninth century. According to the records of the day,

the state was fabulously wealthy; it received tribute from the white Berbers and its renown spread from Cairo to Baghdad.

When Ghana lost its power in the thirteenth century there was a period of political confusion followed by the rise of the Empire known as Mali or Melli. Mali had its origins somewhere before 1000 A.D. and in time exceeded Ghana in area and power. The rulers of Mali were in constant and friendly relations with the Muslim potentates of North Africa and exchanged embassies with the Sultan of Fez. Ibn Battuta, an Arab traveler who visited the state in 1352, left a detailed account of his travels in which he testified to the fine administration of the state, its prosperity, the courtesy and discipline of its officials and provisional governors, and the respect accorded the judicial decisions of its sovereigns. This empire founded and directed by Negro people was governed by a family of rulers who exercised power from the time of its small beginning through its rise and decline.

One of the most famous of the Mali rulers, known as Mansa Musa, made a spectacular pilgrimage to Mecca and to various places along the way. Mansa Musa was celebrated in the Catalan map of Africa which was made for Charles V by a Jewish cartographer in 1375. It shows the Atlas Mountains broken by a pass used by merchants going to the land of the Negroes. At the center of the Sahara appears the figure of a Negro monarch enthroned, with a sceptre in one hand and a nugget of gold in the other. He is being approached by a white traveller. The inscription reads: "This Negro Lord is called Mansa Mali, Lord of the Negroes of Guinea. He is the richest and most noble king in all the land."

As the Mali empire declined, the rival Songhays came to power and produced two notable rulers, known as Sonni Ali and Askia the Great. It was under Askia's rule that the Sudan's two most noted cities reached the height of their fame. These cities were Jenne (or Djenné) and Timbuktu, both on the Niger. Jenne was somewhat obscured by the fame of Timbuktu, but Bovill says it was a commercial and intellectual center of first importance. Leo Africanus visited Jenne in the early sixteenth century and reported of the area that "the inhabitants are rich, and have plenty of wares. Here are great store of temples, priests and professors, which professors read their lectures only in temples, because they have no colleges at all." He found the people of this region excelled all other Negroes in "wit, civility and industry."

Leo visited Timbuktu in 1526 and found there a "great store of doctors, judges, priests and other learned men," and he reported that the manuscripts and written books out of Barbarie were sold for more than any other merchandise. Askia, the Great, a Negro king, is said to have made of Jenne and Timbuktu intellectual centers to which black and white scholars came to complete their education. To the university or

Mosque of Sankoré in Timbuktu came scholars from Cordova, Fez, and Cairo, and some of the scholars from Jenne and Timbuktu were installed as professors in Morocco and Egypt.

Later visitors to Timbuktu were sometimes disappointed because they found no great buildings and little outward evidence of the city's former importance. There was little timber or building stone in the area, and the clay used in building quickly deteriorated. When late in the sixteenth century Timbuktu was sacked by Moors and Spanish renegades from the North, the Negro and Arabic scholars were sent into exile and their libraries were stolen or destroyed. One of these scholars, Ahmed Baba, wrote that he had fewer books than any of his friends and they robbed him of 1,600 volumes. He was the author of twenty books, one of which was a biographical dictionary of the distinguished men of the Sudan.

After this area was overrun by the Moors, these states declined and became disorganized. With the exploration of the Western hemisphere and the expansion of the slave trade to the West these kingdoms were shut off from the rest of the civilized world. They survived for a period of time but they were more or less bottled up in the center of the continent while Europe came into her own. The frontiers of civilization, now no longer in Muslim but in Christian hands, left Africa off the line of march and pushed westward across the Atlantic. Yet throughout this entire period, travellers, whether Muslim or Christian, remarked on the character of the Sudanese Negroes as people who were noted for their industry, who loved peace and justice, and who had a rare gift of human sympathy for the stranger who came their way.

4. The Land of the Fathers

There were other sophisticated cultures of Africa, notably on the East Coast, but the ones of most immediate interest for this study were in those areas of Africa from which the black ancestors of most American Negroes came. Some of the Negroes brought to North America came from the Congo, others were brought from inland by Arab traders, and a few came from the Sudan and other areas. However, the great majority of them came from West Africa in the area between the Senegal River and Angola, where the Portuguese and later the French, Dutch, Brandenberg, British, and American trading companies exchanged cloth, guns, rum, and other merchandise for their human cargoes.

The first slaves taken along the West Coast by the Portuguese and by John Hawkins were kidnapped, but these were few in number. Obviously it would have been impossible for a few Europeans to arrive in ships and kidnap the millions of Africans that were brought to the New World. After the slave trade got well under way, it was a business enterprise made possible by the cooperation of African chiefs and kings with the slave-trading companies. Many of the traders would not have been above kidnapping their victims, but they actually had little opportunity. The African chiefs and kings jealously guarded their rights in the matter, and Europeans generally were not permitted inland. Some of the more unscrupulous ship captains occasionally enticed an unsuspecting African aboard his ship, but the kidnapping and raiding of villages was generally done by Arab traders from the interior or by other Africans.

Even among the non-literate peoples of the Guinea Coast, the area from which most of the slaves were taken, there were peoples whose rulers had to be reckoned with by European traders and by European governments as well. When the slave trade was finally abolished early in the nineteenth century, Europeans for the first time began to make direct contact with the various African rulers somewhat farther inland. Almost invariably they were astonished at the complexity of the cultures which they found.

Among the most highly developed peoples of this region were the Ashanti of the Gold Coast in what is now Ghana. Numerous records of the slave dealers refer to the "Shantees" who were said to be very intelligent but extremely proud and difficult to handle. After the close of the slave trade the British government was involved in six wars with the Ashanti before they were subdued. It was said of one of the Ashanti kings that he never fought an unjust war, never broke a treaty, never failed to respect an ambassador, and never violated a flag of truce. All of this was more than could be said of many of the British officials with whom he had to deal. Some of these officials recognized the worth of the Ashanti rulers, and in the treaties and official documents of the times the Ashanti king is referred to as "Your Majesty" and the Queen Mother as "Your Royal Mother." A British writer of the period referred to one of the Ashanti kings as a "man of high character, honorable in his dealings, peaceable in his disposition, and forbearing with his enemies, a man of sound sense and one who regarded his plighted word as sacred."

A later British writer made it clear that persons who assume that African Negroes are naturally servile can hardly have observed African peoples before European contact. He refers to the solemnity and dignity of an Ashanti court of justice where the chieftain or king sat with his councillors and judges to hear the suits of his subjects. In fact one of the major characteristics of African societies, reported by many investigators, is the dignity of their courts of justice and the consequent respect for law.

The Ashanti had a complex and well organized government. They were a highly stratified society with royalty, nobles, gentry, commoners, pawns, and slaves. Women held a high place in the society, and the Queen Mother had her own court in which cases were tried. A woman could inherit and hold property that her husband could not touch. When the Ashanti signed a treaty of peace with the British, one of the king's official representatives was an Ashanti princess. When a British official asked why he had not been told of the role played by the Queen Mother, the Ashanti elders replied: "We supposed the Europeans considered women of no account and we know that you do not recognize them as we have always done."

An Englishman who wrote of the neighboring kingdom of Dahomey in 1849 referred to "the extraordinary innate civilizations which exist among the blacks" and described Dahomey as a country of contrasts in which the vizier who casually decapitates a prisoner of war "studies and understands an etiquette that would do honor to the most civilized court in Europe." The advanced state of this kingdom was not of late development, for, more than a hundred years before, an Englishman taken as a prisoner of war by one of the Dahomean kings had written of "the power and grandeur of this conquering king, which has often surprised me, not thinking to see anything like it in this part of the world."

The markets of Dahomey were pictured as being extensive, the dwellings clean, neat, and quiet, and the cultivation of the soil rivalling that of the Chinese. The approach to the capital was along a broad clear road as wide as any highroad in England. Other writers tell of Dahomean kings who mounted regular courier service with runners stationed at post houses in all inhabited towns. Travellers were required to carry the carved wooden staff of a chief as a passport. These kings levied taxes and custom duties and made and kept an accurate census. Another Englishman wrote of the Dahomean King Gezo that "his appearance is commanding, his countenance intellectual, and that he is proud there can be no doubt for he treads the earth as if it were honoured with its burden."

The arts and crafts were highly developed in West Africa. There were towns, monetary and trade systems, and well ordered markets. In Dahomey there were organized groups of iron workers, weavers, potters, basket-makers, woodcarvers, brass-workers, silversmiths, hunters, and traders. The Ashanti were famed for their weaving, for their delicate and intricate work in gold, and for the tiny brass weights used in weighing gold dust. The people of Benin were noted for their work in bronze, and they were also skilled workers in wood and ivory.

However, African life should not be pictured as idyllic. Much of life was crude and primitive. Slavery and human sacrifice existed even in the more advanced states. But such practices can never be considered fairly apart from the role they play in the total society nor apart from the times in which they occurred. The human sacrifices in particular were connected with one's conception of the afterlife, and of one's obligations to departed ancestors who needed service in the next world.

In summary, it can be said that throughout Negro Africa the people were found in well-defined social groups, living sometimes in relatively simple fashion under the control of a clan or tribal chief, sometimes in highly developed states and kingdoms under the rule of a powerful king. In every case there were definite rules of conduct including regulations regarding marriage and divorce, the inheritance of property, division of labor, and rules of war. In other words, the African Negro peoples had long ago worked out for themselves forms of social organization and ways of life that represented reasonably satisfactory adaptations to their environments and to one another so that they were able to live in orderly social groups.

It was out of such diverse and by no means unworthy backgrounds that the Negroes came to America. As Africans they had been of various tribes with various languages and cultures. Among them were old and young, rich and poor, slave and free, stupid and intelligent, skilled and unskilled, servile and proud. Some of the larger planters of America came to judge the relative merits of tribal groups in terms of special characteristics. There are references to the sickly Gaboons, the slothful quarreling men of Calabar, the adaptable Whydahs, the handsome and good-humored Congoes, the intelligent but physically weak Senegalese, the proud Fantinians, the Ebbos hardy and stubborn but much addicted to suicide, and the Coromantines of the Gold Coast "all born heroes with not a coward or a rascal of that nation."

But whatever their tribal or national background, or their personal character and skill, slavery leveled them all to a common bondage and a common status. Many of their descendants number Europeans and American Indians as well as other Africans among their ancestors. The degree to which they are still physically and culturally related to Africa is a matter of dispute. But there is no reason why black Americans should not, along with the rest of the world, take pride in the land of their fathers.

5. Negroes in American Life

Negroes were in what is now the United States long before there were any permanent settlements. Free Negroes as well as slaves skilled in the mechanical arts were fairly numerous in Spain and Portugal at the time of the discovery of America, and there is a tradition that at least one Negro came with Columbus, probably as pilot of the Niña. Negroes figured as slaves and servants, and probably as free men, in the exploration and settlements of the Spaniards throughout the period of their early contact with the Western world.

The best known of these black men with the Spanish adventurers was called Estevan or Estevanico. He was with Panfilo de Narváez in the expedition that landed in Florida in 1528. He, with Cabeza da Vaca and two other white men, survived the unfortunate expedition and wandered for years before finally reaching the Spanish settlements in what is now Mexico. Mendoza, then ruler of New Spain, sent the Franciscan monk Fray Marcos de Niza to investigate the survivor's story of the fabled Seven Cities of Cibola and gave him Estevan as a guide. The Negro was sent ahead to gather information, and he actually reached the first of the seven cities. For the Indians of the town, who presumably had never seen people of another race, the appearance of a black man claiming to be the messenger of white men was too much to believe and Estevan was killed.

Fray Marcos on hearing the news of Estevan's death contented himself with gazing on the city from a distance before making a hasty retreat. His report seems to have been the basis of Coronado's expedition in 1540. The tradition of Estevan's death lingered on in Indian lore. Apparently Fray Marcos cited the murder as his excuse for conducting his own investigation from a neighboring hill. It seems generally to have escaped notice that to the murdered Negro, and not to the more cautious friar, belongs the honor of having discovered the fabled, if ultimately disappointing, city.

Both "black men and red men" were with Coronado when he set out on the famous expedition in 1540. That there were a considerable number of Negroes in the New World at this time is suggested in reports of Negroes in Mexico who "elected a king," of Sir Frances Drake's Alliance with a "tribe of self-freed Africans," and of John Hawkins' use of a Guinea Negro, educated in Portugal, as an interpreter. Negroes also played a role in the settlement of Brazil and other Latin American countries and in the West Indies. It is possible here to deal only with Negroes in what is now the United States.

As we have already noted, the Negroes brought to the American colonies came mainly from West Africa where there were many skilled workmen. It seems likely that the slaves represented a fair cross-section of native life. The rich and more powerful were likely to escape unless they were prisoners of war. But at the lower end of the scale, the traders rejected the obviously unfit, many died enroute, and the whole process was highly selective. Certainly some of the slaves were well-born and it has been estimated that perhaps as many as one percent spoke—and some of them wrote—Arabic.

Note has already been taken of the "Black Gentlemen" who visited England and the Continent as guests or wards of the slave trading companies. One black gentleman by the name of Job ben Solomon was brought as a slave to Maryland. Ironically, young Job had gone to the River to sell two of his father's slaves when two Mandingo Negroes kidnapped both him and the two slaves and sold them to the slaver. Job was able to read and write Arabic and, through a series of incredible but well-documented episodes, he was ransomed and taken to England. He was returned to his homeland through the efforts of what he later called his "dear friends," the Royal African Company which had long held the monopoly of the British slave trade.

The first Negroes in the American colonies were probably sold as indentured servants rather than as slaves, and four years after the first Negroes arrived, Negro church members were reported in the settlement. Some thirty years later there were free Negroes in the colony—one of them, Anthony Johnson by name, had land assigned him. He is known to have had servants of his own because another Negro accused Johnson of holding him in indenture "longer than he should or ought." Johnson won the case, and it thus appears that in one of the earliest records we have of a legal decision confirming life servitude in the colonies, both owner and owned were Negroes.

In evaluating the role of Negroes in American life it should be remembered that they came under the handicaps of an alien culture, alien religion, and alien language, of a different race, and under bondage. By the close of the colonial period there were some fifty or sixty thousand "free persons of color" in the States. Among these persons were some of exceptional ability, and even among those who were still slaves there were individuals who were able to overcome to some degree the handicaps of their bondage. Limitations of space preclude any discussion of the role of the exceptional Negro. Books dealing with these persons are listed in the Notes and References for this chapter. The purpose here is to point out some of the contributions made to our national life by the Negro peoples as a whole.

For the most part the contributions made by Negroes fall into the same general categories as those made by white persons. There have been, and are, novelists, poets, actors, musicians, painters and sculptors, doctors, lawyers, preachers and teachers, chemists, biologists, historians sociologists, and psychologists as well as businessmen, and other workers at all levels. Moreover, Negroes have served in all American wars and in spite of segregation and discrimination, they have done so with the same courage and loyalty as other Americans.

There are, however, certain areas in which Negroes have made distinctive contributions without which American culture would be much poorer. The most familiar of these contributions have been in the arts. The United States is a relatively new country and almost its only claim to indigenous folk material is that created by Negroes. Our heaviest debt is in the fields of music, folklore, and the dance. The Uncle Remus stories were straight out of Africa, and numerous other Negro folk tales are now being collected. In music there are the work songs, the blues, ragtime, jazz, rock, and the spirituals. In recent years, as racial barriers have weakened, an increasing number of Negroes have found their places in opera, on the stage, and as entertainers on radio and television, and in movies.

Negroes have also excelled in boxing, baseball, basketball, track, tennis and in a variety of other sports where racial barriers have been less a hindrance than in some other fields.

Given the circumstances, it was inevitable that the Negroes' chief contribution was in the form of manual labor. In an earlier day in the absence of machinery the country could have been developed only as human beings were available to do the heavy labor necessary. Although we honor the pioneers who endured toil and sacrifice to open up the frontier, the equally important toil of black men is often discounted by whites and disparaged by Negroes. The fact that the Negroes had no choice in coming to this country and that most of them did not labor as free men makes greater, not less, the country's debt to them for the part they played in laying the foundations of our economic life.

The American colonists were unable to force the Indians to work for them. The Indians were on their own home ground and had the advantage over the Europeans both in their knowledge of the territory and in their numbers. The African Negroes were unfamiliar with the land and were too conspicuous by their color to escape easily. Many of the Negroes had been relatively skilled workers in their home territories, some were familiar with the care of animals, and all were accustomed to the discipline of daily responsibility.

Langston Hughes in one of his poems boasts of the black man's service to mankind throughout history, "I've been a slave," he writes, and goes on to say that he built the pyramids, kept Caesar's doorstep clean, brushed the boots of Washington, and made the mortar for the Woolworth building. These may have been lowly tasks but they were very necessary ones. There are people who claim that this is a white man's country and that Negroes must "earn the right" to be considered first class citizens. If we are to base rights on the activities of one's ancestors, as many of these people seem to do, then there is no group in the United States that has more fully earned such rights than the Negroes. Except for the Indians, their ancestors were among the earliest Americans. As James Baldwin reminds us, "if the Negro had not done all that totin' of barges and liftin' of bales, America would be a very different country and it would certainly be a much poorer country."

There is another contribution that is generally overlooked. We are frequently reminded that nowhere else in the world has any large Negro population advanced more rapidly in education and economic status than have American Negroes. This is true, but the implication usually is "see how good white people have really been to you." Actually, nowhere else in the world have Negroes done so much for other Negroes. In most areas of the world where Negroes are in the economic if not the numerical minority, a Negro who rises to the top usually ceases to be a Negro in the sense of maintaining identification with the black masses. He has sometimes become a part of an intermediate buffer group as was formerly the case in South Africa, or for all practical purposes, he may become identified with whites as in Brazil and in the French territories. He then often has felt no more obligation to the Negro masses than any other member of the white community. It was a sort of brain drain out of the Negro masses.

In the United States a Negro has usually been defined legally and socially as anyone admitting to, or known to have, a Negro ancestor, and some form of segregation was found almost everywhere. Therefore, no matter what the education, social, or economic achievement of persons so identified, their lot was in large measure cast with the Negro group. As a consequence the educated and more economically secure Negroes became the leaders and the champions of Negro opportunities and Negro rights. They have thus played an extremely important role in uplifting and upgrading those Negroes still burdened with the aftermath of bondage. As preachers, teachers, lawyers, doctors, editors, and business men, these leaders have pulled and tugged at the Negro masses and have, through various organizations and agencies as well as by individual effort, sought to secure for all Negroes a chance to become self-supporting and self-respecting participants in the national life. This is not to ignore the existence of class distinctions among Negroes or the fact that some privileged Negroes have sought to dissociate themselves from their lowlier, and often darker, brother. But countless men and women, from important national leaders to local ministers and teachers, have had an enormous influence in uplifting the Negro masses and in so doing have contributed to the general welfare of the nation.

There was a time when it was assumed that Negroes could do little for themselves. They were in fact often denied the opportunity of exercising either the rights or the duties of citizenship. They were not allowed to vote, to serve on juries or school boards or even to patrol their own neighborhoods as policemen. In the South they were dependent on their "white friends" to plead their cause and the price of survival was often servility, or as Paul Lawrence Dunbar put it "the wearing of the mask" that hid their real feelings. Later it was recognized that Negroes could make a contribution to Negro life. Only within recent years have both whites and Negroes begun fully to appreciate the fact that the latter could make a contribution to the community as a whole.

As women have often been inhibited by their consciousness of themselves as women, Negro scholars and artists have often been so conscious of their Negroness that they had little freedom to express themselves as persons. Only when all racial barriers are removed can Negroes be at leisure from themselves and thus free to make their full contribution as citizens of, and to, the total community.

The Way
We Came

1. The Relevance of History

In a world of rapid change many people feel that the past is irrelevant. But the past is always prologue to the present and we can fully understand our differences only as we come to know how these differences arose and why our maps of reality vary so greatly. History must constantly be rewritten not because the facts of history change but because contemporary accounts are always affected by the perceptions of the people who record them, and the perceptions of the historians of any period are influenced by the cultural milieu within which they operate.

There is also the tendency to read history backwards, that is, to project into the past ideas, attitudes, and values that emerged only at a later date. We have seen how this pattern affected our conceptions of Africa and how it played a part in distorting the role of Negroes throughout history. Much of our own history is distorted in the same way. Many white people of the South cherish the illusion of a time when the land was filled with kindly masters and contented slaves, and they read back into the history of their region a "southern way of life" that really was the way of only a very few of its most privileged members. Many white northerners once indulged in a self-righteous supposition that only the South was prejudiced—a supposition that was rudely shattered when the black masses changed from southern sharecroppers into northern ghetto dwellers. Many Negroes compare the history of black people not with the white poor, who always outnumbered the black poor, but with the more privileged white minority. Militant black youth read back into history their own angry impatience with discrimination and cannot believe that any black slave ever felt kindly toward a white master, or that any white person could ever have been just and honest in dealing with blacks.

This chapter then is an attempt to lift out from our past as a people some of the major factors that helped to make us what we are today, and that account in some measure for our differences. It can, of course, be only selectively interpretive, and the reader who wishes really to understand how we got this way should read not only the histories written from different points of view but also the biographies, especially the autobiographies, of the persons who played significant roles in the making of our history. A number of such histories and biographies are listed in the Notes and References for this chapter.

2. The Black Thread

In his *Epic of America* James Truslow Adams speaks of the landing of the twenty Negroes at Jamestown in 1619 as the beginning of the black thread that has run through our destiny. We have already noted that these were not the first black men on the soil of what is now the United States, but apparently they were the first ones who became a part of the American people.

A number of geographic, historical, social, and economic factors entered into the development of the slave pattern, the definition of what constitutes a Negro, and the position accorded the black man in our history. The way the black people were brought to America, the background from which they came, the nature of the slave trade, and the various conditions of settlement in the New World were all important factors that helped set the patterns of race relations that still affect us today. Some of these factors were discussed in earlier sections and their influence on the prevailing black image was noted.

Slavery was unimportant in the colonies for almost a century and such regulations as were made usually applied to slaves and servants alike. Many of these white servants had no more choice in coming to the colonies than did the Negroes. Some of them were "free willers" or redemptioners who sold their own services for a period of years to pay debts or for their transportation across the Atlantic, but others had been kidnapped or spirited aboard the ships by unscrupulous captains. There were children bound for service by their parents or guardians, and thousands of the children of the poor were kidnapped and indentured through no choice of their own. The colonies also became the dumping ground for criminals or persons imprisoned for debt, some of whom were described by the Virginia House of Burgesses as "the worser sort of people of Europe."

Throughout the early period there were notices of the sale at auction of white servants as well as Negro slaves, and both could be rented for a period of service. Long after the deportation of convicts from England ceased, the redemptioners continued to come. There were numerous advertisements of Irish servants to be sold on board the ship, and Washington once referred to the sale of a shipload of Germans. Sometimes Negroes and whites were sold from the same block. Samuel Sewall in 1714 advertised several Irish maid servants, an Irish man servant, and "four or five likely Negro boys."

Although the first Negroes seem to have been treated much as the white indentured servants were, there were various factors that operated to the Negroes' disadvantage. The white servant usually knew his master's language, and servant and master came from the same general cultural background. Frequently the servant had been trained for some trade or skill and, in any case, he was familiar with European housing, clothing, food, and general behavior. The white servant could generally be counted on to identify with the colonists in the event of Indian attacks or slave uprisings. At the end of his indenture he was frequently given a gun, tools, and sometimes land. Since he fitted into the general cultural pattern and lacked any physical badge of his former status, he was easily absorbed into the population and his origin was soon forgotten.

In contrast, the Negro came from a non-European culture, he was as ignorant of the master's language as the master was of any African way of speaking, and he knew nothing of European ways. Those brought from Africa were "heathen" and therefore not due the obligation that the white colonist felt toward a fellow Christian. Always there was the physical difference that not only set the slave apart but which prevented the freed Negro or his children from escaping the stigma of the slave status. Finally, as practically all Negroes known to the colonists were slaves, or the descendants of slaves, it was easy to assume that slavery was the natural and appropriate status for Negroes. It became increasingly difficult for the Negroes to gain their freedom. They had no advocate and no established protection under English law.

As a consequence of these and other factors there was an increasing differentiation in the treatment of the servant and the slave. The white person was seldom indentured for life, and in almost no case did the child of an indentured person take the status of the parent except for a period necessary to repay the master for care during the child's dependent years. Servants were taxed by the poll, and the contracts under which they served, not their persons, were listed as a part of the owner's estate. Slaves, on the other hand, came to be treated as chattels and might be sold or disposed of by will. More important, the children of a woman servant were free, whereas the children of a slave woman became the property of the person who owned the mother.

Another factor of importance lay in the reasons for settlement. The Spanish and Portuguese at first sent explorers and adventurers who came without their women. They either married or simply lived with Indian or Negro women, and they accepted their hybrid offspring as their own children. This was a continuation of the pattern already established in Spain, and especially in Portugal, where the position of an individual was determined more by his religion, education, and economic status than by his color.

These patterns were alien to the British colonists and in conflict with the purpose of their settlements. The English settlers came primarily to make homes. They either brought their wives with them, sent back home for brides, or bought the indentures of single women servants in order to take them as wives. If they were to achieve their ideal of establishing homes and community patterns like the ones they had known in England, they must not be swamped by an alien culture or have their children brought up by alien women.

With the increase in the number of Africans, the laws affecting them became more stringent. Intermarriage of whites and Negroes was frowned upon and ultimately forbidden, and a rigid taboo came to be held against the relationship of white women with Negro men. The relationship of white men with Negro women was not approved, but it was generally condoned if not too flagrantly open. These patterns although not deliberately planned and probably not fully understood, functioned to create a society in which white dominance was assured. The strong taboo against the relations of white women and colored men meant that practically all children of mixed ancestry were born to Negro mothers. And as interracial marriages were either forbidden or carried serious negative sanctions, such children were born out of wedlock and hence took the status of the mother. The whole pattern thus resulted in all persons of mixed ancestry being classed as Negroes, a pattern that persisted and became the foundation of a biracial social structure.

3. Race and Sectional Patterns

By the beginning of the eighteenth century, the attitudes toward slavery were closely correlated with geographic factors and the consequent social and economic needs of the colonies. The slave was least profitable in the New England area where the climate was severe and conditions led to the development of towns. It was here that the abolitionist movement was strongest, but the New Englanders were the slave carriers and owed much of their wealth to the slave trade. According to Lorenzo Greene, the wealth of many of New England's famed families came in large measure from the slave traffic. Cornelius Waldo, maternal great-grandfather of Ralph Waldo Emerson, Peter Fanueil, who gave Fanueil Hall to Boston, and George Cabot were only a few of the noted Bostonians whose fortunes came in part from the slave traffic. Brown University received its name from the Brown brothers who were slave merchants as well as gentlemen and scholars.

The middle colonies were settled by small farmers and traders, many of them German or Dutch, who worked alongside their servants. They found it more to their profit and liking to have white servants who would ultimately settle on land of their own and thus help along the "peopling of the country." This attitude toward slavery was reinforced by the presence of the Quakers who never felt easy in their minds about "traffic in men-body."

Granted a general acceptance of the institution of slavery and the availability of slaves, a slave system was practically inevitable in the southern colonies. The large grants of land, the type of settlers, the mild climate, the suitability of soil and climate for crops such as tobacco, rice, indigo, and cotton, which made profitable the year round use of unskilled labor—all of these led to an ever increasing slave population and a growing defense of the institution.

After the invention of the cotton gin in 1793, the United States soon became the most important source of raw cotton in the world, and there was a feverish rush to open up new lands and secure slaves. As the frontier swept south and west the differentiation between slave and free areas became increasingly marked. Two systems of labor, two economic patterns, and two organizations of society stood in competition for political and economic leadership of the nation. The northern states by their urban industrial organization were subject to the stimulation of outside contact. In the South, climate, geography, invention, habit, and historical accident had served to create a plantation pattern that shaped masters, slaves, and non-slaveholding whites to its own ends. The Negro, and the white South, which for so long controlled his destiny, were products not only of the slave system but of the plantation with which that system was intimately bound.

The North was prone to think of the South in terms of the slave owner, and to the South the North was typified by the abolitionist. As a matter of fact the slave owners were a small minority of the white population of the South, and the abolitionists were not only a minority in the North but were often regarded by their neighbors as fanatics if not fools. White mobs broke up abolitionist meetings in New York and Philadelphia, set fire to buildings, and fought off the firemen. Many eastern colleges were strongholds of pro-slavery feeling, and anti-slavery speakers were hissed at Harvard and hooted at by young law students. Some professors of theology in northern institutions justified slavery from the New Testament and held that slavery was an institution of God.

Although historians do not agree as to the role of slavery in precipitating the Civil War, there was certainly much more involved than the institution of slavery and the question of states rights. Whether consciously or not, the South fought to preserve its social structure and a way of life intimately bound with it. There were many white persons in the Confederacy who were opposed to slavery and undoubtedly most of the free Negroes were. Yet at the time of the Civil War there were nearly four thousand free Negroes who owned slaves. Some of this was "benevolent bondage," that is, the free Negro bought some relative, but many of the Negroes, especially the ones who owned large estates in Charleston and New Orleans, owned slaves for the same reason as the whites, and those in the cities sometimes profited by buying and selling slaves. On the other hand, two of the slave states fought on the Union side.

The dislike of slavery did not necessarily carry with it a concern for the slave, and the northern and western states had no notion of welcoming any number of freed Negroes. As late as 1866 only six of the northern states allowed Negroes to vote, and all except one of these were in New England where there were very few Negroes. Even after the freedmen of the South were enfranchised, a number of the northern states voted down proposals to extend the franchise to the relatively few Negroes within their own borders. In fact, until the Fifteenth Amendment was ratified in 1870, fifteen of the states that had fought on the Union side continued to restrict their suffrage to white males.

It was of the greatest significance to the Negro's future that even his freedom was handed to him by the back door. Both the emancipation and the subsequent enfranchisement of the freedmen were emergency measures, the first considered necessary for the winning of the war, the second, a political weapon for keeping the defeated South in subjection. Frederick Douglass said in 1865 that the Civil War was begun in the interest of slavery on both sides. The South was fighting to take slavery out of the Union, and the North was fighting to keep it in the Union,". . . both despising the Negro, both insulting the Negro."

W. E. B. DuBois in his *Black Reconstruction* held that to suppose the Union armies as a whole or the northern states as a unit were fighting primarily in the interest of human freedom is to cherish a romantic illusion. He said that the sentiment of many Union soldiers, especially those from the Middle West, was expressed in the marching song:

> To the flag we are pledged, all its foes we abhor
> And we ain't for the nigger, but we are for the war.

Unpleasant as this record is it should not be forgotten, for it can serve as a sober warning of the consequences of polarization in the nation today. Had freedom come to the slaves as the result of a fundamental sense of justice on the part of the majority of people in either North or South, the Negro's place in the nation might have been very different from what it came to be.

4. The Black Man's Burden

There has been much dispute about the role of the Negro throughout the period of slavery and during the time of war and Reconstruction. Some people have contended that Negroes were naturally servile and dependent, and that as slaves they were loyal and attached to their masters; that the "Black Mammy" often showed more devotion to her white charges than to her own children, and that the black woman often welcomed the sexual advances of white men and was proud of her half-white offspring. On the other hand, many Negroes today fiercely resent such an interpretation and insist that Negroes were always resistant to slavery, that they were in a constant state of rebellion and that they hated and despised their white masters.

We are much more likely to arrive at an approximation of truth if we remember several things. In the first place, neither whites nor Negroes were all alike. In the South they were caught up in a vicious and inhuman system, but within that system individuals had a certain latitude of behavior and both whites and blacks behaved in all sorts of ways. Some whites were brutal, cruel, and sadistic. Others were as decent as such a system allowed them to be. Some blacks were fiercely independent and preferred death to slavery. Many slaves on the Middle Passage took suicide as a way out, and there were certainly far more slave rebellions, insurrections, and "self-emancipations" than most people realize. There can be no question, however, that the majority of slaves who were born and brought up on the plantations made the best of their lot as inevitable, if not right. It is only when cultural alternatives are offered them that most people think of breaking away from their usual patterns. Negroes today who repudiate all the more accommodating slaves as "Toms" fail to realize that had they all been Nat Turners or Denmark Veseys, the black race in America would never have survived, much less multiplied.

This accommodation had nothing whatever to do with race. All human beings are in large measure molded by the culture in which they grow up, their specific position in the cultural setting, and the general social patterns of the time. Only the exceptional human being, whatever his race, is able to rise very far above his cultural milieu. Throughout human history, the prophets and seers have moved ahead of their time, but ordinary people, black or white, have tended to adjust to realities and to accommodate themselves to the roles assigned them. In all societies human beings tend to develop personal relationships appropriate to their positions in the system of which they are a part. For centuries what now appears as the subjugation of women was accepted by the great majority of women as the natural lot of their sex. As a matter of fact, they learned to use and exploit their subordinate position to their own advantage, and even today there are women who prefer it that way. Many slaves did likewise and until very recent times so did some Negroes, especially in the deep South. So, too, did many European peasants.

Those who think primarily of the fact that the slaves were often cruelly treated and were not paid for their labor miss the main point. The tragedy of slavery lay in what the system did to the minds of the whites as well as the blacks. Both W. E. B. DuBois and Frederick Douglass understood this. Douglass in *My Bondage and My Freedom* told of numerous injustices and unbelievable cruelties to slaves, but he also reported that his feelings "were not the result of any marked cruelty" in the treatment he received. As a child the only whippings he had were "such as any heedless and mischievous boy might get from his father" and he speaks of "the kind mistress at Baltimore who was almost a mother to me." He told of slaves from different plantations arguing about the relative kindness and superior qualities of their masters. They seemed to think, he said, "that the greatness of their masters was transferable to themselves. To be a slave, was thought bad enough; to be a poor man's slave, was deemed a disgrace indeed."

DuBois, who wrote endlessly of the evils of slavery, could also say, "The victims of Southern slavery were often happy; had usually adequate food for their health; and shelter sufficient for a mild climate. The Southerners could say with some justification that when the mass of their field hands were compared with the worst class of laborers in the slums of New York and Philadelphia and the factory towns of New England, the black slaves were as well off and in some particulars better off." He went on to say that their working hours and lack of education was little different from that of the English factory laborer or the Irish or German peasant and that in contrast with these free white laborers "the Negroes were protected by a certain primitive sort of old age pension, job insurance, and sickness insurance."

This is not to minimize the brutalities and injustices of the slave system but to put them in proper perspective. If the evils of slavery had been primarily a matter of physical abuse and economic deprivation, both blacks and whites would have recovered from the effects long ago. The real crime of slavery was what it did to the minds of men, and it is from this burden that the nation still suffers today.

Certainly most slaves wanted to be free and with the coming of the war many escaped to the Union armies. In the beginning, however, there was no guarantee of freedom if the Union armies won, and some free Negroes who had tried to enlist in the Union forces were refused. As the Union armies advanced and the idea of freedom spread, the slaves behaved in all kinds of ways. Some sided with the Union armies, others hid the family valuables and protected the master's family. Booker T. Washington, who remembered the coming of freedom, reported that the slaves who had been treated with anything like decency often cared for the families of their masters, grieved over those killed in battle, nursed the wounded, and even supported the indigent members of the former master's family after emancipation. DuBois said that "perhaps never in the history of the world have victims given so much help and sympathy to their former oppressors."

These perfectly human reactions varied with personal character and disposition, the quality of the relationship with the master, and the particular hopes held out by the Union soldiers. All of which is simply to say that the Negroes were human beings and that they behaved in perfectly human ways. If they had all behaved in the same way, or if there had been no accommodation to their status and no personal ties with the people with whom they had lived since infancy, they would have been unlike any other human group known to us.

5. After Freedom

Although the war resulted in settling the question of freedom, the conflict itself and the Reconstruction procedures enormously increased the problems of adjustment since they added bitterness, hatred, and economic ruin to the complete disruption of the social system. There is little agreement as to the real motives underlying Reconstruction policies, and in no area are the maps of reality more diverse.

Emancipation resulted in a complete disruption of the labor system in the South where climate, geography, invention, and historical accident had created a plantation pattern that dominated life in the region. The majority of the white people had owned no slaves, but the plantation owners had been in social, economic, and political control, and the attitudes and habits, laws and customs were dominated by the plantation pattern. The whole economic system was geared to slavery. Whereas the North had invested in factories and machines, the South had invested in land and slaves.

At the end of four years of grim Civil War, millions of white people bitter from defeat and millions of black people newly freed from slavery found themselves in a devastated land. Most of the fighting had been on southern soil and in many areas there were rainwashed fields, neglected homes, and financial ruin. Livestock and farm machinery had disappeared, and many railroads and public buildings had been demolished. Confederate money became useless and something to paste in scrapbooks. The people, black and white, were reduced to a "pitiable, primitive, almost barbaric level."

Had the slaves been white, and had they been freed by consent with compensation to the owners—as occurred in other parts of the world—it would still have taken generations to overcome the handicaps of ignorance and the stigma of inferiority or to achieve a satisfactory economic, educational, and social status. The poverty, the economic and social chaos in the South, the bitterness, hatred, and frustration incident to war and Reconstruction furnished the setting in which the Negroes began their new life. For the most part they had had little or no opportunity to handle money or to know the meaning of thrift or self-direction. The slave system had prevented the development of stable family life and had taken from parents the responsibility for their children.

Many household slaves and others who had been in more or less intimate association with the better class of white people had developed qualities of character which made them responsible citizens eager for education and self-improvement for themselves and their children. There were others who had known the white world only through their contact with ignorant and brutal overseers. When the external controls of the slavery system were removed, such persons frequently drifted to the cities to live in idleness and crime. It was inevitable that many of the newly freed slaves should carry over into freedom the patterns and habits that had been directly fostered by the slave system. In some measure, they were the kind of habits that characterize any people who are poor, ignorant, and untrained. In spite of the fact that every white person knew some Negroes who were honest, decent, industrious, and responsible, the tradition grew that all Negroes were dishonest, lazy, irresponsible, and immoral.

The social and economic conditions were such that some new way must be found by which the white and Negro people could earn a living. The white landowners were without money to pay wages and in need of labor. The masses of Negroes were landless and homeless and in need of work. The freeing of the slaves had not changed the crop system or the kinds of skills needed for growing cotton, tobacco, rice, or sugar cane, nor had the change in status affected the deeply ingrained habits of dominance and subordination or of ruler and ruled. The adjustment made was probably the only one possible under the circumstances. The former slave became a tenant of the type later known as a sharecropper.

This pattern of adjustment left the Negro sharecropper little better off economically than he had been under slavery. The system of "furnishing" whereby the planter provided the tenant with his house, tools, work animals, and even his food and clothing to be paid for later out of the tenant's share of the crop, left the sharecropper in psychic as well as economic dependence. Under such a system there was almost no opportunity to develop initiative, independence, foresight, or habits of thrift. Moreover, the raising of cotton demanded hand labor so that the women and children were also involved. In time white sharecroppers outnumbered the black ones, and for generations the South had a large population of black and white tenant farmers who lacked education, whose health was poor, and who literally lived a hand-to-mouth existence, never knowing until the crop year's end whether they would break even, come out still more deeply in debt, or, rarely, have a little extra to call their own.

Reconstruction can be thought to have ended in 1877 when the last federal troops were withdrawn from the South. But what was even more significant for the Negro was the fact that he was abandoned as a ward of the nation, and the country as a whole gave up any attempt to guarantee the freedman his civil and political equality. From 1877 to 1901 the Negro lost one right after another.

In his *Strange Career of Jim Crow*, C. Vann Woodward points out that, contrary to the common idea, segregation was not a primary characteristic of the period immediately following Reconstruction. The various factors are far too complex for any extended discussion here, but from roughly 1885 to 1915 one southern state after another succumbed to pressure for segregation laws that were not to be changed until the 1950s. Basically three things were involved. On one hand were the actual segregation laws requiring the separation of the races—it often amounted to exclusion of the Negroes—in schools, trains, waiting rooms, eating places, and almost every aspect of life. Along with this went disfranchisement brought about by various devices and subterfuges ranging from "grandfather clauses," to white primaries and literacy tests. And accompanying these was the old justification used for slavery, now revived and elaborated, of the Negro's racial inferiority and inability to participate fully in the white man's civilization.

These pronouncements on the inferiority of the Negro were as common in the North as in the South and were supported by the writings of many sociologists and psychologists as well as in the history and literature of the period. Moreover, they were matched by a succession of Supreme Court decisions that in effect curtailed the rights of the freedmen and enabled states and localities to enact repressive laws.

Woodward notes that the steady erosion of Negro rights was not due so much to a change in general feeling as it was to relaxation of the groups that had held such feelings in check. All the elements of fear, jealousy, hatred, and fanaticism were present in the South and in those areas of the North that came in contact with the black population. But these forces had been held in check by northern liberalism, the Southern radicals represented by the populist movement, and upperclass conservatives in the South who had opposed segregation laws as unnecessary and foolish. There were efforts on the part of Negroes themselves—and there were still efforts by some southern whites and northern philanthropists. But on the whole the North turned its mind to other things, and control in the South more and more moved into the hands of those who were determined at all costs to keep the Negroes "in their place."

6. From Sharecropper to Ghetto

The upheavals of the 1960s can be understood only in the light of earlier events. In 1910 nine-tenths of the Negroes still lived in the South, and nearly half of this number lived in the more than two hundred and fifty "Black Belt" counties in which Negroes constituted fifty percent or more of the population.

With the beginning of the First World War in Europe, the steady stream of immigrants to this country ceased, and many of those already here returned home to render military service. With this foreign labor supply cut off and an increased production of goods demanded by the war, the Negro became important to the industrial North because his labor was needed. Labor agents went south and shipped colored workers north by the carloads. From cotton fields and coal mines, steel mills, dock yards, and kitchens, they poured into St. Louis, Cleveland, Cincinnati, and Detroit, but most of all to Chicago and New York. They soon made Harlem the most populous Negro area in the world.

In the South, low wages, an unsatisfactory tenant and sharecropping system, the boll weevil, crop failure, lynching, disfranchisement, segregation, and poor schools all gave impetus to the movement. In New York, Harlem absorbed the incoming groups; there was relatively little friction, and Negroes ultimately acquired millions of dollars worth of property. In many other cities the conditions were not so favorable. The housing problem became acute, schools were overcrowded, and the whole school system was upset by the influx of children who had been in the poor, short-term rural schools of the South. White neighborhoods resisted the appearance of black families, labor difficulties arose, vice and crime increased, and many of the race problems thought to be peculiar to the South appeared in the North.

It was, however, not until the Second World War that the greatest mass migration from sharecropper to ghetto took place. Negroes had steadily lost ground during the depression years. In 1940 three-fourths of them were still in the South, the majority of them in the Southeastern states which had been designated by a President's Commission as the nation's number one economic problem. There was already underway a major social, economic, and mechanical revolution involving a change in farming practices that resulted in the steady displacement of the sharecroppers. These factors in addition to those associated with the war brought about a wholesale migration of Negroes to the cities where they were bottled up in the overflowing ghettos.

Nothing in their life in the rural South had fitted Negroes for living in an urban, industrial setting. The only schooling many of them had received was five or six months a year in a one- or two-room school without library or other facilities. Many of their teachers had themselves been the victims of poor schooling and limited cultural opportunities. The sharecropper cabins were bare of any of the things that would stimulate a child's imagination or encourage learning. Their diets were generally deficient in both protein and vitamins, and many of them had been the victims of hookworm and pellagra.

The cotton complex could not have been better designed to destroy initiative, ambition, and foresight, and it developed no transferable skills. Making the crop was a monotonous and laborious year round job that was profitable only if the hand labor of women and children was employed in the chopping and picking. For most families there was no way to get ahead even if there had been the will and ambition to do so. The cotton economy was always a debt economy, and the outcome could not be predicted until the crop was made and sold. There were always the hazards of the weather, the boll weevil, and the unpredictable price of a non-edible commodity sold in an international market. If you raised pigs or potatoes you could at least eat what you did not sell. If the price of cotton plummeted, there was nothing for either landlord or tenant. Often the landlord himself operated on money borrowed at an exorbitant rate of interest which was passed on to the tenant. So when mechanism pushed him off the farm, the sharecropper was without education or job skills useful elsewhere, and with none of the experiences, practices, or habits essential for successful urban living.

Of course not all southern Negroes were sharecroppers, but the great majority of those who moved to the northern ghettos had been unskilled workers in agriculture, in day laboring jobs, or in domestic and personal service. Almost all of them had been the victims of poverty, poor schooling, lack of cultural opportunities, and limited medical services.

Other immigrant groups, even with a language handicap, had pulled themselves up from the ghetto, and the question is often raised as to why the Negro could not do it too. But circumstances were entirely different. Aside from the handicaps just mentioned, there were others. The great influx of immigrant groups from other countries came at a time when there was a demand for unskilled labor and when "getting ahead" was primarily a matter of ambition, persistence, and hard work. Job training was often a matter of apprenticeship, and many of the immigrants had already developed skills that were usable in the new setting. Many had acquired habits of thrift and were used to urban living. They were often reasonably well educated even when they knew no English. Many were from stable, disciplined families that had "everything but money."

In contrast, the Negro migration came at a time when the demand was for skilled workers. Moreover, while there was often prejudice against the European immigrant, they were rarely, if ever, subject to the discrimination that confronted Negroes. The Negroes were usually denied admission to labor unions, were not admitted to apprenticeships, and were completely shut out from many jobs or paid lower wages than whites. When a Negro did make some advancement, he was often unable to move into a better neighborhood because of segregation and discrimination in housing.

7. 1954 and After

On May 17, 1954 the Supreme Court of the United States handed down a ruling to the effect that compulsory segregation of the races in public schools is a denial of the constitutional rights of Negroes. In a May 1955 decree the Court ordered the implementation of the 1954 ruling "with all deliberate speed." This latter decision permitted account to be taken of local conditions affecting the manner and timing of the carrying out of the Court's order. Lower federal courts as well as later rulings of the Supreme Court have interpreted the 1954–55 decrees as invalidating the existing state and other laws that had long made school segregation mandatory in seventeen states and the District of Columbia.

The most significant aspect of the Court's ruling was its official and specific recognition of the individual's right to be treated as a person, not categorized by the color of his skin or by the fact that one or more of his ancestors had a given racial origin. The Court had ruled that race is not a relevant factor in determining which public school a child may attend. By implication, therefore, the Court had said that race is not a relevant or permissible basis for classifying or categorizing individuals for purpose of defining or limiting their rights. Consciously or unconsciously, both whites and Negroes sensed that the issue was more than that of desegregation in education. The action was seen, therefore, as a direct challenge to a long established way of life.

The Court's ruling naturally aroused both hopes and fears. To many Negroes it appeared as a sort of second Emancipation Proclamation, in a sense really implementing for the first time the original one of almost a century before. To many whites, especially in the deep South, May 17 was referred to as "Black Monday," to be thought of as a day of infamy and betrayal. To the majority of thoughtful people, however, the Court's ruling seemed an inevitable next step. It was indeed, as many of its critics argued, based to some extent at least on the findings of psychologists and other social scientists. The Court had stated that it had at its disposal certain facts about human beings and human behavior not generally available to the Court that had made the "separate but equal" ruling of 1896. It is significant that the 1954 ruling was unanimous.

There had already been steps in the direction of desegregation. Everybody knew that the separate facilities were rarely, if ever, equal. The Court had ruled earlier in cases involving graduate schools that the state institutions must admit Negroes unless facilities and faculty in the separate Negro schools were actually equal. There had also been a number of Executive Orders, beginning with the Fair Employment Practice Act of the Roosevelt administration in 1941. Most notable and far reaching was President Truman's establishment of a Committee on Civil Rights in 1946 and his Executive Order in 1948 declaring it to be the policy of the President as Commander in Chief that there shall be equality of treatment and opportunity for all persons in the armed services without regard to race, color, religion, or national origin.

Following the Court rulings of 1954–55, neither Congress nor the

President took any initiative regarding the implementation of the order. Instead a large group of Southern senators and congressmen issued a statement known as the Southern Manifesto which, while careful to use the words "by lawful means," referred to the action of the Court in such terms as to be an open invitation to defy the law. While there was compliance in a number of states, others sought various ways to evade the law, and in the deep South there was open and official defiance.

Not until the governor of Arkansas ordered the National Guard to prevent the desegregation of a Little Rock high school in 1957 was there any executive action. Within the next two years the United States Congress finally took affirmative measures and passed four significant pieces of legislation dealing with voting rights, school desegregation, fair employment, and public accommodation. In the 1960s further action was taken by Congress, by Presidents Kennedy and Johnson, and by the Supreme Court, but not until 1970 were most of the segregation barriers removed. Even then the great majority of black children were still in segregated schools. When in 1969–70 Federal Courts began requiring immediate compliance, there were complaints from some communities about not being allowed "enough time." Negroes, however, felt that the "deliberate speed" had been mostly deliberate. A black child who entered the first grade in 1954 would have been through college before the ruling was implemented in many areas.

Although many white people complained of the Negro's "sudden demands" and deplored not only the violent actions of the late 1960s but the non-violent efforts that had preceded them, a look at the record shows two things. First, Negroes had been making their attitudes known for a long time in a reasonable and quietly understated way, and second, they had not only worked within the law but for more than ten years following the 1954 ruling, Negro leaders had managed to keep the protest non-violent. And they had done all this in the face of defiance of the law on the part of white officials, verbal violence of middle class whites, and physical violence at the hands of the cruder whites who sensed the generally permissive atmosphere.

One needs only to go back to the published record to realize that Negroes had long tried to communicate to the world what most whites were obviously unwilling to hear. It started long before this century with outspoken statements like Frederick Douglass' *My Bondage and My Freedom*, and Paul Laurence Dunbar's poem "We Wear the Mask." It was continued in the early years of this century with the writings of W. E. B. DuBois and, though in a gentler vein, of James Weldon Johnson. In 1929 Robert R. Moton, although writing from the South, spoke out bluntly, if politely, in *What The Negro Thinks*. Negroes know, he pointed out, that white people are expected to be "good citizens," but black people are supposed to be "good Negroes." He also made it plain that Negroes told white people only what they felt it expedient for whites to know and that whites who think they "know the Negro" are fooling nobody but themselves.

In the early 1940s a concerted effort was made by Negroes and some of their white colleagues to get across to the white world the Negroes' dissatisfaction with things as they were. Within a short period the Myrdal studies that resulted in the now classic *An American Dilemma*, along with a number of related monographs, were published. The American Council on Education's studies of Negro youth and The Office of Education-sponsored *National Survey of The Higher Education of Negroes* appeared. These were all joint efforts of white and Negro scholars that spelled out in more than a dozen volumes the story for anyone who wanted to know the truth.

There were also specific Negro efforts. In 1942 in Durham, North Carolina, a representative group of Negro leaders from the South set forth their interpretation of what the Negroes in the South wanted. They asked for a new "Charter of Race Relations" that included such things as the abolition of the poll tax and all-white primaries, the right to serve on juries, the use of Negro police in Negro neighborhoods, the equalization of salaries for white and Negro teachers of the same education and experience, equal length of school terms for white and Negro children, equality in the distribution of school funds, the admission of Negroes to hospitals and labor unions, equal pay for equal work, and the use of qualified Negroes on school boards.

Perhaps nothing could point up more clearly the deprivations of Negroes a generation ago than these "askings"—they were not listed as "demands"—which for the most part were things that white persons took for granted. While the men who wrote the report stated clearly their opposition to compulsory segregation, their "Charter" was based on the "separate but equal" concept because it represented a long step beyond the existing situation and it was the only goal that then seemed attainable in the immediate future.

A short while later in another publication entitled *What The Negro Wants* fourteen Negroes representing various shades of opinion and all sections of the country, gave their ideas of what Negroes wanted. The general point of view of the group was summed up in this fashion: "Negroes want to be accepted by our American society as citizens who in reality belong. Negroes want what good men want in every democratic society. If they wanted less they would not deserve the status of citizens."

White people in the 1960s who reacted with shock and surprise at growing Negro impatience and the increasing violence of the protest movement were seemingly unaware of two more efforts of older Negro leaders to head off the rising storm. In October, following the May 1954 decision, a group of nearly one hundred Negro educators and civic leaders met and drafted what they called "a statement of invitation to sober and intelligent cooperation" in working out the problems involved in the Court decision. Although the statement was released to the national press it was, as Charles Johnson remarked, "one of the most ignored public invitations on record."

In spite of the defiance of the Supreme Court ruling on the part of leading white citizens in the South and numerous acts of violence, the Negroes made still another effort. In January 1957 a group of Negroes from the South met in Atlanta. They expressed their faith in the law-abiding white citizens of the South and again offered their cooperation. "We cannot," the report stated, "in clear conscience turn back. We have no moral choice but to continue the struggle, not for ourselves alone but for all America." They called upon all Negroes to assert their human dignity and to reject segregation, but they were also urged, no matter how great the provocation, to dedicate themselves to the motto: "Not one hair on the head of one white person shall be harmed." But this offer, too, was ignored by the white world.

During the early 1960s the Negroes' struggle was centered on civil rights and the desegregation of public facilities. Integration was still the goal and there were still heroic efforts to keep the protests non-violent. But white people still failed to get the message. Massive white resistance continued in some areas, and there was increasing defiance on the part of southern governors and mayors. Police dogs and fire hoses were used to break up peaceful demonstrations that included the aged as well as women and children. Civil rights workers were murdered, and Negro homes, churches, and places of business were bombed or burned.

Martin Luther King's non-violent campaigns were the last chance for white people and they missed it. With King's leadership gone and with a "Now Generation" of young blacks who lacked both patience and experience, many Negroes turned away not only from non-violence but from the whole concept of an integrated society. Many of them were ready to pull down the walls of the Establishment even if they perished in the attempt. The older Negro leaders who had managed to keep the Negro protest non-violent were rejected by many whites and repudiated by many increasingly impatient and militant black youth. The northern ghettos exploded, and the black struggle became entangled with the revolt of youth, the war on poverty, and the war in Vietnam.

Two things should be remembered: One is that credit should be given to the long, patient, and often heroic efforts of the older leaders and the old established organizations such as the NAACP, the Urban League, and The Southern Regional Council. Without the pioneering work of these organizations, many of the present open doors would still be closed. The second is that the country owes a great debt to the Negro leaders who so long managed to keep the protests non-violent. Those who blamed Martin Luther King for leading marchers and, as they thought, "stirring up trouble," failed to realize the degree of unrest and bitterness among Negroes that, had it not been channeled in this way, would have erupted in violence long before it did. "Good" white persons have not accepted responsibility or blame for the actions of sadistic whites who have bombed and burned, driven Negroes out of newly bought homes, North and South, and who did not stop short of murder. Yet these same people have held all Negroes responsible for the violent reaction of ghetto dwellers and black youth who have despaired of achieving equality as citizens by peaceful means.

8

Race, Class, and Poverty

1. What Does It Mean To Be Poor?

Although the United States is today the richest nation the world has ever known, there are within its borders millions of individuals and families to whom poverty is a way of life. This poverty has become a major concern to everybody—to the poor themselves, to those who are always hovering on the borderline of poverty, and to the rest of the population who must carry the burden of those who are unable to care for themselves or be cared for by their families. Racial discrimination is a factor in poverty, and poverty has many ramifications in the problems of human relations. Any meaningful discussion of race relations therefore must involve a more general discussion of the problems of poverty.

Poverty is always relative. It is never merely the absence of things, and it cannot always be defined in terms of money. Some of our pioneer ancestors who pushed into the West lived for a time in sod houses that were not much more than large-scale burrows, and their clothing was sometimes made of animal skins. Many of them had fewer material things than the poorest poor of today. Yet they were not really impoverished in the sense in which we now use the term. Their way of life was chosen, not imposed by circumstances beyond their control; it was temporary; and it was a means to what they saw as a better life in the future for their children, if not for themselves. Thus whether or not one feels himself to be poor is an important factor in the impact of poverty. When a life far below that available to the majority of people is forced upon one there is a feeling of being poor even though one may have more than he once did.

Moreover, the previous experiences and inner resources of the people involved are important to any definition of poverty. Many European immigrants who came to this country were able to have a reasonably good life in spite of material hardships. The kind of poverty that afflicts millions of people today in the United States, as well as elsewhere in the world, bears no resemblance to the poverty of these immigrants, or to the "genteel poverty" of once well-to-do families who have come upon relatively hard times. Nor does it have anything in common with voluntary poverty which involves a choice in what one shall do without. Modern poverty is degrading not only because the poor lack the essentials of a decent life but also because there is no choice.

There are different estimates of the levels of income by which poverty in the United States should be defined. The specific figures chosen are not important to the overall picture. For the purposes of this book, people may be considered poor when they are unable to meet their own basic needs of food, clothing, shelter, and medical care at a level that enables them to be self-sustaining and productive members of the community.

It is true that the poorest of American poor are much better off in a material sense than the impoverished in many parts of the world. We do not have the swarms of beggars that fill many cities of the world; there are no people who regularly sleep on sidewalks or in the doorways of our cities; and there is no mass starvation. But in whatever terms we define poverty, there are millions of Americans who are living at levels of deprivation that prevent them from being productive members of the community. There are other millions who live just this side of poverty with no margin of safety.

Poverty almost always means malnutrition with a long train of consequences. Contrary to popular ideas, there are millions of Americans to whom hunger is a way of life. One of the directors of the Tuft's New England Medical Center called the health of the poor in this country "an ongoing national disaster." Poor Americans are four times as likely to die before the age of thirty-five as the average citizen. The lack of prenatal care of the poor increases the likelihood of premature births, and mental retardation occurs ten times more often in small premature babies than those born at full term.

There is also shocking malnutrition among the children of the poor. A survey of 12,000 poor people in four states representing the East, South, Upper South and Southwest, showed one in three children under six to be anemic and showing other effects of inadequate protein and vitamin intake, with black children the chief sufferers. Kwashiorker, once thought to occur only in underdeveloped countries, was found in some places along with scurvy, rickets, and parasitic infections. There is reason to believe that this continuing inadequacy is associated not only with infant mortality but with mental retardation. The mentally retarded then add to the list of the permanent poor, and such persons may themselves become the inadequate parents of the future.

The poor must always live hand-to-mouth. Thus any small crisis can precipitate larger ones and spread as ripples in a pond. Frequent illness keeps the children out of school, thus increasing the likelihood that they will get behind and ultimately drop out. Even with free clinics, the family may lack bus fare or the money to get prescriptions filled. There may be nobody to leave the other children with while the mother seeks medical help for herself or a sick child. Or a trip to the clinic may mean loss of wages for the day. The sort of problems handled routinely by persons with adequate incomes become major crises in the lives of the poor who have no margin.

The poor pay more for goods and services than do other people. Rents charged for slum housing unfit for human use are sometimes two or three times the rent charged for decent housing in other neighborhoods. According to one consumer report, most of the household articles in Washington's low income neighborhoods were often from one-third to twice the price of the same or better merchandise elsewhere. There is no reason to suppose that the situation is significantly different in other cities. In low income areas, shop windows filled with television sets, furniture, and clothing, offered on easy terms that conceal their inflated prices, are a constant temptation to the poor and uneducated who are least able to understand the factors involved. When they get behind with their payments—and any minor crisis can lead to this—the merchant may repossess the goods even though two-thirds of it may have been paid for, and he may then continue to collect for the full amount. Other creditors may garnishee the debtor's wages, thus leaving nothing for necessities, and the garnishment may result in the loss of an all too precariously held job.

The loan shark preys even more heavily on the poor. The borrower not only pays an exorbitant rate to begin with, but there is often an added fee for investigation and insurance. When the note comes due it is often "flipped," a device by which the borrower pays over and over for "investigation" and insurance by having these costs added each time the note is renewed. In the end many persons find themselves paying two or three times the original amount of the loan. Congressional investigations have found that organized crime gets a big piece of the income from loan sharking. Threats of injury or death to persons who fail to pay up are not uncommon and make it difficult to get people to testify in court about their treatment at the hands of loan sharks.

To be really poor then means there is never enough food, clothing, or medical care. It means living in run down tenements or in shacks in which there is no plumbing or in which the plumbing fails to work. It often means stifling heat in summer and bitter cold in winter. It means crowded quarters and no privacy. It means utter dependency with no control over one's own life. It means long bus rides to a clinic where one may wait all day and then be told to come back tomorrow. It means waiting in welfare offices and being asked probing questions about one's personal life. It sometimes means burning the light all night to keep rats from biting the baby. It means going down, not up. It means that one lacks the power to cope. It means life without hope and, in the words of the Indian proverb, "Life without hope is like nectar in a sieve."

2. Who Are the Poor?

There is a widespread belief that the majority of the poor are able-bodied people who are just lazy and don't want to work, women who bear children out of wedlock or who have babies just to get welfare checks, and that most of them are black. Actually, none of these suppositions is borne out by the facts, though obviously some persons in each of these categories will be found among the poor. The majority of persons who are poor either do work, or they are unable to do so because of conditions beyond their control. And while a higher proportion of Negroes than whites are poor, in actual numbers the white poor far outnumber those who are black.

The largest single category of the poor is made up of people who are too old, too young, too sick, or too disabled to work, and the people who are tied down by the necessity of caring for the old, the young, the sick, and the disabled. It is estimated that more than eight million of the poor are over sixty-five. Over a third of the poor are children who might be said to have had the misfortune to be born of the wrong parents. Sometimes the parents are ignorant, unskilled, ill, or disabled; sometimes the family is broken by death, divorce, or desertion. Sometimes there are too many children in the family and there isn't enough to go around. In any case the poverty cannot by any stretch of the imagination be the fault of the child. Among poor adults, about a third have themselves suffered a disability, or there has been the premature death of the breadwinner or a breakup of the family.

A second category is made up of people who are not equipped to fill available jobs. Many of these people live in the areas where mines, mills, or factories have closed, or where farms have been mechanized leaving the sharecroppers stranded. Often when these people move elsewhere they find no market for their old skills, and many of them, because of limited education or other factors, are unable to acquire the new skills necessary. Some of them have simply been "deskilled" by automation and the increasing complexity of our technology.

A third category is made up of people who are able and willing to work but who are unable to find jobs. It is a popular illusion among the affluent that anybody can get a job who wants one. They point to the "Help wanted" signs in shop windows and in newspaper ads, or they cite their own inability to get a maid or some one to do odd jobs. All too often though, the better paying jobs call for skills the unemployed do not have, and the jobs open to the unskilled may be so irregular, so poorly paid, or so distant from the unemployed person's home that they offer no solution. Moreover, there are a variety of artificial barriers to employment over which the individual has no control. There are barriers of race, sex, age, residence, religion, education, and seniority. There are some jobs open only to members of unions and some jobs obtained only by apprenticeship which may be highly restricted in favor of those already on the inside.

The fourth category is made up of people who for various reasons have simply given up and who have escaped into lives of crime, delinquency, narcotics, alcoholism, mental illness, or chronic dependency. They, indeed, "won't work." They have lost, or never had, aspiration, hope, ambition, or the ability to manage their own lives. Some of these persons are youths who have grown up in a ghetto where the "successful" people are not the hard—and low paid—workers, but the dope peddlers, gamblers, bookies, or others who live by their wits. Affluent families also have their quota of alcoholics, drug addicts, and irresponsible individuals, but these persons can be kept out of the public eye and do not usually become public charges. The unfortunate poor have no such protection.

There is a fifth category that often involves one or more of the others, but it may in itself be an effective barrier to employment, that is, minority status. Although this pattern began to change in the late 1960s, it is still true that to be an Indian, a Mexican-American, or Puerto

Rican, and more especially a Negro, often means that there is an additional block to entry to the labor market. The special problems of the black poor will be treated more in detail in a later section.

Far more numerous than is generally supposed are the working poor. It is estimated that almost fifty percent of poor families are headed by a person who works regularly and for long hours, but whose wages are too low to maintain a decent standard of living. Often they are employed in jobs that pay by the day or the hour. Such workers not only lose wages for any days they are sick but also for holidays or days when bad weather makes outdoor work impossible. Such workers generally do not get vacations with pay, and if business is slack they may be "laid off" for days, in which case their income stops.

Some of the working poor once were able to earn an adequate wage but are now too old to do heavy work or to adjust to jobs requiring new skills. Many of them are women who are the sole support of their families, and almost all of them have too many people to support. The poor tend to have large families—this is in part at least a function of their poor education and of poverty itself—and they often help support, either temporarily or permanently, other relatives who are unable to care for themselves. In spite of the increase in welfare loads, there are large numbers of the poor who for one reason or another do not receive any public assistance, and many of these persons are cared for by relatives who are among the working poor.

The poor are generally invisible. Those who live in rural areas are often in isolated places. They are migrant workers, people on Indian reservations, in mountain coves, abandoned mining towns, "the left overs" from the old sharecropping cotton areas, or "turpentine camps" on pine-tree plantations. The shacks of the rural poor do not show up from a jet plane, and they are not visible from the highways and even if they were, would not be noticed by people in cars that are speeding by at sixty-five or seventy miles an hour. The city poor are crowded into ghettos of the central city, again out of sight of the more affluent people who have taken to the suburbs. It is easy to forget about, or be impatient with, people who are nameless, faceless statistics, and who take on meaning only as we think of the effect of poverty programs on our taxes.

3. The Cycle of Poverty

The saying that money breeds money can be matched with an equally true statement that poverty breeds poverty. Many families have been on welfare for generations. Although there is no agreement about the usefulness of the concept of culture—or more properly subculture—of poverty, the studies and formulations of Oscar Lewis offer insights into what is meant by the cycle of poverty. Once such a pattern comes into existence it tends to be perpetuated from generation to generation because of its effect on the children. By the time children are six or seven years old, they have usually absorbed the basic values and attitudes of their subculture and are not psychologically geared to take advantage of changing conditions or increased opportunities.

The reasons for this seem fairly obvious. With no example of the importance of education before them, and with no stimulation at home, these children enter school totally unprepared for a learning experience. They soon drop out or cease to learn altogether. Most of them are further handicapped by inadequate nutrition. A child who had only boiled cabbage for last night's supper and no breakfast is hardly likely to learn much even if he is motivated. He is likely also to suffer illnesses that often are induced by poor sanitation and other factors.

In one city a woman known simply as Willie Mae, long since deserted by the only man to whom she had been married, lived with her unmarried daughter in a shack unfit for human habitation. The two women had borne a total of fourteen children by various fathers, their only source of livelihood for all of them being a welfare check that barely kept them alive. To say that such people are immoral, lazy, irresponsible, and unwilling to work gets us nowhere until we begin to ask how people get that way. When we see these children growing up in the condition in which they now live, we know that unless there is some drastic social intervention they will repeat the pattern. Willie Mae and the daughter have moral standards by their own definitions. They know nothing of birth control and they think abortion is murder. Both women profess to love their children and have refused to give any of them up for adoption to people who could give them better care. How could the Willie Mae's, themselves reared under similar conditions, have developed a sense of responsibility, sexual restraint, ambition, or work habits and skills that would enable them to provide for themselves, much less be responsible for other human beings?

As people become more aware of the white poor and of the fact that poverty is not going to just disappear, however prosperous we get, many people come to think that the white poor, as well as the black, are mentally inferior and that it is wasteful to give the poor, especially if they are both poor and black, the same quality of education in the same schools as the more privileged, and supposedly more intelligent children.

Actually, of course, there is no proof that whole categories of people are born inferior. Certainly heredity plays a role in mental competence, and some individuals are clearly of lesser ability than others. However, almost everything in this book points to numerous factors, not inherent in the individual's makeup, that affect his lifetime potential, and new evidence is constantly appearing. Malnutrition of the pregnant woman, poor nutrition in infancy and early childhood, the lack of a stimulating environment even in early infancy, lack of motivation, the self-fulfilling prophecy, and the stigma of inferiority—these and numerous other factors are already established as causes of retardation and the consequent inability to become a self-sustaining member of society.

Among other less well known factors affecting the children of the poor are lead poisoning and visual defects. It is estimated that as many as a quarter of a million children each year get lead poisoning from ingesting the flaking and peeling lead-based paints found in the old houses and furniture in slum tenements. The poisoning leads to mental retardation and other neurological handicaps that cause the affected children to be written off as retarded or slow learners. Other children are presumed to be retarded when their real problem is defective vision. In one poverty area over sixty percent of the supposedly retarded children had visual defects serious enough to impair their ability to learn. Some of them could not even see the writing on the blackboard.

It is obvious to anyone who takes a close look at the permanent poor that if the cycle is ever to be broken, something must be done about the children—not only to protect those that are born to poor parents but to reduce their number. One of the characteristics of the poor family is the large number of children, but the notion that the poor want large families and have children just to get welfare checks is not borne out by the studies made. Most of the families interviewed did want children but not the five or six or even eight and ten often found among the poor. In some cases they did not know how to limit their families; some thought it was wrong to do so; many simply lacked the self-discipline for consistent birth control practices.

The poor are not necessarily less "moral" than the more affluent, although they may well have different ideas as to what constitutes morality. The sexual practices of many middle-class persons hardly leave them in a position to lecture the poor to whom sex may be the only pleasure available. The lower-class girl, particularly the lower-class black girl, is more likely to become pregnant, to bear the child, and to keep it or leave it with a relative, than is the middle-class girl who uses a contraceptive and, if she should become pregnant, either obtains an abortion or retreats to a home for unwed mothers and gives up the child for adoption.

Breaking the cycle of poverty will not be easy. The really poor have so many strikes against them that the hope of their being able to do anything about their own problems is unrealistic. Such factors as general ignorance, lack of education and training, poor health, and lack of incentive or motivation are all interdependent, and they are cumulative in that parents who are poor, ignorant, untrained and unmotivated bring up children who learn these things as a way of life. Moreover by our methods of dealing with poverty we practically guarantee that it will not only continue but increase.

For a civilized nation, and especially the world's most affluent nation, to allow millions of children to be brought into the world and grow up under conditions that practically guarantee that they will never become effective human beings or productive members of the society seems incredible. Many of these children are doomed before they are born because of the malnutrition of their mothers. Apparently it is much simpler to write off people as naturally inferior than it is to get at the basic social factors that prevent the poor and the deprived from realizing the potential that is there.

4. Race as a Factor in Poverty

Although the cards are clearly stacked against the poor in general, the black man has all the handicaps of his white counterpart plus a great many that are peculiarly his own.* Other sections of this book point up the manifold ways in which segregation and discrimination have served to stand in the way of the Negro's normal participation in American life. Here we need only summarize some of the ways in which prevailing racial patterns have helped to keep the great majority of Negroes poor. There are, of course, Negroes who have achieved middle-class status and middle-class incomes, a few have become affluent, and many are better off financially than the whites with lowest incomes. The fact remains that circumstances beyond their control have strongly affected the Negroes' economic status.

With the exception of a few free Negroes and more favored slaves, the majority of the black population entered the nation as citizens in the 1860s with limited skills, no material possessions, no economic resources, no formal schooling, and no jobs. Such deprivations are cumulative, for each generation suffers from the handicaps of the parents who bring them up. Even today Negroes average fewer years of schooling than whites, and what they have is often of poorer quality. There is

*The cards are stacked against all minority groups including Indian and Mexican-Americans and Puerto Ricans. Because this book is primarily concerned with the relations of white and Negro it is the Negro's handicaps that are given attention here.

still serious job discrimination in many industries, and blacks have been almost completely shut out from some apprentice programs. Many labor unions have excluded Negroes or accepted them only in token numbers. The great majority of Negroes live either in the South where opportunities are limited or in Northern ghettos that are far removed from the places where the jobs are.

Negroes suffer not only from unemployment but from underemployment, that is, many of them are employed at wages so low as to leave them below the poverty line, no matter how hard they work. The minority poor are "hired last, paid less, and fired first." Even in the late 1960s the unemployment rate for blacks was generally twice as high as that for whites. Among teen-agers in central cities the rate for white youth reached as high as twelve percent, but for black youth it rose to thirty percent. For every dollar an employed white male earned, his black counterpart was paid only eighty cents. The same discrepancies existed in wages paid black women and youth. The discrepancy was actually greater the higher the level of education. The college educated Negro has generally earned less than half the amount of the white college graduate. In fact, until very recently the Negro college graduate could expect to earn on the average only as much as the white person who left school after the eighth grade.

A high proportion of the black poor work hard and for long hours. It is the concentration of black men in low paying jobs rather than unemployment that keeps them and their families in poverty. Many of these persons would actually be about as well off on the welfare rolls as they are working full time at the menial jobs available to them. Although as we have noted, the white poor far outnumber the black poor, the proportion of blacks in poverty is three times as high as that of whites. As will be indicated later, this fact affects the income of Negro business and professional men and has important ramifications throughout the Negro community.

Educational facilities for Negroes are still inferior not only in most southern states but in northern ghettos as well. The black child's chance of finishing high school is less than that of the white child and, as will be noted later, he not only stands a poorer chance of getting into college but is more likely to attend a college of inferior quality. Health also remains an important factor. In the 1960s Negroes could expect to live something like eight years less than whites. This shorter life expectancy has serious consequences in depriving the Negro family of a parent and in the erosion of lifetime earnings growing out of the shorter life span.

Apart from the continued discrimination in employment, Negroes suffer the most economic deprivation in housing. Because of segregation and racial bias, there are really two housing markets—a free one for whites and a very limited and restricted one for Negroes. Senator Javits in his book *Discrimination USA* reported that as a result of discriminatory practices less than two percent of all FHA financed housing has been available to Negroes, yet in urban renewal sixty to seventy percent of the displaced families were non-white.

The black man is blocked at every turn. In the typical ghetto situation he pays an exorbitant rent for substandard housing. Unlike his white counterpart he cannot buy or rent a house or apartment just anywhere even if he had the means. His job opportunities are limited by racial barriers and by the cost and time involved in getting from his ghetto residence to the places where jobs are available. The churches and schools available to his children are generally poor, and recreation and cultural facilities are closed to him by custom, if not by law, and are generally too far away to be of much use.

Many of these ghetto dwellers, or their parents, were earlier victims of discriminatory agricultural practice. With the mechanization of farms, the unskilled agricultural worker and the sharecroppers were forced off the land. In 1960 more than forty percent of Negroes in the urban North and West were born in the South. The subsidies the Federal government paid (and still pays) to wealthy individual and corporate landowners did not include anything to relocate and teach new skills to these displaced workers who now make up many of the ghettos' unemployed or low-paid unskilled residents.

5. Poverty and the Affluent Society

Although the problem of poverty is ancient and practically universal, there is something particularly shocking in the fact that in the most affluent society ever known to man there should be millions of people who are ill-clothed, ill-housed, ill-fed, and lacking in adequate medical care. Poverty today is what has been called a structural problem. There is, of course, still an individual factor. Few people are completely pawns in a situation over which they have no control at all. But the less endowed—for whatever reason—are really trapped in an economy that has no place for them and which is controlled by forces beyond their reach.

No individual is responsible for automation or the changing patterns of industry that may cost him his job. He is not responsible for the structural patterns of our cities that have come about as the affluent move to the suburbs leaving the central cities to the poor. He is not always responsible for the fact that a good education was beyond his reach. He is not responsible for the changing social patterns that mean there are no longer relatives, friends, or neighbors able to help out in sickness or misfortune. He is not responsible for poor transportation, skyrocketing medical costs, the business cycle, depressions, or the general affluence that leaves him relatively poorer. He is not responsible for inflation which has robbed the dollar of its value and, if he is old, may have made the dollar he saved in his younger days worth forty cents or less in buying power in his old age.

Many of the factors that lead to poverty are pictured in other sections of this book: the structure of our cities that shut the poor, and especially the black poor, into ghettos while the more prosperous move into the suburbs; technological development that has not been matched by means to preserve the dignity and welfare of human beings; economic patterns that make rejects of the less efficient; educational systems that have left large numbers of persons without the basic tools for living in a literate and complex world; a judicial and penal system that has a built-in double standard and that actually fosters rather than prevents crime; a business system that discards workers at sixty-five, combined with a medical system that keeps people existing physically long after they have deteriorated in mind and spirit; and a welfare system that is punitive rather than preventive and reconstructive.

The real problem is not so much the deliberate cruelty of individuals, though of course this exists, but the cruelty of systems—political, economic, educational, judicial, penal, and cultural. Our social patterns and structure and our institutional arrangements are such that the poor and the not-poor live in different worlds, have different sets of experiences, and therefore different maps of reality. The problem is compounded in a multi-racial society when the members of minority groups are singled out as "they." For while the white poor sometimes can and do escape from poverty and become accepted as one of the not-poor, the people who are of a different physical appearance can never lose their group identity which is the source of the labels other people attach to them.

A major obstacle to the elimination of poverty is the punitive attitude toward the poor. It is as if we said: "if you are poor it must somehow be your own fault; therefore we will make life as difficult for you as possible so you won't be encouraged to go on being poor." We resent people who do not conform, who embarrass us, or who cause us trouble. This punitive attitude is not really directed toward reform or change but to see that people "pay the price" of their sins or their folly. This attitude is bad enough when directed toward criminals but we can at least rationalize that punishment may be a deterrent to crime. There is no such justification of the punitive attitude toward the unfortunate. The most inhuman aspect of the punitive attitude is that of punishing children as a means of control over the parents. This begins with the practice in many communities of refusing access to birth control information or contraceptives to unmarried women or those not living with their husbands. The rationalization is that to provide such information would be "encouraging immorality." But what we are really saying is that if a woman insists on "living in sin" we will punish her by forcing her to take the consequences, that is, to bear a child. Such punitive action neither protects the right of a child to be wanted and cared for nor the welfare of the society, because such children stand a good chance not only of becoming public charges but of becoming delinquent and ultimately criminal.

This punitive attitude also shows up in the feeling that the poor——regardless of the cause of their poverty—should not enjoy any of the good things of life that other people take for granted. They should not have children, and if they are ignorant of birth control methods or if they have been taught that such methods are wrong, they should refrain from a normal sex life. They should not have television sets—presumably they should sit in their crowded apartments, often unheated in winter and stifling in summer with nothing to do. In other words, the poor who have had less than the average of education, training, and guidance, and whose lives are generally barren, are supposed to exercise more self-control and are expected to be more moral than people of superior background and training who have access to a variety of stimulating and rewarding activities.

Among the indignities visited upon the poor are the methods used in the investigation and checking of their eligibility for public assistance. The now discarded rule that aid to dependent children could be granted only if their were no adult male in the house, even if unemployed, led to the desertion of families by men who were unable to get work. In some communities unannounced inspections were made, sometimes in the middle of the night, to make sure that the child was actually living with the mother and that there was "no man in the house."

Critics of these procedures pointed out that a high percentage of welfare costs went to employees, a major portion of whose time was spent checking on the eligibility and conduct of the welfare recipients. We accept a simple declaration on tax returns with only a limited number of audits, and it is generally conceded that most ordinary people are honest in their returns. In fact, tax evasion appears to be more common among the well-to-do than among the poor. Why then do we assume that the poor are less honest than other people? Undoubtedly some of them will cheat, but the takers from the public purse range up the entire social and economic ladder as is amply documented elsewhere in this book.

We maintain a double standard regarding the poor in other ways. We pay out billions of dollars in a variety of subsidies to business corporations and wealthy individuals from oil companies, shipping companies, contractors of various kinds, including payments to large landowners for not raising cotton and other crops. These subsidies have been justified as being for the public good though some of them have long since become merely handouts that it is politically inexpedient to end. Yet the idea of subsidizing the sharecropper displaced by automation, or the aged ruined by inflation, is regarded as a welfare handout that would encourage the poor to be lazy and irresponsible. The suggestion that if you could pay a wealthy landowner for not raising cotton why you couldn't also pay the poor not to have children was met with shock and disbelief.

There seems to be a good deal of evidence that many of the things supposed to aid the poor have been, in fact, a means of binding them more tightly in their chains. Labor unions have fought for the rights of workers, but have generally excluded the poorest of them especially if they were black. Minimum wage laws have excluded the people who needed protection the most. If a poor family on inadequate welfare tried to better their condition by taking any odd jobs available, the welfare payments were cut by the amount earned—a penalty of one hundred percent for trying. We built public housing and then put it out of the reach of the people who needed it most. In the 1960s we tried to halt inflation by means that admittedly would increase unemployment that we hoped could be held to "tolerable levels." But whatever the levels it meant that the poorest and least efficient workers were among those sacrificed. Some of them would go under for good, taking a whole family unit with them. The elderly were told that increasing social security would cause more inflation, but they were the ones whose savings for their old age had already been so eroded by inflation as to leave in want many who thought they had provided adequately for the future.

Of all the burdens which progress has placed on the poor, those of urban renewal and highway construction have perhaps been the cruelest and most devastating and, as in so many other cases, the heaviest burden has fallen on the blacks. This fact can be brought home most vividly by the events in one city. Nashville, Tennessee, has been generally regarded as better than the average city in the treatment of Negroes, even though most of them still lived in a separate world, so much so that an urban renewal project in one area and a highway cutting through another area took little account of the needs or the welfare of the black community. Of the two, the highway program was probably the more devastating. As work on the highway cut through the area where three predominantly black colleges and universities were located, a staff writer for the *Nashville Tennessean* told the story as he saw it.

To those men, women, and children—mostly Negroes—building the highway meant giving up a home already paid for and going into debt for another. It meant making the nearest route to school, church, and market twice as long as it used to be in a neighborhood where almost everyone, especially the old, still walks wherever he goes. It meant destroying businesses or separating them from their customers to the point where the businessman's future livelihood was in jeopardy. It meant forcing grade school children on their way to school to walk across a concrete arch spanning six lanes of interstate highway.

To be sure it was a neighborhood with many poor homes where land could be had cheaper than elsewhere, but there were also good homes destroyed, in this city with a distinct housing shortage. Among the displaced people were school teachers, the owners of a restaurant, a service station, and a barbershop. There was a nurse, a retired dentist, doctors, an insurance agent, a school principal, a U.S. Marine, and an engineer for the U.S. Department of Agriculture. There were also countless poorer folk to whom the area was home and who had to seek new places to live and work. The more prosperous who could assume the higher interest rates on new mortgages were able to buy homes elsewhere. But what will happen to the housemaids, the widows, the retired persons, the waitresses, the factory workers, and the day laborers? Some of them will relocate in housing projects a long way from their jobs. Some will move in with relatives and friends in areas fast being made into ghettos as more and more displaced blacks must find new homes.

If this were an isolated story of events in one town it would not be worth the telling, but it is a story retold in city after city as more and more highways cut their paths through the areas where land is cheap and the people lack power to protest effectively. When the highways are finished some people will rejoice in the progress that enables them to get quickly and comfortably where they wish to go. And some people who were lucky or who had advance knowledge of where a clover leaf was to be built will profit handsomely from the increased price of their land.

Of course many middle-class whites have lost their homes to the highways or to urban renewal and not all of them were adequately compensated, but it has been the poor, and especially the black poor on whose backs the major burden of this progress has been laid. And the burden for many is even greater than this story reveals. Can any middle-class person really understand what owning even the shabbiest home means to the black man or woman who paid for it over the years by working at the lowest wages as janitor, yard man, house maid, or porter? They are now too old and too poor to buy another home when the price they received for the old one was not much more than the down-payment required for a new one at today's prices. In an insecure world, the home that to an urban renewal appraiser was only a shack, to its poor black owner represented not only a major achievement but the realization of a life-long dream and a tenuous thread to status and self-respect.

Poverty is a complicated and many faceted problem, and there is obviously no simple solution. The National Advisory Council on Economic Opportunity in its 1969 report made the point clear in saying "no single strategy—for malnutrition, illness, family stability, housing, education, employment, neighborhoods, or income—will succeed." It will take all of these and more. Even then there will always be some people who for one reason or another cannot care for themselves. In a modern industrial society, technological advances, the manipulation of economic forces, wars, and depressions, as well as booms, and inflation, are as far beyond individual control as are tornadoes, hurricanes, earthquakes or tidal waves. In such a world a society must assume collective responsibility for the individuals who are the victims of such forces.

9

Race,
Crime,
and the Law

1. The Problem of Lawlessness

All societies that we know anything about have found it necessary to deal with individuals who do not conform to accepted ways of behaving as the society in question defines them. The problem is accentuated in a complex society with many subcultural groups, because the core of common values may be small, and not all people will have the same definitions of right and wrong. These facts were brought out sharply in the 1950s and 1960s when the Supreme Court rulings on desegregation were widely disregarded and even defied by middle-class white people who did not consider their actions wrong. These same people had strong negative reactions to the various protest activities and to what was generally referred to as the crime problem. They saw the main issue as the maintenance of law and order. Other people saw the issue as a complex matter that involves the securing of rights and justice for all, and the alleviation of the social ills that created conditions conducive to crime. Nowhere were the maps of reality of different groups more out of focus than in this area.

It is beyond the scope of this book to go into the intricacies of civil and criminal law, the varying definitions of crime, or any detailed analysis of the causes of crime and delinquency. In its simplest terms a crime is any act prohibited by criminal law and punishable by law. For our purposes here, it is important to distinguish the major categories of behavior that are of significance in race relations. These categories are what are usually designated as ordinary crime, white collar crime, and organized crime. There are also serious questions regarding the unequal protection of the law, preventive and corrective versus punitive measures, and the relation of law to the system of values that underlies the conceptions of justice and order.

2. Ordinary Crime

The kind of lawlessness with which most people are concerned involves the direct safety of their persons or their property. Although, as will be documented later, greater injury to both persons and property occurs through white collar and organized crime, people are less aware of these activities, and because their effects are indirect, such crimes may arouse little concern. Crimes of violence such as assault, rape, murder, theft, and burglary are dramatic and immediate in their effects, not only on the victims, but on the people in general who hear about them and feel threatened by them.

There is a general impression that such crimes have increased much more than other types of crime, that the danger is everywhere, and that the people who commit such crimes are usually strangers to the victims. There is also a common belief that low-class persons, particularly low-class black persons, are more lawless than other people. All of these propositions are of doubtful validity and at best are only partial truths. Such beliefs have important consequences for intergroup relations especially those involving Negroes and whites.

In a 1967 report the President's Commission on Law Enforcement and the Administration of Justice made it clear that the law violations of the poor, and especially of the black poor, are much more likely to be reported than are the illegal activities of business men, labor union officials, government officials, policemen, physicians, lawyers, or middle-class youngsters. Moreover, some laws are strictly enforced while others are ignored. Often not only the kind of crime a person commits but the social statuses of both offender and victim may enter into whether an act is designated as criminal. Even when an arrest is made, the outcome may be the result of negotiations by the offender or his counsel with representatives of the judicial system. Some authorities go so far as to say that criminality is a status conferred upon certain persons, for certain acts, at certain times, in certain places.

People tend to think of the danger to their persons and property as coming from strangers, particularly the persons of another class or race thought of as "they." But the Uniform Crime Reports and other studies show that the risk of assault, rape, and murder from family members, friends, and acquaintances is almost twice as great as it is from strangers on the street. More than three-fourths of all murders involve relatives or other persons known to the victims. Moreover, a person's likelihood of being killed in a car crash is almost fifteen times the chance of his being murdered by a stranger. And most crimes of violence are intraracial rather than interracial, that is, whites assault, rape, and murder other whites, while Negroes commit these crimes against other Negroes.

It is true that the common serious crimes happen most often in the slums of large cities, especially in racial and ethnic ghettos. But these patterns have generally remained the same regardless of the race or nationality of the people involved. When any given immigrant groups have lived in such neighborhoods, they have had a high crime rate. When these people moved into better areas their crime rate decreased, but there was a high rate among whatever other ethnic groups took their places in the slums. Poverty in the modern city usually means segregation in slum areas where there is frequent contact with drunks, prostitutes, beggars, thieves, dope peddlers, and hardened criminals. Because of unemployment and low wages, the "successful" man is often the gambler, the racketeer, or the narcotics pusher. Thus while poverty itself is not a cause of crime, it often creates conditions that foster particular kinds of crime.

An examination of the prevalence of white collar and organized crime and the differential treatment of crimes committed by people of different races and social levels does not bear out the assumption that either Negroes or lower-class whites are basically more lawless than other people. They do commit different kinds of crime. That is, most of what is called ordinary crime is committed by the urban poor and as a high proportion of the poor are black, the Negro rates are higher than the whites. However, the difference becomes very small when comparisons are made between whites and Negroes living under the same conditions. The Crime Commission is of the view that if really equal opportunity prevailed, the large difference now found between the Negro and the white arrest rates would disappear.

3. White-Collar Crime

People generally have reacted strongly against crimes of violence committed by the poor, and during the ghetto riots of the 1960s there were many people in favor of shooting looters and even those suspected of looting, though such police action would be essentially executions without trial. There has been much less concern for the lawless activity of persons of the more affluent social and economic classes, generally termed white-collar crime. But apart from organized crime, the cost of which runs into billions, the cost of crime committed by middle- and upper-class persons of all ages is many times greater than that of all of the lower-class crime that is usually thought of as the crime problem.

Employee theft, shoplifting, embezzlement, and other forms of crime involving business, cost the public billions of dollars a year. The manager of one of the largest bookshops in the country says that a quarter of a million dollars in their stock is missing each year—a loss euphemistically labeled "inventory shrinkage." In the grocery trade, loss by employee theft and shoplifting is estimated to be almost equal to the total amount of profit. The general public, of course, pays for such losses in higher prices. It is estimated that direct stealing, manipulation of accounts, and other such criminal activities cost the public the equivalent of a two percent sales tax each year.

Shoplifting and employee theft are not limited to lower class people or poor neighborhoods though these are most often reported. Many of the employees involved are white collar workers, and the shoplifters include college students, middle class youth, and housewives of good standing in the community who are seldom reported to the police. Employers generally prefer to handle employee theft, and the white collar shoplifter is often let off with a warning. The parents of a middle-class youth caught shoplifting are often indignant at the implication that their child is a thief. If the parents are good customers the theft may not even be reported to them.

The amount of loss through business crimes is even more staggering and such criminal activity occurs at all levels of business and government. Business crimes most frequently take the form of misrepresentation in advertising and in the financial statements of corporations, embezzlement and manipulation of funds, short weights and measures, adulteration of foods, tax frauds, home improvement frauds involving the sale and repair of cars and appliances, illegal repossessing of goods, exorbitant rents, and the violation of housing codes. Bribery, payoffs, collusion, and taking advantage of inside information is widespread. One study estimated that one year as much as five billion dollars changed hands in kickbacks, payoffs, and bribes.

There is a prevailing belief that such illegal business practices are not "real crime." Many businessmen have developed "game rules" that make business crime seem routine and shrewd rather than wrong. A *Wall Street Journal* staff reporter pointed out that the fines imposed on corporations for law violations were often so low compared to the profits that could be made by violating the law that the chance of being caught and fined was regarded by some firms as simply a good business risk.

Furthermore, white-collar crime and especially business crime is handled differently from lower-class crime. The lower-class criminal is handled by policemen, prosecutors, and judges, with penal sanctions in the form of fines, imprisonment, and even death. Business crimes are handled by inspectors, administrative boards, or commissions, and their penal sanctions often take the form of orders to cease and desist, sometimes a fine, or the loss of a license. Only in extreme cases is there a prison sentence, usually very light.

This differential treatment is supported by the general community conception of crime, by the business community's self-conception, and by the interrelatedness of interest of government officials and the business community. There is a general reluctance to impose criminal sanctions on the offenders, especially if they occupy executive or managerial positions and hold places of trust in the community—as they often do. The list of persons convicted of such crimes includes people at every level in every business and profession as well as local, state and federal officials. And such persons are often prominent in church, civic, and community enterprises.

Aside from the fact that white-collar crime costs the country more in monetary loss than does ordinary crime, both are forbidden by law and the law stipulates penal sanctions for each, though often proportionately heavier ones for ordinary crime. It is clear, therefore, that white-collar crime is not morally neutral. Most fraud involves preying upon the weak and ignorant. Violations of food and drug laws may cause serious injury and even death; embezzlement is simply a form of theft; tax fraud involves cheating the government and indirectly defrauds other taxpayers. Moreover, such antisocial conduct, by whatever name it is called, is the more reprehensible when it involves privileged members of the community.

4. Organized Crime

As the term is commonly used, organized crime refers to economic enterprises organized for the purpose of conducting illegal activities or operating legitimate ventures by illegal methods. Organized crime has traditionally controlled such activities as gambling, loan sharking, prostitution, and drug distribution. Distillers, wholesale liquor companies, retail liquor stores, taverns, and night clubs are often controlled by mobsters either directly, or indirectly through respectable fronts. Racing tracks, juke boxes, vending machines, loan companies, trucking companies, and even such enterprises as laundry and linen supply houses have been invaded by the mob. As labor unions grew and their welfare funds became significant, they also became the object of mob interest, and today almost any business may find itself under pressure from mob activity. The methods used by organized crime range from maiming or murdering people who resist their demands, to threats of bodily harm to their families or friends, or the ruin of their businesses.

Although many people refuse to believe that organized crime is really pervasive, or a threat to the community, studies show the cost in money to be tremendous, and the danger to the entire fabric of society very real. The annual cost in money is estimated to be at least in the range of seven to ten billion dollars and may be much higher. The social cost is even greater. Through bribery or blackmail of officials ranging from policemen to the higher reaches of government, and the infiltration and control of legitimate business, labor unions, and other organizations, the mob corrupts and intimidates law enforcement officials, legislators, and judges and attempts to elect to public office individuals favorable to its activities. Mob money is frequently obtained by blackmail or for "protection," and it is used to pay policemen for noninterference or as campaign contributions.

Organized crime is possible because of public ignorance and apathy, and because of the cooperation, willing or unwilling, of business concerns, police, and government officials at all levels. Criminals would not be able to make huge profits from various illegal activities if Americans did not buy their products or patronize their activities. Illicit gambling, prostitution, and the trade in narcotics thrive because they meet public demands. Politicians of questionable integrity remain in office because the electorate allows it and sometimes returns to office persons known to be guilty of criminal activity. The President's Crime Commission puts the matter bluntly: organized crime flourishes in America because enough of the public wants its services, and most citizens are apathetic about its import. It will continue as long as America accepts it as inevitable and, in some instances, desirable.

The toleration of organized crime has important ramifications for law and justice and for the relations between middle class society and the poor, especially the black poor. The May 1963 issue of the *Annals of Political and Social Science* points out that preachment of law and order are a bitter joke to those who most often see organized crime in action—that is, the urban poor and the blacks. When police are corrupted and law enforcement is arbitrary, when the laws are violated by the respectable members of the community, and when people guilty of criminal activities rise to prominence and power, the very basis of society is in danger because people no longer honor or respect those values in which they profess to believe.

5. The Unequal Protection of the Law

It is clear that there are different standards of law enforcement for different kinds of crime. One authority says bluntly that the prison population reflects only that part of the criminal world that isn't smart, rich, dishonest, or lucky enough to stay out of jail. The poor and ignorant who do not know about good lawyers, bargaining techniques, appeals, and technicalities stand a much greater chance of being arrested, tried, convicted, and punished than do persons of higher social status. Even when the crime is the same, as in the case of murder, it is the poor man, and especially the poor black man who ends up on death row.

There are other ways in which a man is penalized for being poor. Although technically a man is considered innocent until proven guilty, a poor man unable to raise bail may spend weeks or even months in jail awaiting trial, while his more affluent fellow townsman, accused of the same crime, goes free until the time of his trial. The effect is even harsher if the poor man's family is left without support. He is thus punished before he is tried, even when he may ultimately be proven innocent.

An even more unjust practice is that of requiring an offender to "work out" his fine at an absurdly low rate of pay. As late as 1968 there is on record the case of a youth convicted of a theft that netted 87 cents. He was fined $50 and assessed another $71.80 in court costs. He was unable to pay either the fine or the costs and was sentenced to the work house to "work out" the total at the rate of $2 a day.

The daily newspapers document endlessly these discriminations practiced by law enforcement agencies and apparently supported by public opinion. In one newspaper was the report of two men who had broken into a store and were caught as they emerged with a carton of cigarettes. Although the men were unarmed and offered no resistance, they were each given seven years in the penitentiary. In the same newspaper was a seemingly unrelated report of a businessman found guilty of income tax evasion. In spite of an income totalling six figures, he had not even filed a report for the preceding five years. His only excuse was that he had been "too busy." He was given a moderate fine and a suspended sentence.

Since the 1954 Supreme Court ruling on school segregation white adults of all ages have bombed or burned dozens of Negro churches, schools, homes, and places of business. They have taken the lives not only of adult Negro and white civil rights workers but of one fourteen year old boy and four young children attending Sunday school. In most of the cases, the states where the crimes occurred made no serious effort to apprehend or to punish the criminals. On the day Martin Luther King, Jr. was buried five young Negroes set fire to a rundown service station that was known as a Ku Klux Klan hangout. Nobody was hurt and the damage came to less than one hundred dollars. Three of the Negroes were boys in their teens and the other two were twenty and twenty-one. The youths were tried and each was sentenced to twelve years in prison.

Inequalities of the law are, of course, not new, as evidenced by the anonymous jingle of ancient lineage,

> The law will punish man or woman
> Who steals a goose from off the common
> But turns the greater felon loose
> Who steals the common from the goose.

Such inequities persist because in the eyes of many people stealing a purse is worse than robbing a bank, and the bank robbery is worse than fraudulent breach of trust or manipulation of the stock market, either of which can cause the public the loss of a half million dollars. This attitude has important ramifications for race relations because in upper level business crimes, the offenders are usually not only middle-class but white, whereas the offender in ordinary crime is usually poor and often black. One Negro bitterly remarked that black people would know they had arrived when they began to be indicted for fraud and income tax evasion rather than for snatching purses and playing the numbers.

6. The Black Man as Victim

The black poor have been subject to the same, or greater, differential treatment as the white poor in the administration of justice, but Negroes at all social and economic levels have been penalized in various other ways by the very legal forces that were supposed to protect them.

The Tuskegee Institute Reports estimate that between 1865 and 1955 more than five thousand Negroes met their deaths at the hands of white mobs, and countless others lost their lives at the hands of individual white men or through "legal lynching." Many of these persons were not even accused of any crime, and only a fraction of them had been guilty of anything more than misdemeanors. In any case they were not granted the due process of law supposedly guaranteed to every individual and, although the persons responsible for the deaths were generally known to authorities, not one was ever convicted. Most of them were not even tried. Although lynchings as such no longer occur, there have been numerous "unsolved" murders of Negroes since the 1954 Supreme Court decision on segregation.

It has long been a widespread practice, particularly in the South, to have three standards of justice as far as Negroes are concerned. If a white man injures a Negro he is likely to go free or to receive a very light sentence. If, however, a Negro injures a white person the severest possible penalty is usually exacted. If both injured and offender are Negroes the crime often is not taken very seriously, and if it occurs within the Negro community it may be ignored altogether. This pattern makes for greater disorder within the Negro community and penalizes law-abiding Negroes who are often forced by segregated housing to live in areas where crime is rampant. In any case, the inequities can only breed contempt for the law as an instrument of justice.

Although the cry of police brutality has been used indiscriminately, there is no question that Negroes, north and south, have been subjected to intimidation and harassment and even bodily injury and death at the hands of officers of the law, often with the flimsiest of excuses. In 1945 a Negro accused of stealing an automobile tire was beaten to death by a sheriff and his two deputies. The sheriff justified his action on the basis that the Negro had "used insulting language" and had reached for a gun, although the Negro was handcuffed at the time and was in the custody of three officers. No evidence was offered that the man even had a gun. None of the three officers was ever punished.

But the harassment of Negroes is not limited to the South, and the victims are not always poor. Repeatedly, Negro doctors and other business or professional men have been accosted by police, ordered to pull their cars to the curb, and addressed as "boy" or "nigger." If any protest was made they ran the risk of being booked for insulting a police officer or resisting arrest. Most of them were not even violating any traffic rules—the police were merely suspicious of a well-dressed Negro in a good car. These occurrences have been documented over and over by Negroes from New York to San Francisco, and they are by no means all in the past. Louis Lomax in the *Negro Revolt* stated: "I don't know a single Negro who doesn't get a flutter in his stomach when approached by a white policeman."

7. Violence as a Form of Protest

The decade of the 1960s saw in the United States the widespread development of protest as a weapon for forcing social change. Whether such protests were regarded as crimes or as a legitimate means of dramatizing the inequalities of the law and the violation of human rights depended on the differing maps of reality of the persons making the judgments.

Although the protests had certain basic causes in common, they took a variety of forms. There were the non-violent sit-ins and marches designed to call attention to and dramatize discrimination against Negroes; the planned civil disobedience programs, originally nonviolent; the ghetto riots triggered by a variety of causes; the anti-war and anti-establishment demonstrations that also took a variety of forms; and in the later part of the decade the student protests that swept from one end of the country to the other. Each of these protests had its own history and its own special grievances though some of them were either initiated or supported by national organizations or groups outside the areas involved.

The general widespread revolt against authority and the campus disorders are treated in a later chapter, although both at times clearly involved violations of criminal law. Attention here is given primarily to the ghetto outbreaks that began in the 1960s and which involved rioting, looting, and burning. Most of these disturbances occurred in predominantly Negro ghettos, and the varying interpretations of the behavior of the rioters, the community involvement, and the actions of the police and other law enforcement officials have important consequences in human relations, particularly in the black-white confrontation.

Most of the recent ghetto rioting has been done by blacks, and it is generally assumed that they are more aggressively militant than the white poor who greatly exceed the blacks in numbers. This may well be true and, if so, there are a number of factors that could account for the difference. Poor Negroes have suffered all the disadvantages of the white poor plus many others that the white poor escape. Moreover, many present day Negroes have a deep sense of grievance about the past. They know that their disadvantages are compounded by the cumulative effect of the lack of educational and economic opportunity suffered by their parents and grandparents. It is much harder for blacks to escape from the ghetto and from poverty than it is for whites who are not penned in by segregation and job discrimination. Therefore, the black poor probably includes a great many naturally intelligent and aggressive persons who, if they had been white, would have reached higher economic levels and hence would have long since escaped from the ghetto and from poverty and lower-class status.

The President's Commission pointed to a number of factors that entered into the explosive mixture that erupted in violence in the ghettos. Among these were the pervasive segregation and discrimination in employment, education, and housing that results in the exclusion of great numbers of Negroes from the benefits of economic progress; black in-migration and white exodus from the central cities that results in the concentration of impoverished and poorly educated blacks in the deteriorating inner city; the concentration of Negroes in the black ghettos where segregation and poverty converge to destroy opportunity and result in crime, drug addiction, and dependency with consequent resentment.

Added to these factors were the frustrated hopes and unfulfilled expectations of the Civil Rights movement; a climate that tends toward approval and encouragement of violence created by white terrorists and directed against non-violent protest; the open defiance of law and federal authority on the part of white officials resisting desegregation; the feeling of powerlessness that led some Negro groups to believe that there was no effective alternative to violence as a means of redressing grievances; the resentment toward police as instruments of white repression; and the widespread belief in police brutality and a double standard of justice. Finally, there was a new mood, with many roots, that led young blacks to an enhanced racial pride and a lessened willingness to submit to a system in which they felt they had no part.

There are other factors that must be taken into account if we are to understand the rioters. In a perceptive book on *Crime, Law and Society*, Frank E. Hartung points out the role of a self-conception that allows an individual to admit his criminal acts to himself without damage to his conception of himself as a worthy person. As we have already noted this self-conception is an important factor in middle-class criminal behavior, that is, these persons recognize their acts as illegal though they do not admit that they themselves are "criminals." Business and professional men, government officials and others justify their illegal activities by labeling them "shrewdness," or "common business practice," or by defining the law as "bureaucratic nonsense" or "interference." The officials at all levels of government who defied court rulings regarding school desegregation had definitions of their behavior that enabled them to violate the law and not only to retain their self image as worthy persons but even to take pride in their actions.

The same self-justification appears in the activities of ordinary middle-class citizens. When radar speed detection devices were installed, thousands of motorists bought anti-radar devices to outwit the highway patrol and evade the law. The middle-class people who engaged in this maneuver would be astonished and indignant at being labeled criminals though they would admit that their behavior was illegal. Their perception of their behavior is such that they can engage in it without damage to their conception of themselves as worthy and even law-abiding persons. At the same time, they can give high priority to "law and order" and can be righteously indignant about "welfare chiselers" and "crime in the streets." This is a common middle-class map of reality.

What the average middle-class person does not realize is that the lower-class person, the slum dweller, the "welfare chiseler" and especially the lower-class black, each has his own set of perceptions and definitions that enable him to evade certain laws and behave in ways that are contrary to middle-class standards but which are quite consistent with a lower-class worthy self-image. The trouble is that the lower-class person's perceptions and self-image are based on lower-class standards and values, while the laws are made and enforced by people whose standards and values are middle-class. Until we understand the different maps of reality involved, and how they are arrived at, we are not likely to make much progress toward our avowed goal of equal justice before the law.

Many people have expressed surprise that in the wake of the riots the looting was by no means limited to the riffraff or to criminals. Many of the persons had jobs, and some of them were above any ordinarily defined poverty level. Although there were many complex factors involved, much of it can be explained in the light of two phenomena common to our own and to many other cultures. For convenience these may be labeled selective honesty and the special situation syndrome. The two are often related and sometime overlap. While there are many uncorruptible individuals, irrespective of race or class, who remain honest under all circumstances, there are many others whose honesty is selective. As in the case of the definitions of "criminal" discussed earlier, they may either rationalize their dishonesty as not wrong under the circumstances, or they may simply define the terms differently for different situations.

It is common knowledge that many otherwise honest people cheat on examinations, pad expense accounts, lie about a child's age to get him in the movie free, or help themselves to "souvenir" towels or silver from hotels. Such behavior is often rationalized on the basis that it is somehow less reprehensible to steal from a corporation or the government because they "won't miss it" or "they charge too much anyway."

In the ghetto when people felt that they were regularly overcharged or otherwise cheated—and often they were both—stealing was a way of getting even or getting what one had a right to anyway. The lack of any meaningful personal relationship between landlord and tenant, shop owner and customer, or official and citizen gave no basis for identification. "The Man," therefore, could be put in the category of the enemy against whom anything goes. Here was a chance for the turtle to outrun the rabbit or, if you were the rabbit, to outwit the fox.

The special situation syndrome has many of the elements of selective honesty but its chief characteristics is just what the name implies—a special situation abrogates the usual rules. The breakdown of law and order for whatever reason creates a special situation in the minds of many people. Any disaster—fire, flood, earthquake, or war—brings out the compassion and concern of some people, but to others it is an excuse for the loosening of customary restraints, and looting is an old and widespread pattern in such cases.

There is also the general contagion of mob action which certainly is not racial as such. White mobs form as readily as black ones and their actions are just as irrational. Mob action is usually irresponsible but not always vicious. There are numerous examples of people in groups behaving in ways that would be unthinkable on the part of a single individual. We need only recall football crowds, panty raids, the Fort Lauderdale youth bashes, or American Legion and Lodge conventions to see mob psychology in action.

In the riot areas there were all these conditions—selective honesty, a special situation, and mob psychology—plus smouldering resentment and a sense of injustice. In some cases there was deliberate retaliatory activity. Some people who lacked inner discipline and established personal standards simply responded to the removal of external restraints. Some people saw the chance to get things they felt had been unfairly denied them. The carnival air described by some observers indicated that, in some cases at least, there was created in the minds of many people the kind of special situation in which all rules of ordinary behavior are suspended.

There is another factor that is of white society's own making. By lumping all Negroes together as an undifferentiated "they," and by the perpetuation of a segregated social structure, the white world has almost guaranteed that even well-to-do Negroes of middle-class habits will feel to some degree a sense of identification with all other Negroes. Thus while responsible Negroes deplored the riots and certainly did not participate, many of them could not help feeling a degree of sympathy and identification with even the most lawless and irresponsible blacks. If you have been treated like Br'er Rabbit you can't help feeling some satisfaction when Br'er Fox gets what's coming to him. The black man's "we" is a normal response to the white man's "they" or, as someone has put it, when the chips are down all blacks are black. If this is true, it is the white world that has made them so.

8. Law and the System of Values

There are few things that create a greater sense of bitterness and unrest than a sense of injustice for which there is no redress. The earlier sections of this chapter have documented the gross injustices in our legal and judicial systems that heavily penalize large sections of our population, notably the poor and the black, with the black poor being doubly penalized. We have not always realized that it is not only the victims of injustice who suffer—there are important ramifications that threaten the whole social fabric.

Franz Alexander and Hugo Staub in their book *The Criminal, the Judge, and the Public*, point to three things that make rebellion, and if pushed far enough, revolution, almost certain. These three are punishment that is undeserved and hence unjust; punishment that is too severe for the offense committed; and deserved punishment that is not forthcoming. Sentences passed upon the innocent and those that are too severe for the offense committed have an effect upon the psychology of the people involved that leads to an unwillingness to accept the established order and its laws. This sense of injustice is increased if there are privileged people who escape punishment for their wrongdoing. Furthermore, when punishment is too severe for the offense committed the punished individual feels that he has overpaid his debt, that society has put itself in the wrong, and therefore its laws need not be respected.

Although this book was published in Germany in 1929 its relevance to our present situation seems obvious. There can be no disputing the fact that many Negroes have been unjustly punished and that they have often been severely punished for trivial offenses. Because these two things have happened to many Negroes, and can happen at any time to any Negro, there is a strong sense of identification that makes it easy for any Negro to see "Whitey" or "the establishment" as an enemy to whom nothing is owed and whose laws need not be respected or obeyed. Moreover, when the relative freedom from punishment of the middle-class white law violators is added to the picture, one has all the ingredients for defiance and rebellion. As Alexander and Staub point out, the internal policeman of conscience is eliminated by overly severe punishment and there remains only external force for the enforcement of the law. Thus unduly harsh punishment or inconsistency in law enforcement do not deter crime but rather create tougher and tougher criminals.

The authors further state that the feeling of responsibility toward one's self develops only in free societies. In the totalitarian states, whether Communist or Fascist, the individual no longer has free choice or control over the direction of his own life. When Negroes are not permitted to become fully a part of society, sharing in both its duties and its privileges, they cannot develop that inner feeling of responsibility that is essential to a free society. And since the social fabric is really all of a piece, the total society is threatened when any substantial part of it is excluded from the democratic process.

It is hard to see how Negroes could have any respect for law when civil rights workers have been arrested for "trespass" when they insisted on being served at supposedly public lunch counters, for "breach of peace" for sitting in the front of a bus, for "parading without a license" for carrying picket signs, and for "criminal anarchy" for distributing leaflets. When to such actions as these are added the police harassment of Negroes, the "verbal violence" of influential whites, the physical violence of other whites and the murder of Negroes accused. of nothing more than civil rights activity or "getting out of their place," it is a miracle that black people have any respect for law at all.

There are other ramifications. When a society through its legal processes sets up laws with penal sanctions, and then both the legal apparatus and the public condone the violation of these laws by the more privileged members of the community as not being "real crimes," respect for law as well as a sense of justice can be seriously impaired. Such practices bring all law into disrepute; they provide a convenient rationalization for other types of law violation; and they give substance to the claim of hypocrisy on the part of "the establishment."

One of the severest indictments of the inequalities of our system of justice comes from a Judge of the U.S. Court of Appeals of the District of Columbia. Writing in the *New York Times Magazine*, Judge Wright documents numerous circumstances in which the law protects the privileged but offers no such protection to the poor, as if, he says, an assault is more serious when it happens to one of "us" than to one of "them." The system is such that the poor are likely to perceive the law not as protection for life and property but as an instrument of oppression. He describes our so-called equal justice as being the kind of mockery pictured by Anatole France when he said, "The law, in all its majestic equality, forbids the rich as well as the poor to sleep under bridges on rainy nights, to beg on the streets, and to steal bread."

There is a common notion that law enforcement agencies are entirely too lenient with criminals. There is no question that some of the more sophisticated types are able to escape the law though these are more likely to be the big operators rather than the ordinary man. But students of the problem point out that there is far graver danger to society when it fails to follow scrupulously that hallmark of civilized law known as due process. More than one Supreme Court justice has reminded us that the very existence of government is imperiled if the government itself becomes a lawbreaker and an obstructor of justice, as it does if it gains confessions and other evidence by violent and unlawful means.

There are no simple solutions to the problems of crime. It is obvious that the problem must be attacked from many angles at once. There must be preventive measures, correctional systems that correct and reclaim rather than turn first offenders into incorrigibles, a complete restructuring of the whole penal system, better courts, speedier trials, the upgrading of police training, and perhaps most of all the recognition on the part of business and government that there cannot be a double standard—a lax and permissive one for the powerful and a harsher and more exacting one for the powerless, whether black or white. In the words of Judge Learned Hand, "If we are to keep our democracy, there must be one commandment: Thou shalt not ration justice."

10

The
Black
Experience

1. The Blight of the Color Line

The blight of the color line can best be expressed in a series of deprivations. Some of the most serious of these have been discussed in earlier sections of this book, and others are more fully documented elsewhere in this chapter. But the fundamental fact in all of them is that from the early days of slavery to the present, the country has operated as a dual rather than a unitary system. The separation of black and white in churches, schools, community and recreational facilities, civic affairs, business, and government has meant that Negroes were in, but not of, the community.

The most far-reaching aspect of the black experience lies in the fact that Negroes were robbed of any cultural identification with their African heritage yet denied the right to become Americans in the fullest sense of the word. Other immigrant groups usually came in families with cultural and linguistic patterns relatively intact. Moreover, most of them were from European backgrounds. As time went on they moved from the status of hyphenated-Americans into full integration into the national life. Although they might maintain sentimental ties with the country of their origin or that of their ancestors, they ceased to be Italian- or Polish- or Irish-Americans. They belonged.

The Negroes were not only brought in chains, but they came for the most part as individuals cut off from family ties and even from others of their own language and cultural community. So completely were they shut off from their original homelands that only in recent years have many Negroes thought of themselves or their ancestors in this country as Afro-Americans. Yet they were never allowed to forget that they did not belong and were really a different order of being. Negroes were always "they" and were seldom included when people said "we Americans," or "we southerners," and they were not considered full participants in "our way of life," although that way of life was heavily dependent on their service. Many Negroes who wanted desperately to be considered simply American spoke of never being allowed to forget their "two-ness." W. E. B. DuBois in his *Souls of Black Folk* written in 1903 spoke of it as "two souls, two thoughts, two unreconciled strivings, two warring ideals in one dark body."

Many Negroes claim that no white person can ever really understand the black experience and this is doubtless true. Two whites tried to do so by temporarily passing as Negroes and have written accounts of the experiments—John Howard Griffin in *Black Like Me* and Grace Halsell in *Soul Sister*. Each of them found the experience shattering in its impact. In some ways the sudden reversal in roles increased their sensitivity to events, but on the other hand there was always the knowledge that the blackness was only assumed, that the experience was temporary, self-chosen, and could be terminated at will.

One of the most devastating aspects of the black experience is that it begins so early. Not only during slavery, but in all the years since, black parents have been under the necessity of teaching their children how to be black in order that they might survive in a white man's world. Many adults of today remember the harshness of the lesson taught by a parent who knew all too well the dangers that confronted the black person who got "out of his place." More privileged parents often tried to shield their children as long as possible from the harsher realities of a divided society. "But how," one such mother asked, "do you explain to two little boys why they can't use the swings in the park, or go into the restaurant for lunch, or use the restroom at the filling station?"

Some children learned what it meant to be black through the unconscious cruelty of white children who reflected the racial bias of their parents. It came to W. E. B. DuBois in New England when a white child new to the school, haughtily refused the bright card he offered in what had been a merry exchange. Countee Cullen in one of his poems recounts the experience of an eight year old who smiled at a white boy. All the black child could remember of the long visit in Baltimore was the response of the white child who "poked out his tongue and called me 'nigger'."

Even more revealing are the stories black men tell of their experiences when brutal white men undertook to teach the black child a lesson about "staying in his place." One man in his middle twenties tells how he learned what it meant to be black when he tagged along behind his father through the corridor of a southern courthouse. The day was hot, and when he saw a water cooler the child reached up intent only on getting a drink. Before he could get the water a passing white man knocked him off his feet. "I was five years old," he says. "How could I know that the water cooler was only for white people?"

And what must be the ineradicable scars left on the black children who in 1963 were in the church where four of their friends were murdered by bombs set off to explode during Sunday school? Or the first graders who saw the hate filled faces and heard the screamed insults of white adult men and women protesting the desegregation of a public school? Or the children who—as late as 1970—saw angry white adults overturn the school bus that had transported the youngsters to what had been an all white school?

These brutal lessons were not limited to the South. Malcolm X in his autobiography tells of having the windows of his Nebraska home shot out by Ku Klux Klansmen, and when the family moved to Michigan the house in which they lived was set afire by two white men. The family lost all they had and barely escaped with their lives.

Sammy Davis, Jr. did not realize the full meaning of the color line until as a sensitive and patriotic young serviceman in World War II he encountered a half dozen white soldiers who insulted and harassed him in every conceivable way.

When the other deprivations recounted here and elsewhere are added to the shock and trauma of such youthful experiences, one begins to get some glimpse of what it has meant to be black in America. As one Negro expressed it, "It isn't that these things happen every day to everybody; but you always know that they do happen, and that at any time they can happen to you." To be sure, conditions have improved to some degree nearly everywhere and many barriers to participation have been removed. But if these cruelties and injustices appear to white people as old, unhappy, far off things, long since on their way out, it should be remembered that they are a part of the life experience of most adult Negroes and of many younger ones as well.

2. Separate and Unequal

Aside from the blighting experience of learning to be black in a white world, Negroes have been subjected to inequities and exclusions that operated in at least five major ways. They limited the Negroes' education, restricted their economic and occupational freedom, excluded them from many civic benefits and cultural opportunities or permitted them only an inferior sort, placed restrictions on their social mobility, and laid upon them like a heavy hand the inhibiting stigma of inferiority. They denied to Negroes full participation in the duties as well as the rights of citizenship, and forced them to live in a divided world in which many of the values and goals deemed appropriate for whites were placed beyond the reach of black men.

It is true, of course, that not all Negroes have been affected in all these ways to an equal degree. There have been great local and sectional variations in the severity of the segregation patterns, and there have been some significant changes in recent years. The fact remains, however, that the great masses of Negroes have been hemmed in and held down, both through the exterior force exerted by the dominant group and by their own attitudes and habits resulting in large measure from the enveloping pressure of their continued low status.

Basic to all other deprivations has been the denial of equal educational opportunity. One of the bitterest complaints of recent years has been that of black parents in northern ghettos as well as in southern communities about the quality of education provided for their children. These deprivations have a long history. Before the Civil War few slaves had any schooling, a condition they shared with most of the poor whites. With the establishment of public schools throughout the former slave states, there soon developed a dual system in which the Negroes' educational opportunity was almost without exception inferior to that of the white youth in the same area. Until the Supreme Court decision in 1954, separate schools were required by state and local laws in seventeen states and the District of Columbia, and the great majority of adult Negroes living today were the products of these separate and inferior schools.

As long as the separate schools existed Negro children generally received far less than their proportionate share of school funds. Even in the best of counties the Negro child often received less than half as much for his education as was spent on the white child in the same county. In the earlier years many of the schools for Negro children in rural areas had only a six month term, a fact that led one Negro educator to say that white people must think Negro children very bright to expect them to learn in six months what it took the white child nine months to learn. Of course, the black child actually lost one year out of every three apart from the inferior quality of his school.

This discrimination against Negroes was not limited to grade schools. In many of the poorer counties, or those in which there were few Negroes, there were no public high schools for them, and they were not permitted to attend the white high schools. This deficiency continued at the higher education level. Although there were Land Grant Colleges for Negroes throughout the southern states, these were generally far below the level of the Land Grant Colleges for white students and even more inferior to the State Universities which were open only to whites. In fairness to the much criticized white churches, it should be noted that in many areas of the South for many years the only high school and college facilities available to Negro youth were sponsored and supported by various religious denominations, including some of those whose entire membership consisted of white southerners.

With a few notable exceptions the colleges for Negroes have long been lacking in almost everything necessary for first rate work. Library and laboratory facilities were limited, and faculty salaries were low. The students who came from the segregated and generally inferior public schools were often unprepared to do even low quality college work. Most of the public institutions were at the mercy of state legislatures or boards of trustees that were predominantly and often exclusively white and who took it for granted that Negro schools required less than white ones. It was out of these colleges that many of the Negroes came who were to be the teachers of the next generation of black children.

The people of other sections find it easy to lay all the blame for discrimination on the South. The discrimination against northern black children at the public school level was generally a function of the residential patterns. However, contrary to the belief of many northern college administrators, until relatively recent years only a few hundred southern Negroes each year attended northern colleges, and most of these were graduate students. On the other hand, several thousand northern Negro youth were attending the all-Negro colleges of the southern states. Some of them came South because it was cheaper, and some undoubtedly found the competition less severe. However, northern prejudice played the major role. The students cited their obvious unwelcome on the northern campuses, discrimination in the use of dormitories and eating places, and their exclusion from social life. Those who wanted to teach or go into one of the professions found more doors open to them in the segregated life of the South than in the supposedly more liberal North. Until 1950 the number of Negroes on northern college faculties could be counted on the fingers of one hand.

Many of these conditions have been improved at both the public school and the college level, but even today proportionately fewer Negroes than whites get to college. Whites outnumber Negroes in the population about ten to one; as college students, the proportion is nearer thirty to one. Moreover, of the approximately 200,000 Negro youth in college in the mid-sixties, half were in the predominantly Negro institutions in the South. More than one half of these colleges were privately supported and more than three-fourths of the private institutions were church related. Although practically all colleges and universities in the South as well as in the North are now open to Negroes, the enrollment of black students in most of them is small. Even when they are ostensibly welcomed, these students often feel left out of things and not really a part of the institution. The demand for separate dormitories and exclusive black departments are in part a reflection of this feeling.

The majority of Negro students from the South enter college with a handicap. Even the brightest ones—and there are many who have high native ability—have often been denied the breadth of experience and the good academic background available to many white students. Many of these black students come at a tremendous sacrifice to themselves and their families. A teacher in one of the better private Negro colleges in the South found that half of his students were the children of ministers, teachers, social workers. skilled laborers, and businessmen. The other half were the children of maids, porters, waiters, tenant farmers, unskilled laborers, and factory workers. In a state college the proportion from the second group would probably be much higher. Many people think of Negroes as lacking ambition, but how many white parents at this economic level have helped one, and sometimes two or three, of their children through college?

If any "reparations" are owed Negroes for past wrongs, their first claim should be on the federal, state and local governments that have done so much to shortchange blacks in the past, and that are still doing so at both the public school and the college level. The small investment of the states and the federal government in these black youth is indicated in the fact that as late as 1960 the average expenditure per student in the Negro colleges was only a little more than sixty percent of that of students for the nation as a whole. Although the Negro colleges enroll over half of all black students, the average state appropriation for current expenses for the Negro colleges was less than three percent of the total appropriation for higher education, and the Negro colleges got less than one percent of the Federal expenditures for colleges and universities. These small amounts are all the more striking in view of the fact that almost all of these institutions are suffering from the cumulative deprivations of earlier years.

Segregation of the black students at all educational levels is still the rule, north and south. Moreover, if we are to correctly appraise the significance of this long history of inequality in education, we must remember that deprivations of any kind are cumulative in their effects. The great majority of middle-aged Negro parents, teachers, college professors, ministers, doctors, lawyers, and businessmen of the 1960s and 1970s were the school children and college students of the tightly segregated society of the 1930s and 1940s. These early deprivations are still a factor in the health, the efficiency, the earning capacity, and the self-confidence of many adults, and in the kind of life they have been able to provide for their own children.

3. Economic and Cultural Deprivation

Economic and cultural deprivation go hand in hand, and both are related to poor educational opportunity. Many of the economic handicaps of Negroes were pointed up in earlier sections, but it should be emphasized here that an important factor in the Negroes' deprivations lies in their treatment as a group. Of course, some Negroes have achieved success, but regardless of personal qualities and effort, the black person is always identified with a supposedly inferior group, and many blocks are laid in his path solely because of color.

It was a century after emancipation before any appreciable number of Negroes began to obtain other than menial jobs outside the segregated Negro community. In the South they were sharecroppers, day laborers, and in domestic and personal service. Job opportunities were almost as limited in the North. Only in the late 1950s did black persons really gain a foothold as sales persons and clerical workers in non-Negro establishments. Labor unions long excluded them and not all apprenticeship programs are freely open even now.

By the late 1960s many white business firms were employing Negroes and offering job training. On the surface this appeared to constitute a removal of racial barriers. But black men were seldom found in the higher executive positions or on boards of management. The persons hired were often token or "showcase" blacks. Government studies made in northern industrial cities showed that in the late 1960s there was still only a limited use of Negroes in white collar jobs, and they were in the lower paying clerical and technical categories. In 1966 Negroes constituted more than eighteen percent of the population of New York City, but they held only slightly more than six percent of white collar jobs and less than three percent of management and professional positions. Conditions were equally bad, and sometimes much worse, in other cities.

Negro business and professional men have been handicapped by the fact that most of their customers and clients are still in the lowest paid occupations. There are, of course, notable exceptions, but if one's clientele is poor, this fact obviously limits what they can pay for goods and services. Moreover, the Negro business has generally lacked capital and access to sources of credit. As more affluent Negroes move out of the ghettos, they are likely to do their shopping at the big department stores and supermarkets where stocks are more varied and prices lower than the smaller Negro firms can provide. The Negro businessman must be located where his customers are, and he may find rents disproportionately high and insurance difficult to get except at an exorbitant rate. Urban renewal and highway programs may shut him off from his customers. He may lack experience and the benefit of the give and take with successful businessmen of the community.

Until the public accommodation acts of the 1960s, the questions of where to stay when travelling, where to eat, or even where one might find a drink of water or toilet facilities were daily problems to Negroes. In many areas social and cultural opportunities were equally restricted. As late as 1953 two-thirds of the Negro population in thirteen states were without access to library facilities of any kind. Throughout the states where separate schools were required, museums, parks, playgrounds, theaters, and concert halls were also generally closed to Negroes. In many northern areas such facilities were technically open but were located so far from the poorer Negro residential areas as to put them completely out of reach.

Reference was made earlier to housing restrictions and to the serious health and nutritional problems of the black poor. In many areas of the South there was a serious lack of access to medical services. Some white doctors refused to accept Negro patients, and there have been cases of seriously ill or critically injured black persons being refused admission to the only hospitals in the community. There is still a shortage of Negro doctors, and in many areas Negro physicians were denied hospital privileges and the stimulation of association with their white medical colleagues. Some state and local medical societies refused membership to Negro doctors regardless of their personal or professional qualifications. It was not until 1968 that the American Medical Association took a formal stand prohibiting racial discrimination within its constituent chapters.

The continuing deprivation of Negroes was summed up in President Kennedy's Message to Congress in February 1963: "The Negro baby born in America today, regardless of the section or state in which he is born, has about one half as much chance of completing high school as a white baby born in the same place on the same day; one third as much chance of completing college; one third as much chance of becoming a professional man; twice as much chance of becoming unemployed; about one seventh as much chance of earning $10,000 a year; a life expectancy which is seven years shorter, and the prospect of earning only half as much."

And that baby born in 1963 will be the relatively young adult of 37 when we reach the year 2000.

4. Techniques of Subordination

Once the pattern of dominance and subordination was established, numerous techniques were developed to support it, and an elaborate set of rituals grew up and functioned as a sort of etiquette of race relations. Such procedures are seldom, if ever, consciously planned. They are not even understood by many people who practice them. They become taken for granted as natural and right and are handed down from one generation to the next as a part of the accepted way of behaving. Of course the whole pattern of segregation functioned as a technique of subordination in that it set Negroes apart and limited their access to goods and services open to the rest of the community. However, there were many specific patterns that were explicit expressions of the superiority-inferiority value system. Many of these patterns have changed or are in process of change, but they are still common enough or recent enough to be a searing aspect of the black experience.

One of the most nonrational of these patterns, once common everywhere in the South, was the refusal to use ordinary courtesy titles in addressing or referring to Negroes. While the use of first names is now extremely common in all kinds of situations, in the past a reciprocal use of first names implied both equality and intimacy. A one-way use implied subordination of some kind based on age, status, or similar factors. Parents, teachers, employers, or adults in general addressed children, pupils, servants, and lower level employees by their first names, whereas these persons used proper titles of respect for parents, teachers, employers, and older people. The refusal of white people to use proper titles for Negroes carried the implication that they were classed either as servants or as children.

The ramifications of these patterns were numerous. Some school superintendents in the South were known to walk into a classroom and address the Negro teacher by her first name, in the presence of the children. Respectable, educated women, even if they were grandmothers, might be addressed by their first names not only by white adults but by any white of any age or status. This lesson was not lost on Negro children who constantly saw their parents, teachers, and ministers treated in this fashion.

Although modern Negroes generally resent the "Aunt" and "Uncle" once used by children in middle- and upper-class white families in addressing older Negroes, these were terms of respect though clearly within a paternalistic pattern. Close friends of the parents were often addressed in the same way. More bitterly resented, and with reason, is the practice, still all too common, of addressing adult Negro males as "boy." Outside the deep South this pattern is most common among sheriffs and policemen who are themselves lower class, though any Negro who works as a janitor, porter, or waiter may be so addressed by many white people. However, neither status nor place of residence is any guarantee of immunity.

The terms used in reference to Negroes were sometimes deliberately insulting and sometimes unconsciously so. "Coon," "burrhead," and "Nigger" were known to be contemptuous terms, but many people used "darkey," "picaninny," and "Negress" without being aware of their offensiveness to Negroes. Some Negroes compared the use of the term Negress to lioness, but it could have been as easily compared to actress or princess. The term was not unusual in the West Indies. Many Negroes today see in the pronunciation "Nigra" an insulting connotation though many white persons are wholly unaware of offending and may not even realize that they are mispronouncing the term. It is often the result of slovenly speech habits. The same persons are likely to drop their final g's in words such as coming, going, or doing.

One of the still persistent forms of subordination is in the spelling of the word Negro without capitalization. It was for a long time considered proper by reputable publishers although there seems to be no basis for it other than persistent usage. The *New York Times* set the pattern for change in 1930, and most American publishers of books, journals, and newspapers capitalize the word though a few still insist that the lower case is "correct." The lower case is more common in British publications. A copy of the unabridged *Oxford English Dictionary* of fairly recent vintage still shows Negro spelled without the capital though Malay, Indian, Eskimo, and every other such group whether identified as national, tribal, linguistic, religious, or within any other ethnic category, is capitalized.

Taboos on shaking hands or eating with Negroes were once widespread as were the rules against sitting together in trains, buses, or in public waiting rooms. Many public places were off bounds for Negroes under any circumstances unless they were there in the role of servants. When they were admitted to theaters, they frequently were placed in special sections and might have to enter through alleys and rear doors. In many buildings they could use only freight elevators. Until the passing of public accommodation laws Negroes might be refused admittance to hotels, restaurants, theaters, and other places of amusement or entertainment. In many public places there were no restroom facilities open to them, and in some cases there were three facilities, for white men, for white women, and for colored men and women. Wherever they went in the South they were forever reminded of their inferior status by "white only" signs.

The ritual nature of all these patterns is apparent, for they often involve psychic rather than actual physical separation. All kinds of exceptions could be made so long as the symbolic aspects of the situation were observed. A woman who would not shake hands with a Negro or sit by one on a bus or in church would allow a Negro nursemaid to care for her baby. Persons who would not dream of eating with a Negro would employ Negroes to prepare and serve their food, make their beds, and care for their clothes. Segregated waiting rooms often had only a sign to designate the white and colored sections with no actual physical distance between the two. The use of titles and the use of first names are, of course, purely symbolic expressions of relative status.

5. The Middle-Class Dilemma

White people in the United States have long classed all Negroes together. They do all share to some extent the black experience, but actually, Negroes take their statuses from two positions, sometimes referred to as caste and class. The terms are only partially accurate but are to some degree useful. Negroes have had two reference groups based on their position within the Negro community on the one hand, and their position within the larger, predominantly white, society on the other. The two reference groups have varied in importance not only in time and place but with the degree of the Negroes' dependence on the white world. Many Negroes, particularly in the South, for self-protection, if not for survival, attached themselves to some white family from whom they could expect protection in return for deference. In many communities all Negroes were more or less forced to live their public life with one eye on what the white community would approve, or at least tolerate. At the other extreme today are the militant youth who not only repudiate any interest in what the white world thinks but who profess to scorn the whole of so-called white civilization.

Although class lines are fluid and never clearly or sharply defined, there are some rough distinctions that can be made. The great majority of Negroes fall into the category of the lower class, but these persons are by no means all alike. There are differences in the lower-class poor of the rural South and those of the northern ghettos. There are the shiftless and irresponsible ones and those once described as poor but honest, or as Drake and Cayton put it, in their *Black Metropolis* the lower income group can be divided in the "shadies" and the "respectables." The problems of the poor, and especially those of the ghetto, were more fully discussed in the chapter on poverty. It should be emphasized here, however, that the lower class and the poor are not necessarily synonymous. There are many Negroes, especially outside the disorganized ghettos, who are poor by any standards and who may have little or no education yet who are scrupulously honest, clean, moral by conventional standards, who maintain a stable family life, work hard, and try to give their children a chance for an education and a way of life better than their parents had.

Middle-class Negroes, however defined, face a dilemma that today has grown increasingly acute. Because of education, background, and training they share in many of the values and goals, the interests and ambitions, of their white counterparts. On the other hand, they share many of the handicaps and frustrations and suffer many of the deprivations and humiliations, of the black masses. It is not surprising that they have responded in a variety of ways. They are no more all alike than are middle-class whites, but there is an extra dimension to the choices they must make.

The most comprehensive—and controversial—study of the Negro middle class was made by E. Franklin Frazier, a sociologist and himself a member of the black middle-class. In *Black Bourgeoisie* written in 1957, Frazier makes it clear that his description does not fit all middle-class Negroes. Those falling outside the group he distinguishes as Negro intellectuals and artists and many ordinary people who are neither superficial nor self-seeking, and who are concerned with helping the Negro masses.

Frazier was unsparing in his criticism of the ones he labeled the black bourgeoisie. These persons, he said, had made a break with their cultural past. They were without cultural roots in either the Negro world with which they refused to identify, or the white world which refused to accept them. Thus lacking a cultural tradition, rejecting identification with the Negro masses, and suffering the contempt of the white world, they had, he contended, developed a deep-seated inferiority complex and in order to compensate had created a world of make believe.

The behavior Frazier describes is not unlike the behavior of the new rich or the newly emancipated. It is in some ways merely an exaggeration of the behavior of many white families on their way up and a reflection of the superficiality of many American values. Booker T. Washington documented this kind of behavior on the part of newly freed slaves who wanted to learn banking and discount before they had mastered the multiplication table. It appeared in the superficialities of much of the social and political life in the early day of Liberia, and it can be seen in the flamboyant extravagance of some of the leaders and their wives in certain of the developing nations. It appeared in the behavior of the poor white who gained some power after the Civil War and in the emerging "lower classes" in Britain.

Frazier, who was a competent sociologist, laid the blame on self-hatred. Other students identified it as one of the "marks of oppression." The factors are doubtless more complicated. For one thing, it is not limited to people of any one race and therefore can't be wholly racial. It would seem to occur partly because it is much easier for the newly arrived to see and take over the superficial aspects of patterns previously reserved for the privileged. Form is more easily followed than substance. Certainly not all middle-class Negroes fitted into Frazier's category. The phenomenon was almost certainly related to the caste-like restrictions that forced Negroes into a segregated world. Omitted from the main stream, shut out from community participation, ignored by the white world, this type of exaggeration and overcompensation is understandable.

It is true that in some cities many of the more affluent Negroes have established their own suburban gold coasts and have shown as little concern for the poor Negroes of the ghetto as have affluent whites. At the time Frazier wrote, things were comparatively quiescent, and many Negroes had achieved a relative, if precarious, security and, like most white people in similar circumstances, were reluctant to rock the boat. They had come up the hard way and were not eager to be identified with the black masses. Indeed some of them asked, "Does the white man who comes up the hard way identify with the white poor? Or is he not more likely to move to the suburbs and say of the poor he leaves behind, 'I worked hard for what I got; let them do the same.'"

Middle-class Negroes have been criticized for their superficial values, their emphasis on clothes and big cars, and their preoccupation with "society." But middle-class Negroes are no more all alike than are middle-class whites. It is those who show off who attract attention. Moreover, Negroes generally have had less choice than whites have had in the way they spend their money. Sammy Davis in his autobiography *Yes I Can* sums up the matter by asking, "How else can they spend it?" Negroes can drive it and they can wear it, but too often they are not free to spend it the way whites do. Therefore they buy all the things they shouldn't because they can't do half the things they should.

It has been much harder for the successful Negro than for his white counterpart to cut himself off from the lower-class masses. Segregation patterns in churches, schools, and social life, as well as in housing, limited the Negro's freedom of association. Also, occupational and educational handicaps meant that almost any successful Negro had relatives in the kind of jobs that only lower-class whites would consider, and color was always a badge that proclaimed lowly origin and identification with a disadvantaged group. Although Negroes had developed a social hierarchy in which a light skin and "good" hair were aids to upward mobility within the Negro group, as far as most of the white world was concerned they were all just Negroes.

More recently two other factors have compounded the middle-class dilemma—the rise of the black power separatist movement, and the growing criticism of middle-class standards and values. The two, of course, are related in that the black militants not only emphasize black separatism but profess scorn and contempt for Western civilization in general and middle-class values in particular. The result has been what Louis Lomax calls "a deep schism within the Negro race." This has shown up in the Negro colleges in which there has been the same kind of dissent of black youth against black administrators and faculty as has been found among white students in white colleges. And some of the more militant black youth have been as scornful of the black middle-class adult as they have been of the white world.

Some of this is a matter of difference in basic goals, but much of it is a difference in specific goals and in the means by which certain ends are to be achieved. A part of it is the difference in youth and age. All Negroes are confronted with the fact that no matter what their education, background, or economic status, they are not fully accepted by the white world, and they are all subject at one time or another to various stresses and strains that even the lowliest and poorest whites escape. Involved in it all are questions of integration versus separatism, the emphasis of blackness or *Negritude*, and identification with Africa and the "Third World."

Louis Lomax in *The Negro Revolt* remarks that Negroes have remained marginal members of what has been called the Atlantic civilization because only doors on the periphery were opened to them. "We cannot change our color," he says. "Instead, our efforts have been directed toward achieving what must be called 'cultural whiteness,' although we and our ancestors made substantial contributions to that culture." But he feels that "the Negro individual has no hope of final or secure identification except with the general American social structure."

Carl Rowan not only justifies the middle-class Negro's integration with the white (or total) community but insists that this is necessary for the welfare of the Negro people as a whole, including the poor. Saunders Redding is even more blunt. Writing in *Prejudice USA*, he maintains that the unique thing about the present civil rights revolution is that its purpose has not been to overthrow the basic structure of society but to move the black man from outside it to a place within it. "Basically," he says, "the Negro wants no one put out—he simply wants in."

6. The Mark of Oppression

As we have documented earlier, the Negroes' experience in the United States has been such as to rob them of a worthy self-image. The crime of slavery was that too often it made the black man a slave in mind as well as in body. Since the days of slavery, Negroes have lived in a world in which the inferiority of their position pressed upon them negatively in the form of omissions and positively through the overt reminders that they did not really belong. The Negro child was denied a feeling of identity with the white world and yet was provided with no other worthy or meaningful identification. In such a marginal and fractured world the black child tried to find his way. He was assumed to be innately inferior, and looking about the only world he knew, he often accepted this judgment and made no effort to prove himself otherwise. Negro scholars have recognized this self-contempt and self-hatred as the most devastating mark of oppression.

It may be appropriate here to note that Jews and Negroes have taken different roads to survival, the choice, however unconsciously made, growing out of the necessities of the peculiar position of each. Jewish parents pushed their children to study and work hard and to excel as a means of survival in a generally hostile world. But Negro parents knew all too well that to demonstrate superiority especially among lower class or inferior whites was to invite disaster. They worried about the child who was too bright, too questioning, or too ambitious for of all things an inferior white person couldn't stand was an "uppity nigger" who didn't "know his place." The record of thousands of lynchings and countless murders and "legal lynchings" recorded elsewhere in this book is grim evidence that this protective device was all too often necessary to survival. The premium was not on creativity, intellectual achievement, or even material success but on fitting into the protective coloring of deference, docility, and humility. And contrary to the accepted white pattern it was more dangerous for Negro males than for Negro females to be smart or to try aggressively to get ahead.

Kenneth Clark in *Dark Ghetto* points out that human beings whose daily experience tells them that almost nowhere in society are they respected and granted the ordinary dignity and courtesy accorded to others, will begin to doubt their own worth. Children who are consistently rejected begin to doubt whether they, their family, or their group are worthy of respect. These doubts, Dr. Clark believes, become the seeds of a pernicious self- and group-hatred, the Negro's complex and debilitating prejudice against himself. The resident of the ghetto is bombarded by the myths of the American middle class, through television, motion pictures, and other media, yet confronted by his own harsh world of reality. He can never be sure whether his failure reflects personal inferiority or the fact of color.

Given the history of the relations of black and white, it was perhaps inevitable that Negroes as well as whites should come to associate the dark skin, broad nose, and crinkly hair of the Negro not only with ugliness but with inferiority. In this case all classes of Negroes were involved, and for a long period, class distinctions within the Negro group were strongly affected by color.

During the period of slavery Negroes with any observable degree of white mixture often had a distinct advantage over the blacks. Whether or not they were related to the master—and this was by no means always the case—they were more likely to be used as house servants, taught trades, or otherwise favored. When they were the offspring of the slave owner and a female slave, they were often taught to read and were sometimes granted, or permitted to earn their freedom. In 1850 more than a third of the free Negroes but less than a tenth of the slaves were of partially white ancestry. Inevitably out of this favored treatment, class distinctions arose within the group, and it was easy to assume that the persons of mixed ancestry were biologically superior as a result of their "white blood."

Another factor entered into the attitude toward color. Not only were the persons of wealth, power, and prestige white, but identification with the standards and values of the white world was in itself rewarding. Although the relationship of white men to the female slaves often involved force or sheer exploitation, there is no reason to suppose that this was true of all such relationships. The slave woman was sometimes motivated by the fact that if she bore children to the white man she could count on better treatment for herself and greater advantages for her children. Furthermore there were known cases of genuine mutual attraction between black and white, as there are today.

In any case, as Frazier points out, a light complexion became a most precious possession. This was true in the West Indies as well as in the United States. In the West Indies there was an even greater emphasis on degrees of whiteness. The lighter persons of mixed ancestry were known as *people of colour* in the English speaking colonies, *gens de couleur* in the French and *gente de color*, in the Spanish. These peoples constituted a separate—though not segregated—group from the darker ones who preferred to be called blacks rather than Negroes.

Eric Williams in his *The Negro in the Caribbean* wrote "A white skin in a society still obsessed economically and culturally by the slave tradition, is an indication of social status and the best passport to political influence. The nearer one is to the coveted white skin, the more likely one is to be accepted in society." C. L. R. James goes even further. Writing of the British Islands he says, "There are the nearly-white hanging on tooth and nail to the fringes of white society—there are the browns, intermediates who cannot by any stretch of the imagination pass as white, but who will not go one inch toward mixing with people darker than themselves. And so on and on and on." Frantz Fanon confirms these attitudes for the Martinicans who, he says, want to be taken for French and who cannot bear to admit their Negro-ness.

In the United States the custom by which any person known to have a Negro ancestor was classed as a Negro, no matter how white he might appear, resulted in a different pattern. The only persons with any Negro ancestry who were accepted as white were those who "passed," by going where they were not known and concealing their identity. Everybody else was a Negro as far as legal and social definition were concerned, but this did not lessen the premium put upon a light (not white) skin and "good" hair.

In his study of the Negro family, Frazier found that a light brown skin was particularly important for women. During the thirties and forties when a large number of such studies were made, the dark woman was under a much greater handicap than the dark male—a fact related to the general patterns of Western culture of attaching importance to beauty and attractiveness in women and to success and achievement in men. Throughout this period middle-class men tended to marry women much lighter than themselves. This pattern worked to the disadvantage of darker women. However, it also meant that in the next generation the daughters of these lighter women tended to be darker than their mothers—a fact that may have resulted in modification of the attitudes that associated lighter color with middle class status and with attractiveness.

However, even within the same family, the parents, often perhaps unconsciously, favored the lighter children. Malcolm X reports that he was the lightest child in his family and although his father was anti-white, he was so affected by "the white man's brainwashing of Negroes" that he inclined to favor the light ones. Most Negro parents in those days, Malcolm writes, would almost instinctively treat any lighter children better than the darker ones. Later on, in Brooklyn and New York, he says he was "among the millions of Negroes who were insane enough to feel that it was some kind of status symbol to be light complexioned." Later he came to share his mother's hatred of the white man who was her father.

"Good" hair was considered as much or more important than a light skin, especially for women. Men could wear their hair short though some men went through the time-consuming and sometimes painful ritual of having their hair "processed." Until the recent emphasis on blackness and "Afro" or natural hair styles, hair straightening was almost universal among black women and "doing hair time" was a dreaded but inevitable chore.

Whites assumed that the Negroes' only motivation for hair straightening was to be like white people. To some extent this was true since "white" standards were dominant in the culture. However, it was to some degree at least simply an effort to be in style. The willingness to follow fashion at any cost does not seem to be limited to any race, either sex, or any time. Western women at various times have affected wasp waists, spike heels, and foot deforming pointed toed shoes. Chinese and Japanese women, who rarely have wavy hair, followed western women in getting permanents. In the 1960s when straight hair became the style, many blond youngsters took turns ironing one another's hair in an attempt to remove any natural curl. Men at various periods have worn powdered and curled wigs, stiff high collars, and heavy suits in tropical weather. So perhaps the hair straightening ritual of the Negro women should be attributed at least in part to this widespread human desire to follow the fashion of the times.

Unquestionably, however, the Negro's concern with skin color and hair texture was in large measure an attempt to conform to what they saw as the desirability of white standards and values. Kenneth Clark saw this preoccupation with hair straighteners and skin bleaches as a tragic aspect of the Negro's acceptance of black inferiority. But he sees in the current rebellion against it an overemphasis that attests to its continued importance. Whether a Negro woman uses hair straightener or flaunts a "natural" style, whether a Negro man hides behind a neat Ivy League suit or wears blue jeans defiantly, each is still reacting primarily to the pervasive factor of race. He still is not free to take himself for granted or to judge himself by the usual standards of personal success or character. It is, Dr. Clark concludes, "still the white man's society that governs the Negro's image of himself."

The blight of the color line was never better expressed than in a 1968 CBS news sequence in the series "Of Black America." Here were shown the faceless, armless, ugly self-portraits drawn by black children. Commenting on these pictures in *Life Magazine*, Mrs. Roy Innis wrote that the greatest crime against the black man is not to be found in lynching or unemployment records, but in "the systematic stripping away of his humanity—of those cultural values that give one a sense of being not only in the world but of it."

Servan-Schreiber makes the same point when he says it is not good for only Americans and Russians to go into space. It inhibits the dreams of children of other nations. A child needs to be able to identify with a worthy model whether it is a parent, a remote ancestor, or even a great countryman. And although most of us do not realize our young dreams, it is important to know that dreams can be realized. Perhaps this is what Robert Frost meant when he said that the greatest of all crimes is "the theft of glory."

11

Why the Blacks Won't Wait

1. The Black Revolution

The black revolution took white America and even much of middle-class black America by surprise. It should not have done so for there had been storm warnings and what Walter White as early as 1945 called "a rising wind." The revolution has many facets and many roots, and it is by no means a unified phenomenon. There are splinters and off-shoots, antagonisms and rivalries. There are wide differences in the conceptions of specific means and of specific ends desired. There are the separatists who want a black nation within a nation; those who want full integration; those who profess to want out; and those who only want in. There are those who still cling to an American dream and those who see their major identification with an African-Asian world. There are those who seek cooperation with whites and those who regard whites with hatred and contempt. There are those who are non-violent and those who declare open warfare on what they consider a hopelessly racist society. Yet in one way or another all of these people are contributing to the black revolution; all share in some degree the black experience; and the most sober and responsible of them warn that we will ignore this movement at the country's peril.

Martin Luther King Jr. in his *Why We Can't Wait*, written in 1964, called it the Negro Revolution—the term black had not then come into general use. He called it America's third revolution and placed its explosive beginning in 1963. This was the year when in widely scattered places Negroes were saying in effect, "We have had it." Even in the deep South where mayors and governors, senators and congressmen, were still saying "never," the Negroes suddenly began interposing their own "now." The factors leading to this apparently sudden upheaval are many and complicated and can be touched on only briefly here.

Dr. King listed these factors as disillusionment over unfilled promises, disappointment in both political parties, the incongruity of the nation's championing of freedom in foreign lands while failing to insure that freedom for its own, the decolonization and liberation of nations in Africa and Asia, and finally the fact that one hundred years had passed since emancipation. The talk and publicity accompanying the centennial served only to emphasize the fact that emancipation had been a proclamation but as yet was not a fully realized fact. Throughout the nation Negroes still faced countless discriminations, openly practiced in many areas of the South, but no less real in the hidden and subtle disguises in which they appeared in the North. Moreover, as Dr. King pointed out, Negroes had grown increasingly aware that they lived "on a lonely island of economic insecurity in the midst of a vast ocean of material prosperity."

The 1954 Supreme Court ruling on school desegregation had seemed to many Negroes a second emancipation proclamation. But like the first one almost a century earlier, this was a proclamation, not a fact, and it did not open the door to the promised land. At the beginning of 1963, nine years after the Court decision, less than ten percent of southern Negro students were attending integrated schools. At this rate it would take another century for education in desegregated schools to become a reality for all children. All kinds of devices had been used either to evade or openly to defy the law, and there was a deep sense of frustrated hopes at the unfulfilled promise of the court ruling.

Events in the rest of the world had their impact on Negro Americans. The 1960s saw the rise of new nations all over Asia, Africa, and the Pacific as European colonial power was replaced by independent governments. By 1963 thirty-four African nations were ruled by Africans, and these black men were taking their places in the affairs of the United Nations. The American Negroes' self-consciousness regarding their own disadvantaged position was enhanced by these events and by the publications of Frantz Fanon who likened American blacks to a colony.

Another factor, little recognized, entered into the picture. Revolt rarely comes when people are in the depths of despair and see no hope. As Carl Rowan expressed it, the Negro has begun to taste freedom, and he longs for more of it. "Men become addicted to freedom," he says, "and the fuller their veins become of it the greater becomes their need of it." Frederick Douglass made a similar comment regarding the slave revolts. These revolts did not always come from those most disadvantaged but from those who had been given some advantages—enough for them to realize that they were really persons and not things. With that realization slavery became intolerable. By 1963 the sharecropper tradition was broken. For a generation since World War I Negroes had been on the move. The number of high school and college graduates had multiplied, and a fair number of Negroes had moved into more favorable conditions. This had the dual effect of making the educated Negro painfully aware that no amount of education or anything else was giving him full admittance into American society, and it made the Negro masses more keenly aware of their doubly disadvantaged position of being both black and poor.

There were other factors such as the worldwide revolution of rising expectations and the flaunting of American affluence in movies, on television, and in the glamorized advertisements in magazines and newspapers. It was an affluence in which the masses of Negroes had little part. Younger Negroes no longer had any contacts with better class whites on the level that at least some of their parents had known. For the most part, the only whites the ghetto youngster knew were those who exploited the blacks. There was also both a generation gap and an economic gap in the Negro community. Black youth were a part of the Now generation, impatient with both whites and the older Negroes who had tried to work out some means of accommodation. There was as much scorn for the "Uncle Toms" as for "Whitey."

There was also the disillusion with the methods used to achieve progress toward full acceptance into American life. Negroes had been admonished to work hard and to make themselves acceptable to white society, but they were still on the outside looking in. The organizations working for their welfare had eschewed violence and had been careful not to go too far. The National Association for the Advancement of Colored People had worked primarily through the courts. The National Urban League had concentrated on job opportunities and economic advancement. The Southern Regional Council, a more definitely interracial and southern based group, had depended primarily on the dispensing of information and efforts to improve the relations between whites and Negroes. It was not that these organizations had not shown courage and initiative, for they had done so to a high degree, but all of them were working within the system and their major goals had been to get Negroes into the mainstream of American life.

Lerone Bennett writing in *The Negro Mood* in 1964 spoke of four life styles—militants who express themselves through protest; moderates who take a middle course between accommodation and protest; accommodators who accept segregation and strive for various modes of individual advancement; and activists who repudiate protest, accommodation, and moderation, and demand action, violent or non-violent. In a completely different category are the Negro nationalists who say the civil rights struggle is useless and demand total separation either in Africa or in America.

In its earlier stages the movement had concentrated on the civil rights struggle with whites and blacks together singing "we shall overcome." By 1966 the emphasis had shifted to black power. As noted earlier, the year 1966 marked the real coming of the blacks with the rejection on the part of many, especially youth, of the word Negro, the emphasis on blackness, the use of African dress and natural hair styles, and a general repudiation of the white world by the more militant blacks. Although the situation was extremely fluid at the beginning of the new decade, one thing was certain—neither the black world nor the white one would ever be the same again.

2. What Do They Want?

White people sometimes ask impatiently, "Well, what do they want?" Any white person can find the answer by asking himself honestly: What basically do I want for myself and my family? The answer, of course, is not to be found in such specific desires as a split level house, a swimming pool, a color television set, a new car, or a boat, but in those basic things that most white people take for granted.

To suppose that all Negroes want the same things and would use the same means to get them is as absurd as to assume that all whites think and feel alike. If one asked what white Americans want he would get different answers from rich and poor, from educated and uneducated, from old and young, from liberal, conservative and radical, from the war protestor and the war hero, and even within any of these categories there would be wide variations. Negroes' views, too, are determined by economic status, education, place of residence, religion, and all other factors that influence the opinions of Americans.

The specific ambitions, desires, and goals of Negroes have changed over time. At any given period in our history Negroes have probably wanted basically what other people wanted, that is, a chance to be themselves, to live their own lives as they wished, to be free to go and come as other people do, and to be free of the hampering restrictions of overcontrol. However, these desires have tended to be expressed within the context of the life about them. In the past, these desires were, as a practical necessity, usually expressed with one eye on what the white world would tolerate and the black world could dare hope for.

Unquestionably there have been gains in the Negro's position, and these gains have been accelerated though there is still a question as to relative progress as compared with gains among whites. In almost every area of life and in almost all communities there have been changes. Negroes can now walk into hotels, restaurants, theaters, concert halls and just about any public place and expect service given with varying degrees of courtesy. Practically all colleges and universities are to some degree desegregated, and even in the states that said "never" there is at least token desegregation in most schools. Negro policemen have become commonplace, and Negroes are serving on juries, city councils, and in state legislatures. Public transportation is no longer segregated, and more and more newspapers are printing news about Negroes and are using ordinary courtesy titles in referring to them.

During the same period there have been comparable changes on the national scene. For the first time a Negro was appointed to a cabinet level position and another to the Supreme Court. Negro models began to show up in advertisements in national magazines, and mail order catalogues began including Negroes in their illustrations. Prominent Negroes were included in White House functions, and the marriage of daughters of prominent white families to Negroes caused only minor flurries of comment. When state laws forbidding interracial marriages were declared unconstitutional, the ruling received only minor press notice.

Wasn't this enough? It was too much in the minds of many white people, but the answer from the black population was an emphatic no. In the first place, nothing reveals the actual discrimination against Negroes more clearly than these "signs of progress." One hundred years after the Negroes supposedly became full citizens, it was counted as progress that they could in some ways and in some places be accorded the rights and privileges which the lowliest white person had long taken for granted.

Furthermore the progress made by Negroes has not been uniform nor has it kept pace with the progress made by whites. Middle-class Negroes have made relatively greater gains than their poorer fellows. While some Negroes were gaining in wealth and recognition, and while universities and business concerns were competing for the highly educated Negroes, no such doors were opening to the black masses. In fact, since there were fewer opportunities for the unskilled, the gap between blacks and whites widened, and poorly trained Negroes found themselves slipping even further down the economic ladder.

Many white people responded to the new demands of Negroes as if a hitherto contented people had suddenly presented a bill for past grievances. Many militant young blacks have scornfully labeled as Uncle Toms, their forebears who tolerated discrimination and were conciliatory in their demands. But Negroes really have been presenting the bill for a long time, and many of the persons now derided by rebellious young blacks were, within the climate of their own day, persons of outstanding courage without whose pioneering efforts the changes of today could not have come about.

In an earlier day Negroes asked for equality within a segregated society because that was all many of them could envision and was more than a white world was then ready to grant. Even in asking for equality of opportunity and separate but equal public services they were generally careful to specify that they were not interested in "social equality." This, of course, was the primary factor in Booker T. Washington's famous Atlanta Compromise of 1895.

As time went on it became increasingly evident that the separate was never going to be equal and that segregation involved the exclusion of Negroes from many aspects of life. As more and more Negroes received college and graduate degrees, the incongruity of the old patterns based on ideas of racial inferiority was more and more apparent. The Supreme Court decision of 1954 was a logical development as were the various civil rights statutes of the later 1950s and early 1960s. As we have noted, 1963 marked the push on the part of Negroes for full civil rights and when these were not forthcoming, with the 1966 march in Mississippi the idea of black power came to the fore. In a matter of months the direction of the civil rights struggle shifted from an integration-oriented movement to what has been called "a cultural and political revolution of black consciousness, self-development, and self-determination."

As the world moved into the seventies there were wide differences in the immediate goals for Negroes and in the means they would employ to gain those ends. Although the militant young blacks made the headlines, they were by no means in the majority, and they were not all agreed among themselves. However, the sharpest divisions within the Negro group were between those who held to the idea of integration within the mainstream of American life and those who felt that some form of separatism was the only way open.

The separatists were usually the younger and more militant groups who generally repudiated the term Negro and insisted on being called blacks or Afro-Americans. Some, though not all of them, identified with Africa, Asia, or "the Third World." Many of them made a point of affecting a natural hair style and often some form of African dress. They asserted their pride in blackness and their rejection of white middle-class standards and values. Beyond this, their specific goals varied. Some of them wanted a separate black nation. Others wished a completely separate black life with all black communities, black businesses, black universities, and black departments within formerly white universities, all of these things to be under complete black control. Some of them demanded that these enterprises be financed by whites in the form of reparations for past wrongs inflicted on blacks.

Some adults encouraged the more militant black youth in their dream of an "impossible revolution" which involved not only black control of black institutions but the "taking over" and remaking in a black image of all the institutions hitherto controlled and dominated by whites. They were to do this "by any means necessary." "The call is now to take over," one such adult wrote. "Perhaps the Age of Blackness is here."

Other blacks were quick to say that while youth should dream "impossible" dreams, the idea of a completely separate black world was unrealistic and the "impossible revolution" was suicidal. The late Whitney Young writing in the August 1970 issue of *Ebony* pointed out that the idea of a black "take over" would first be dependent on the unlikely support of the more than 23 million American Negroes. Moreover, he said, unless 88 percent of the population of this country packs up and moves elsewhere, state and federal governments will continue to be dominated by white people.

Roy Wilkins said that given the position of the American Negro population as a numerical minority of one-tenth and an economic, political, and social minority of much less than a tenth, the only road open to blacks is integration into the general population. Mr. Wilkins does not see this as either complete assimilation or absorption but as adding separate parts to an entity. He claims that the overwhelming majority of the Negro American population, including at least half of those under thirty, still see integration as the goal.

Some of the separatists emphasized the fact that although blacks are a minority in the United States, the darker peoples are a majority in the world. Roy Wilkins called the idea of unity among these people a romantic dream. Even the Africans do not necessarily feel any unity with American Negroes. In fact, the African nations often have difficulty in achieving unity among their own people who have tribal, religious, linguistic and ideological differences as evidenced in events in the Congo, Nigeria and the Sudan.

The late Tom Mboya, Kenya's minister of economic development and planning, warned American Negroes that they could not look to Africa for an escape. "I have not found a single African who believes in a black demand for a separate state or for equality through isolation," he wrote. He called unrealistic the belief that some black Americans had of the ease with which they could throw off North American culture and become African. "The black American should look to Africa for guidance—and for a chance to give guidance—but not for escape. He must merge his blackness with his citizenship as an American."

Other black leaders pointed out that Negro Americans are just as alien in most of Africa as they are in most of Europe. Although some Negroes professed to feel at home in Africa and Malcolm X claimed to have been warmly welcomed by the Muslim Arabs, most American blacks who stayed in Africa for any length of time found that they felt—and were regarded by Africans—not as Africans come home but as Americans abroad. Richard Wright who visited the Gold Coast (now Ghana) in 1954 found himself baffled by many of the customs of the people. Speaking of one ceremony he had witnessed, he wrote, "I had understood nothing. I was black and they were black, but my blackness did not help me." Langston Hughes had a similar experience. Writing in *The Big Sea* he said, "I was not Africa. I was Chicago and Kansas City and Broadway and Harlem." Others noted that the Africans they did identify with were the leaders most of whom were the products of Christian mission schools and of British, European or American universities.

Saunders Redding first became fully aware of his identity as an American while on a trip to India in 1954. He found many Indians color conscious to a degree completely unimaginable even to American Negroes, and their beliefs about America incredible. "Until I came out to India," he wrote, "I had no idea that there was in me so great an urge to defend America or that there were so many dangerous untruths to defend her against." Writing in *Prejudice U.S.A.* fifteen years later Redding insists that whether they realize it or not black Americans are Americans. "In spite of the Black Muslims and the ambivalent appeal of their emotional identification with Muslim Africa," he writes, "the Negro American is no more African than the fairest Anglo-Saxon Protestant is. He is American. His destiny is one with the destiny of America. His culture is the culture of Americans and so are his vices and virtues and problems." Louis Lomax sums up this point of view in the Epilogue to *The Negro Revolt*, "Whatever else the Negro is," he wrote, "he is

American. Whatever he is to become—integrated, unintegrated, or dis-integrated—he will become it in America."

There were others who agreed with the young militants in rejecting integration. Roy Innis took the position that blacks must develop a strong black nationalism before they can discuss equality and integration. Others noted that integration as conceived of by whites almost always meant the absorption of the black minority into the existing white structure without any necessary changes on the part of the whites. They would therefore strengthen black agencies, organizations and institutions as a necessary step in being able to bargain from strength. As one put it, "We must sing black and black together before we can sing black and white together."

Still others pointed to the fact that integration served as a sort of brain drain on the black community. As white universities sought black professors, churches and social agencies sought black directors, and business concerns competed for the exceptional Negro, black institutions had to take whatever was left. Moreover these blacks taken into the white institutions were rarely placed in policy-making positions and were often "showcase" or token blacks rather than fully accepted members of the group.

Apart from the extreme militants, however, there is actually more unity among Negroes than appears on the surface. What we are all for, the editor of *Ebony* wrote in 1970, is really liberation or transformation. Most blacks, he said, are integrationists, separatists, and pluralists all at the same time. They have to be in order to exist in the present situation. They integrate for some purposes on some occasions, separate at other times, and co-exist in a form of pluralism under other conditions. Blacks want control over their own lives and over their own communities even when they operate within an overall framework in which whites dominate. Moreover they would use integration, separation, and pluralism as strategies as the occasion demanded.

In a special edition of *Ebony* in August 1970, the editor equates real integration with what he prefers to call transformation, which would not be simply an absorption of blacks into what they think of as white culture. It would require changes in white people and in the institutions they now control. The important thing is that whether they ask for integration, separatism, pluralism, transformation, or any gradation between or combination of any of these, what Negroes really want is liberation, and that involves the freedom to choose as one wishes. Whitney Young called this the open society.

A long series of national and world events have combined to crystalize sentiment. Resentment that has long smoldered has now become articulate and militant when triggered by seemingly commonplace and trivial events. In the meantime a worldwide revolt against authority and a militant youth movement have complicated the picture. Negroes speak with many voices about the specific ends desired and the specific means considered appropriate to gain those ends. They speak as one in their insistence on the end of discrimination and their right to all the privileges, duties, and obligations of other citizens.

3. The Revolt Against Authority

It is foolish to attempt to understand or to evaluate the black revolution without seeing it in the context of a worldwide revolt against authority. In a sense, what has happened in the United States is only incidentally racial. It is essentially a rebellion of the powerless against the powerful, of the have-nots against the haves, and of the deprived against the privileged. The rebellion of American youth is treated in the following section, but it is only one aspect of the larger problem.

There is, of course, nothing new in rebellion or revolution. Strikes, riots, civil wars, uprisings, and revolts are recorded throughout history. What is peculiar to the present situation is its worldwide nature and the variety of forms it takes. The social history that has brought us to our present worldwide involvement is briefly treated in the final chapter of this book. Here we need only note that it is a part of the revolution of rising expectations and that the instant communication that makes events in one part of the world quickly known everywhere is undoubtedly a factor. If in the twelfth century a good part of Europe could be caught up in the contagion of the crusades—even involving the children —it should not be difficult to see how the idea of freedom from authority has spread so easily and so quickly in an intercommunicating modern world.

Frantz Fanon, who has greatly influenced the black youth of America, likens the powerless everywhere to people in colonies. The essential characteristic of a colony, as he describes it, is that of a powerless people used and exploited for the benefit of the powerful. Following World War II, and with an accelerating pace in the sixties, most of the peoples ruled as colonies of the European powers gained their freedom and set up independent governments. During this period India, Pakistan, Indonesia, Malaysia, a number of Southwest Asian countries, Pacific Islands, and practically the whole of Africa escaped from colonial to independent status. In such a worldwide upheaval, the idea of freedom spreads, hitherto undreamed of alternatives open up, and it would be surprising if many people did not get the idea that freedom meant the right to do whatever one wished. It would also be surprising if those accustomed to power yielded their privileges without a struggle.

Many of the revolts against authority took the form of armed rebellions, but there were also forms of passive civil disobedience, notably in India under Gandhi's leadership. This was the example followed in the early days of the Negro protests under Martin Luther King, Jr. in The Christian Leadership Conference and in the original program of The Student Non-Violent Coordinating Committee (SNCC). The people who most severely criticized Dr. King and the whole civil disobedience movement as being a threat to the rule of law were strangely blind to the far more active and lawless disobedience engaged in by many white officials throughout the South and less directly in the North. The basic philosophy of civil disobedience rests on the concept of a higher law, that is, obeying God rather than man and following one's own conscience, but it also involves willingness to suffer the consequences of such disobedience as a means of inducing change in unjust laws. When carried out in this way—a standard perhaps above the capabilities of ordinary mortals—it becomes a powerful weapon for social change and may have in it the distinction between the martyr and the criminal, though both break the law.

Negroes generally saw a monstrous hypocrisy in the self-righteous pronouncements about law and order and the wrong of choosing which law you would obey, since many white Americans had for a long time chosen which laws they would obey. Certainly no literate person could be ignorant of the fact that the 1954 Supreme Court ruling on school desegregation had called forth massive resistance throughout the South and that elsewhere in the country as a whole, cities and states along with numerous agencies of the Federal government had long ignored certain laws affecting the rights of Negroes. With a few outstanding exceptions, southern senators and congressmen had signed a Southern Manifesto which all but openly breathed defiance of the Supreme Court. Southern governors "stood in the door" to prevent the entrance of Negroes into publicly supported institutions, and state legislatures, city councils, mayors, school boards, and various officials sworn to uphold the law openly defied the authority of federal law and Supreme Court rulings.

In other parts of the world, revolts against authority took various forms. Sometimes the rebelling group was a numerical minority; in other cases a powerless majority opposed a powerful ruling minority. In some cases the two groups might be more nearly even in numbers and were in conflict as to which group would gain control.

As we noted earlier these conflicts were only rarely actual racial conflicts though they may have been so defined either by the press or sometimes by the people involved who thought of their differences as physical when they were basically religious, linguistic, ideological, or political. At the time of the partition of India hundreds of thousands, perhaps as many as a million, people lost their lives in Hindu-Muslim riots although the two groups were not in any way racially distinguishable. The conflicts between North and South Korea, North and South Vietnam, Nationalist and Communist China, the civil wars in the Congo, Nigeria, and the Sudan, the rioting in Northern Ireland, recent disturbances in Malaysia and Pakistan and earlier in Madagascar, and the Arab-Israeli conflict all involve peoples in which the racial differences are either minor or non-existent.

Campus unrest and the revolt of the young blacks in the United States are the subject of the following section, but it may be noted here that an important element in the revolt against authority throughout the world is that of student or other youth groups. As in the United States some of their protests have been directed against government policies and others against institutional arrangements. Even the totalitarian countries have not wholly escaped, though they are in a position to ruthlessly repress any dissent.

Student revolts have long been common in Latin America where students have been more politically conscious than in many other areas. In Japan during 1968 and 1969 more than a hundred campuses were disrupted, a half dozen university presidents were forced to resign, and thousands of students were arrested. Student revolts were widespread throughout France, and the London School of Economics was forced to close for three weeks. Rioting on one Canadian campus resulted in the destruction of a computer complex reportedly valued at more than two million dollars. A United Nations report indicates disruptive dissent among student groups in more than fifty nations.

This rebellious activity in the rest of the world points up the complexity of the problem in the United States. Those who lay all the blame on the racist character of American society overlook the turmoil in countries where there are no racial differences; those who would attribute it all to the Vietnam war forget that countries not involved in Vietnam have their share of unrest; and those who would find the causes in American affluence, permissiveness, and television addiction overlook the conflicts in countries that have none of these things. There is no single cause, and all of the conditions described throughout this book have played their part as background to the general unrest of which the rebellion of black youth is only one manifestation.

4. The Now Generation

The behavior of militant black youth can be understood only if seen within the context of the general revolt against authority and the rebellion of certain segments of the youth population everywhere. There has been much talk of whether this is the most idealistic generation in history or whether the great majority of youth are merely spoiled brats bent on having their own way. The answer, of course, is that modern youth are not all alike. Aside from the wide differences in aims and goals of black and white youth there are differences within each group. The patterns and attitudes of many of the more privileged white youth are particularly relevant in understanding the behavior of black youth.

Only a few years ago educational leaders were complaining about the apathy of American students, their lack of involvement, and their preoccupation with trivialities. Sororities and fraternities were riding high, and young men found their amusement in swallowing goldfish, stuffing telephone booths, and engaging in panty raids. There were sometimes wild parties and after-football activities that were destructive. Most of these activities were regarded as youthful pranks, to be accepted with a sort of benevolent tolerance. When this apathy and frivolity turned to a revolt against the establishment in general and educational authority in particular, both parents and college administrators were taken by surprise.

It is important to note that the protesters are not all alike, and their goals are not the same. The demands have varied from the trivial and self-indulgent to those concerned with the most basic and urgent social problems. Apart from the differences in the grievances and goals of white and black youth, to be considered later, the most fundamental differences are between those committed to revolution and the destruction of institutions, and those who want varying degrees of reform within the system. The first group is in the minority but has shown skill in "radicalizing" other students who do not necessarily agree with their basic revolutionary aims. These revolutionaries are convinced that Western civilization in general, and American society in particular, are incapable of social justice and that their dominant values and interests are evil. Particular protests are not meant to be ends in themselves but means to more revolutionary goals. A part of the strategy of this group is to encourage retaliation so as to win sympathy for their cause. They taunt and bait policemen, destroy property, insult those in authority, and generally act in ways to invite rage, fear, and repression. Their "negative heroes" are the reactionaries and arch-conservatives whose opposition aids the revolutionary cause. To the revolutionary the liberal is an anti-hero because liberal reforms tend to weaken the justification for revolutionary action.

The great majority of the student protesters are not revolutionaries but reformers in the sense that they wish to change rather than to destroy society or its basic institutions. However, many such groups have become convinced that no really significant changes are likely to be brought about by the people in power who have a vested interest in the status quo. They thus see that the only hope of change lies in getting some of the power. This was essentially the condition of the laboring man of an earlier day, and the rise of the labor unions was a means of gaining bargaining power through organizations. In some cases the reformers have been used by the revolutionaries either because the former were innocent and unaware that they were being used or because they had been radicalized by the repressive actions of those in authority in answer to the often deliberate provocation of the revolutionaries. Basically, however, reform groups that have engaged in disruptive tactics have done so not to overthrow the institution but to force attention to their needs or to gain concessions.

Many of the youth on American college campuses are idealistic, and young idealism often tends to a sharp dichotomy of right and wrong, simplistic solutions, and an acceptance of absolutes that may appear as arrogance or self-righteousness. In their demands for certain "rights," a vocal and militant minority have sometimes ridden roughshod over the rights of the majority. On many of the disrupted campuses the demand for freedom of speech meant freedom for the protesters but not for those who opposed them. The "non-negotiable" demands were often arbitrary, sometimes frivolous, and at times destructive of the very values the protesters were avowedly clamoring for. In some cases the students who were demanding that they be treated as adults and given a greater voice in running the institutions were at the same time demanding amnesty for students who had committed lawless acts that, had they not been within the protected environment of the campus, would have quickly brought down upon them the full force of the law.

Many students were ideologically opposed to the militants, and others simply objected to the disruption of their studies. To a large percentage of today's students, their education is something important and dearly bought. Unlike the ones from affluent homes or the recipients of generous scholarships, these students were often earning a considerable part of their own expenses. Moreover the more thoughtful of them were aware of the negative reaction of many of the people on whom the colleges depended for support. These people were raising questions as to why some students were allowed to get away with disrupting classes, breaking windows, and even burning buildings when other thousands of qualified youth were being turned away from publicly supported institutions because of classroom shortages, inadequate facilities or lack of housing. "Why," people were asking, "should not the disrupters be sent home to make room for others who really want an education?"

The resentment was greater because so many of the protests—some estimates indicated fully one half of them—were not concerned with basic social issues but with housing rules and other regulations that the protesters felt were personally restrictive. In one particularly incongruous case one thousand students in a state school rioted to protest the holding of classes on Good Friday. Added to the irony of the situation—and to the number of serious youth who would be turned away—was the fact that public reaction against the disorders resulted in decreased giving on the part of some supporters of private colleges and smaller appropriations by state legislatures.

As Amitai Etzioni pointed out in a discussion of the Columbia confrontation, the students often had a highly unrealistic idea of what "the system" can do. They wished a larger faculty and many other reforms that would have called for a much larger financial outlay, but they were horrified at any suggestion of higher tuition fees, and at the same time demanded actions that would have reduced, if not cut off altogether, other means of support. In other institutions the students have protested the university's investment programs and the presence of successful businessmen on Boards of Trustees, and they have berated state legislatures and wealthy private donors which are the major sources of funds by which universities operate. Many of the protesters were seemingly unaware that every college student today is heavily subsidized by society in one way or another. In many cases, they were making demands that nobody had the power to grant, or that, if granted, would mean a reduction of funds and the consequent end of educational opportunity for thousands of youth.

Although the black and white students had much in common, there were important differences in the demands of the two groups. The three consciously powerless groups of today are the poor, the black, and the young. It is important to note that black students generally fall into all three categories. Moreover, you get over being young, and being poor is not necessarily a permanent condition, but being black is something that isn't going to go away. The one hope for a better life for black people is to make blackness an asset rather than a liability.

In an *Ebony* article on "Negro youth and the 'Now Generation'" Dr. Donald Hopkins holds that black youth are alienated for reasons that are essentially different from those affecting white students. Both groups may feel that there is hypocrisy in the older generation and may feel bitterly about the draft and the Vietnam War—as well they might since the sacrifices are made by youth while their elders make few if any sacrifices. But the black youth are the inheritors of cumulative deprivations and injustices that can produce an overwhelming rage. Although some black students have made some non-negotiable demands that are totalitarian, coercive, and sometimes of the kind that, if granted, would destroy the very equality they seek, they have on the whole been more serious and more responsible than many white students. And since blacks in this country have for generations been the victims of violence and of the arbitrary demands of white people, the rage of the young blacks is understandable even when their actions are not always defensible.

The majority of the militant white youth generally come from the more affluent middle class and their interests and goals often differ in many ways from that of the black youth who usually are poor. White youth who have never known deprivation and who have never had to earn their own living may repudiate the "technological civilization" without being aware of their dependence on it. Dr. Hopkins notes that many of these privileged white youth "speak in highly stylized self-pity of how awful is the society which annually supplies them with $14 billion worth of clothes, cars, and sundry paraphernalia essential to maintaining the generational distinction."

Of course not all middle class white youth are unduly privileged but the extent of white affluence was illustrated when the Chamber of Commerce of Daytona Beach estimated that the 1970 "Easter vacation romp" would bring 60 thousand or more students to the area and that they were expected to spend 6 million dollars.

The black youth who have always been among the have-nots may merely want in on something they have never had, or they may want the freedom of choice about their own lives that has been available to most of the privileged white youth. The more revolutionary of the black students not only reject the white establishment but the traditional black leadership as well, which they may label "Negroes" in contrast to their designation of themselves as blacks or Afro-Americans. The black students on the campuses of the predominantly Negro colleges have often charged Negro administrators of these institutions with being paternalistic and imitative of whites.

In judging the protest of youth, a number of things need to be taken into account. To be merely passive in a day like this can be considered immoral and is certainly dangerous. A people can drift into destruction as easily as they can be destroyed by evil or misguided actions. For youth to be passive today in the face of problems confronting the nation and the world would involve an insensitivity and lack of responsibility that would overshadow any irresponsible or misguided actions they might take in their efforts to introduce change.

Moreover, the establishment, however one chooses to define it, in many ways has only itself to blame. Earlier sections of this book have documented numerous ways in which power has been misused to discriminate against the black and the poor, and doubly against those who are both black and poor. We live in an affluent society that seemingly finds money for everything except tackling the social problems that daily grow more glaringly apparent. Colleges and universities are controlled by boards that are often made up exclusively of affluent men well past middle age. Administrations and faculties have often appeared more interested in research and in their own careers than in excellence of teaching or concern for undergraduate students. Moreover many institutions had so resisted reform and were so outdated in their procedures and so insensitive to the needs of black students in particular, that only shock tactics would have shaken them out of their lethargy and complacency.

This is not to say that all the demands of students should have been met or that violent disruptions of universities should be tolerated. For administrators to grant to immature and inexperienced youth concessions that would wreck the institution or to permit the wanton destruction of property, the prolonged occupation of buildings, the rifling of files, or the manhandling of personnel is to behave as irresponsibly as the students who engaged in such acts. Administrators must also be held responsible for the fact that in many cases changes were initiated only after pressure and disruption. As one student remarked, "The only way we can get attention is by tearing up stuff."

Youth today are caught between the adult world's piecemeal and inadequate dealing with major social problems and their own naive and inexperienced belief in the magic of protest signs, the shouting of obscenities, or verbal affirmations of peace and love. But is it really so strange that many youth should believe in the efficacy of the thoughts of Mao Tse-tung, that Castro has the answers, or that Hanoi is devoted to peace and freedom? If they believe that poverty can be eliminated, peace achieved, and age old social problems solved by some sort of magical means that ignores cause and effect and the wellsprings of human behavior, they have learned these beliefs from their elders. In the news media, particularly on television, they have been exposed since infancy to a constant diet of violence, of a division of the world into good guys and bad guys, and to the implied sanction of violence or any other means so long as it is used for "good" ends. Simplistic instant solutions are offered for everything. Patent medicines, special diets, or exercises promise instant health and vitality; perfumes and cosmetics promise instant beauty and popularity; and books promise instant business success or peace of mind. The under-thirty generation has grown up in a world of push-button magic. How could they know of the labor and sacrifice of the generations of people necessary to make this magic possible?

Adults must assume responsibility for the facts that values have been distorted, that our efforts at betterment have been piecemeal and painfully slow, that there is much hypocrisy in the expressed ideals and sorry performance, and that much of what we have taught youth was not only irrelevant but trivial. The triviality of much of their education is revealed in the ephemeral nature of what they often define as relevance. We have not taught them that true relevance is not found in the immediately useful or seemingly practical but in the fundamental and lasting principles by which life can be directed regardless of change in specific conditions.

The real cause for concern about many white youth may not be their rebellion but their lack of any real sustained commitment that gives promise of being consistent, constructive, and permanent. Whites constitute nine-tenths of the population of this country and, given the inevitableness of the march of time, the white youth of today will be the major part of "the Establishment" a few years hence. If they simply "get over" their youthful fling and settle down, or if they are unwilling to commit themselves to the slow, painful, consistent and persistent labor that is going to be necessary to keep the human race from self-destruction, there will not be any future worth bothering with.

It is significant that many of the black youth have been far more serious in their goals, and more consistent in their performance than the majority of white youth. The "tune in, turn on, and drop out" philosophy that has won many devotees among white youth has had little appeal to the blacks. Few, if any, black faces have been seen in the hippie hangouts, in the Ft. Lauderdale bashes, or in the various versions of Woodstock. The use of drugs among blacks is more a ghetto than a campus phenomenon. As one of their number has put it, "That is not where the black youth is at."

There are, of course, many Negro youth who fit into Frazier's black bourgeoisie and whose ambitions are as frivolous or self-seeking as those of any white. But on the whole the blacks who rebel are rebelling about something very real and fundamental to human dignity and worth. And, in spite of the excesses of some of the more extreme groups, many black youth have shown a concern for and an identification with the deprived masses that offers significant hope for the future. White youth of any persuasion could learn a great deal from their black counterparts.

5. The Search for Identity

In the late 1960s events moved so rapidly as to leave many Negroes and perhaps the majority of whites puzzled and frightened by the demands of the more militant young blacks. The emphasis on African dress and hair styles; the use of the term black instead of Negro; the demand for black power, for separate dormitories and separate black departments in the predominantly white colleges, and for black universities that would sever all connections with the white community; and the repudiation of any interest in integration, were topped off with demands for "reparations," and even for a separate black nation, coupled with threats to "tear the country down" if their demands were not met.

Beneath the rhetoric and the extremes, however, lies something of great fundamental importance that has its roots in the black experience in America. James P. Comer in a chapter in *The Black Power Revolt* makes the point that a degree of black power is an essential foundation for any really meaningful integration into American life. As we noted earlier, when other groups came to this country they usually settled in the same area or sections of a city. They were, as Dr. Comer points out, sustained psychologically by the bonds of their common heritage. They maintained family, religious, and social institutions that fostered group unity. They voted, gained political influence, held public office, and often prospered. Within a generation or two they moved into the mainstream of American life with only a nostalgic interest in the old country.

The Negroes' experience was entirely different. They came from many different tribal groups with different languages and different cultural heritages. During the slavery period they were not only separated from family and fellow tribesmen but were often on isolated plantations where there were only a few slaves. They were thus completely separated from their past and made dependent on the white man. Security lay in identification with the master and his interests. They were never allowed to forget that in the eyes of the white world to be black was to be inferior.

In the past, and up to the present, no Americans were more loyal or more patriotic. No group tried harder. In every war they enlisted even when they faced discrimination, were segregated in labor battalions and denied enlistment in officers' training schools and in certain of the services. Even when they returned wearing medals for bravery, they were in many places not allowed to vote, were denied jobs, and access to many services open to the poorest and meanest whites. They were still dependent on white favor. The black man's struggle for identity, for a sense of belonging, a heritage, and models to emulate, all grow out of the fact that throughout his life he has been shut off from his African past but denied full acceptance as an American.

It is in the light of all this history that one should see the demands of the black militants. It is a demand to be treated as persons, a defiant acceptance of the blackness with which they were born, and identification with Africa because they were rejected by America. Even the demand for separatism is not surprising in the light of the fact that they and their fathers before them were always on the outside looking in as far as most of life was concerned. It is a natural consequence of all that has gone before.

After generations of denigrating or trying to deny the unalterable facts of physical difference, there is everything to be gained by coming to terms with their own physical heritage and accepting themselves as human beings in their own right—black human beings. Basic physical characteristics must be accepted if one is to live a healthy life. As color is the most noticeable and largely unmodifiable characteristic, the acceptance of blackness and the disassociation of color with inferiority are necessary steps toward self-acceptance and self-respect. And such self-acceptance is essential to the acceptance of others.

The use of the term black is psychologically important as a means of giving a positive connotation to a characteristic that for so long was perceived in a negative way. The demand of black Americans for recognition as a group is in large measure a response to the fact that they have long been treated as a unit, and as an inferior one, by the majority of white people. Negroes have long been the bottom rail in the we-they syndrome. Now some of them are saying that they do not wish to be swallowed up in the "we" if it means a repudiation of what they are and the values they have come to think of as peculiarly their own. They do not want their children to be simply darker versions of Dick and Jane.

In terms of basic American standards and values much of this is good. Are we to ask young Negroes to glorify the people who fought for freedom from British rule and deny honor to the black men who fought for freedom against the white men who held them in bondage and traded them as chattels? The demand for courses on African culture, Negro history, art, and literature, the glorification of black heroes, the repudiation of western values and western dress, the turning to Arabic-Muslim culture, the desire to learn African languages—all these are a function of their exclusion from American life and culture.

The blacks would be more than human if such a movement did not involve some irrational elements, excesses, and an ignorance of some of the facts of history. What they now do is in some ways a mirror reflection of what has been done to them. Thus it is not surprising that this search for identity has sometimes taken incongruous forms as in the identification with Arabic-Muslim culture and in the desire to learn Swahili. It is true that the Arabic-Muslim peoples have generally shown less color consciousness than many others, that they freely intermixed with African blacks, and that together they developed a high civilization in the western Sudan. On the other hand, the Arabic-Muslim peoples were the preeminent slavers. They were carrying blacks out of Africa long before the slave trade to the West began. They were important middlemen in that trade, and they continued the trade to the north and east for nearly a century after the slave trade to the west ended. The black men who were with the Spanish and Portuguese explorers of America had been transported across the Sahara and sold as slaves by Arab and Berber traders. In the western Sudan as late as 1900, slavery was basic to the Muslim Hausa's economic system, and the non-Muslim blacks were subject to periodic raids. There is today a continuing conflict in the eastern Sudan between the Muslims in the north and the black tribes to the south, most of whom follow their traditional religions.

Dr. Lorenzo Turner, a black man who has been a distinguished student of Africa and African languages for thirty years, attributes the Swahili enthusiasm to a lack of knowledge of history. In East Africa the Swahili people served as middlemen for the Arabic slave traders up to the middle of the last century and had far more association with the trade in blacks than with the American Negroes, whose ancestors came not from East Africa but from the sophisticated cultures of the West Coast and the Congo. For American blacks to study Swahili to establish cultural identity is a bit as if white Americans of French ancestry were to study Russian as a means of identifying with their French heritage.

However, aside from any practical use that can be made of the knowledge, learning a second language has value in expanding horizons and making one aware of different ways of perceiving and categorizing experience. If the fact that Swahili is an African language has the additional value of enhancing the self-esteem of the learner and if it helps to dispel the notion of Africa as an unrelieved "dark continent," its study can be justified. But it is unfair if black youth in America are led to believe that their ancestors had any real connection with the East African peoples. Their African ancestors were biologically, culturally, and linguistically associated with the peoples we know as the Hausa, the Yorubas, the Ibos, the Ashanti, and others of West Africa.

The demand for the teaching of what is called black history is all to the good, though many of the hastily set up black studies departments can be the means of cheating Negro students out of a good education.

Too many degrees in something vaguely labeled "Black Studies" can reduce the degree holders to the economic equivalent of taking in one another's washing. Carl Rowan points out that although it has not been true that getting an education, using good English, and acquiring some skill and "acceptable" habits have opened all doors to Negroes, the fact remains that few doors are going to be opened without these things. Being "relevant" to the black community may mean many things, but if black people are to be fed, clothed, housed, transported, and given medical attention, black students are going to have to learn to be teachers, doctors, lawyers, merchants, bankers, electricians, salesmen, accountants, journalists, nurses, and social workers, as well as factory workers, farmers, carpenters, and bus drivers.

Black history is needed for white as well as black students at all levels from kindergarten to college, and it should properly be taught as an integral part of history in general. Even more fundamental is a complete overhauling of both curriculum and text books, not to emphasize blackness but to rid them of narrow conceptions, bias, and omissions. The great majority of students, black or white, get through college almost totally ignorant of any history, culture, literature, religion, or philosophical systems that go beyond western Europe with perhaps a smattering of material on ancient Greece and Rome.

Such changes will not be made at once and in the meantime the insistence on the inclusion of African history and the role of Negroes in American life are appropriate to correct a serious and long-standing neglect. Moreover, there is a great need for a few really good Black Studies Departments extending through the graduate level in which the most exacting scholarship should be employed. Any really adequate black history must rest on a lot of research not yet done and on the collecting, editing, and in some cases translating, of a great deal of material now buried in libraries in various parts of the world. Such meticulous scholarly work is necessary to provide the source materials on which ordinary textbooks, histories, and school materials at all levels should be based.

As many of the more experienced and more thoughtful Negroes have emphasized, the American Negro is neither European nor African but is biologically, psychologically, and culturally a little of both. America is the only home he knows, and the American heritage is his heritage even though in many ways he has been shut out from it and denied his place in it. In the long run, all Americans, black, white, Indian, and Oriental, all whose ancestors came to these shores to make their home— and even the Indian's ancestors did not originate here—are a part of the American people, and their ancestral homelands were a source of the American heritage. In fact, as we note more specifically in the concluding chapter, the human species now has a common cultural heritage going back to man's earliest beginnings, and our real identity in such a world must be our species identity.

But there are intermediate steps. Black Americans must come to accept their blackness and their identity as men before they become fully ready to accept their species identity. White Americans must rid themselves of their narrow conceptions and must realize that the civilization of which many of them are so proud is not white civilization at all but a heritage from many lands and peoples on whose collective shoulders we all stand. A proper beginning is a recognition of the long neglected African cultures which are not only a part of the black man's heritage but are in a very real sense a part of the heritage of all Americans.

6. The New Blacks and the White Liberals

Many white persons who have thought of themselves as liberals have been puzzled and sometimes hurt when they, as well as their efforts for racial betterment, seem to be rejected by black persons. Some of the more militant blacks have gone so far as to say that the so-called liberal is a worse enemy to black aspirations than is the avowed racist. Certainly all blacks do not feel alike on the subject, and many of them do maintain a friendly and cooperative association with the whites they have long known and worked with. However, the generally negative reaction is important and needs to be understood. It is not unrelated to the militant's reaction against any black accommodation to the white world and to the rejection of Negroes in the past who worked for such accommodation. These Negroes are lumped together as "Toms" or "white niggers," epithets that correspond to the "nigger lover" once hurled by some whites at any white person who showed any interest in or concern for the welfare of black people.

The present rejection of the white liberal is a stage in the achievement of a sense of identity and is understandable in that context, however uncomfortable and disturbing it may be to the persons so rejected. During slavery and up until fairly recent times, Negroes in the South—and until very recently that is where most of them lived—not only lacked the vote and consequently any political power, but they were in economic dependence on the white man who controlled jobs, wages, the machinery of government, and all other aspects of community life. The safest thing any Negro could do was to attach himself to some white family with sufficient status, economic resources, and good will to protect him. In order to stay in the good graces of his protector, the Negro assumed the appropriate role of a deferent and grateful beneficiary.

It is not surprising that both partners in these arrangements developed the attitudes appropriate to their roles. If the white man "invented" the Negro, the Negro in turn perpetuated the white man's image of himself as a "friend" of the Negroes. It was, of course, a paternalistic pattern, but in the world as it then was, it constituted the Negroes' only protection from less scrupulous whites who had no concern for the black man and no compunction about cheating him, abusing him, or even lynching him. Under these circumstances when Negroes needed help or protection, they turned to their "white friends."

With increased education, economic advancement, and a modicum of political power, Negroes and the more liberal whites began to work together, less as patron and dependent, but still perhaps as senior and junior partners, in various enterprises. In many areas there was still an often unconscious paternalism on the part of the whites and a degree of dependence on the part of the blacks. These paternalistic and sometimes condescending attitudes showed up in various subtle ways of which the white person was often unaware but which Negroes were quick to catch. There was still a good deal of the see-what-we-have-done-for-you, and the Negroes were expected to be properly grateful.

The present day mood has moved from the "Please, mother I had rather do it myself" stage to an often impatient rejection of even the most disinterested proffer to help. Not only are the mice of the world no longer doing what the cats say, but they are thumbing their noses at the cats. This is as true of the nations formerly under colonial control as it is of minority groups. Such nations can seldom, if ever, make it alone, but they are extremely sensitive. They have not yet had time to fully establish themselves or to feel secure in their own freedom. They are generally dependent on the wealthier and longer established nations for both economic help and freedom from outside aggression, but they bitterly resent any interference. This was clearly demonstrated in the reaction reported in a Nigerian newspaper headline admonishing the British—and others—to "stay off of our crisis."

Rebelling groups in the United States include youth, the poor, the blacks, and sometimes women, all of whom are demanding a greater say in what happens to them, greater freedom to do their own thing, and a greater share of the good things of life as a right, not as condescending charity. It should not be surprising therefore that persons who are at the same time poor, black, and young should be most vociferous in their demands.

But there is more involved. The militants who are real revolutionaries actually do believe that liberals are their enemies. It is partly in keeping with the old saying that bad kings are good if they are only bad enough, that is, if their behavior is so outrageous as to create support for their overthrow. If you believe that our present society is so bad that the only hope is to overthrow it completely and "start over"— as some of the militants do profess to believe—then the people who are concerned with reform merely get in the way and delay the confrontation. This is essentially the attitude of the Communists who are committed to revolution as a means of establishing party control, though a corresponding belief is held by many persons who reject the Communist party as such. This is one more case in which it is necessary to understand the premises that underlie overt behavior. There is no use in arguing that a given behavior is wrong because it will tear the society apart if the other person considers tearing the society apart exactly what should be done. The argument must be on whether tearing a society apart is a good or bad means to a good or bad end.

There is still another factor involved. The white liberal often has worked primarily to promote interracial understanding and good will. He seldom has had much power to influence events except in an indirect way. But the new blacks profess not to care whether they are understood, and they scorn the goodwill of whites as being a mere patronizing sop to keep blacks quiet. They are in a demanding not a pleading mood. These demands take a wide range. They include the employment of blacks at executive and administrative levels and, in some cases, that churches and other organizations pay millions of dollars in "reparations" for past injustices to blacks.

Allowing for the rhetoric, there is considerable reason back of many of the proposals, outrageous as they may appear to people who are distressed by anything that disrupts orderly procedures. However, if the actions of the more militant blacks succeed in antagonizing genuinely concerned whites, the resulting polarization, already far gone, could reach levels disastrous for all concerned. Whites have long admonished Negroes to be patient and to give white people time. It is now the whites, particularly the liberal whites, who must be patient and who must step aside while blacks settle for themselves their own problems of identity.

It should not take too much imagination to see why many blacks wish white people would stay out of the way. The problem is twofold. Many whites out of long habit tend to "take over" and either try to run things or else stand by with a sort of benevolent paternalism while they allow the blacks "to learn by making their own mistakes." The second aspect of the problem is within the black people themselves who, because of their long experience in subordinate roles, are insecure in the presence of whites. This insecurity tends to express itself either as a self-conscious deference to white opinion or else as angry rejection. It is in either case an uncomfortable and inhibiting situation. Some one has described it as like having your mother-in-law along on your honeymoon.

There is obviously a dilemma here, and again it is not unlike that faced by the new nations. The recently independent countries are dependent on the cooperation and help of the more powerful nations for economic and political survival, but so is the peace and welfare of the whole world dependent on the economic and political health of all of the nations in the world community. In the same way, the blacks must have the cooperation and help of the white community if they are to achieve their aims. Likewise the health of the nation as a whole is dependent on the health and well-being of its constituent units, however they are formed. Most thoughtful Negroes agree that in the long run it must be black and white together, but they also understand that there must be a degree of black identity and black independence so that the cooperation can be that of equals in dignity and self-respect, if not in numbers.

There is always the danger, of course, celebrated in the fable of the killing of the goose that lays the golden eggs. It is easy to forget that colleges, churches, foundations, businesses, and governments cannot create money on demand. Somebody must earn it, and agencies and organizations must acquire it through gifts or taxes, or investments of gifts and taxes made earlier. Moreover, it is not there merely for the taking. It must be granted or appropriated. Only in a totalitarian country can the democratic process be completely bypassed, and if the United States of America should go totalitarian the people who would suffer first and most are those who now have the least power, that is the poor and the blacks.

These considerations perhaps define the primary role of the genuinely liberal and humanitarian whites in the present crisis. However much the new blacks may scorn them, such whites are needed as never before. They are needed to interpret the situation to the rest of the white community, to work for legislative and structural changes by which injustices and abuses can be eliminated, and to exert pressure on those who have the power to correct the abuses from which the powerless have so long suffered. For while the militant blacks may say they are not interested in, and do not want, the understanding of whites, the black community cannot survive without white understanding and help. And the whites cannot survive without the cooperation and help of the blacks. Whether we like it or not, this is our home. We are all here and there is nowhere else for us to go.

Most thoughtful blacks really know that the destinies of whites and blacks are bound together. Malcolm X in his last years admitted that he had once made sweeping indictments of all white people, but that he would never do that again. "I now know" he wrote, "that some

white people truly are capable of being brotherly toward a black man—
a blanket indictment of all white people is as wrong as when whites
made blanket indictments against blacks."

Whitney Young probably spoke for the great majority of Negroes
when he said that there is no reason why blacks should deny themselves
access to whites who are genuinely committed to their cause. There is,
he says, an important place for whites who are willing to accept peer
relationships with blacks, for those who can communicate with other
white people and who have the influence and power to help white
institutions change. Our fight is one of the long haul, he says, and we
need organizations run by blacks, but with the lasting support of whites
capable of working as equals to change the system that oppresses whites
and blacks alike.

At this point, no one can predict the form this black-white cooperation can or should take. Apartheid would surely lead to oppression.
Pluralism has a not very attractive history in other areas of the world.
Integration has its opponents from both the extreme left and the extreme right. The only things we can be sure of is that black and white
must go on living together and that it will be to the benefit of all of us
if it can be done with justice and mutual respect. Understanding and
good will alone are not enough, but they are necessary ingredients in
any solution to the problems of a multiracial society.

12

The White Experience

1. Thinking White

In an earlier chapter it was emphasized that an individual's behavior is the result of his particular genetic structure in interaction with the particular environment within which he operates. His behavior thus has a history, but it is also affected at any given moment by the circumstances, and the position from which he views the event in question. Because no two persons begin life with identical equipment and no two environments are ever exactly the same, no two people ever perceive the world in exactly the same way. Obviously, therefore, the way people perceive what we call race relations is unique to each individual. In one sense, our perceptions are as distinctively our own as are our fingerprints.

There are, however, certain kinds of experiences that people in different positions share. And in a biracially structured society, just as there is something that can be labeled a black experience, there is some-

thing that can be called a white experience. It is of the greatest importance to an understanding of race relations that we recognize that race
as such is not the major factor in either the black or the white experience. There are no black or white genotypes that determine any particular kind of behavior. There are only black or white individuals whose
racial identification makes it probable that they will be subjected to
certain kinds of experiences that, in general, give to blacks and whites
what we have called different maps of reality. There are thus individuals
who, because they are defined as black or white, in a particular place at
a particular time in history, have had experiences of a particular kind.

It follows that when we excuse people for race prejudice on the
basis that it is "natural," or when we berate a whole people for the sin
of "racism," we obscure the real problem. Throughout this book is
repeated documentation of the fact that more often than not man's inhumanity to man has operated within rather than between races. No
race has any monopoly on greed, selfishness, cruelty, ethnocentrism, or
willingness to use power in the exploitation of the powerless. This
chapter then is about white people not because there are any behavioral
characteristics inherent in the lack of pigmentation, but because in most
of the world today, and in the United States in particular, power and
privilege are largely in the hands of people who are white, or in nations
whose populations are predominantly white. "Thinking white," then
is essentially the kind of thinking that arises out of a position of dominance.

It is true, of course, that not all whites are privileged. Many of
them are as poor and helpless as the poorest blacks, and some of them
are far less privileged than the more affluent members of the black
community. Nevertheless, their identification with the white population
has given them a freedom denied to most blacks. And the denigration of
blacks, especially as it has been expressed in segregation, gives to the
less privileged whites somebody "to feel better than," and thus has
bolstered their all too precarious claims to self-respect and status. Like
the slave who took pride in his master's status, the poor white takes
pride in his race. Often the smaller his own personal achievement, the
more he boasts about what "whites" have done.

Moreover when blacks get into positions of power and dominance
over others, they are as prone as the people of any other race to "think
white" in the sense in which the term is used here. This is not the same
thing as the "Tom" or the "white nigger" to which blacks sometimes
refer. It may have nothing to do either with one's color or with one's
identification with whites or the white world. It is rather the kind of
authoritarian, dominating, and often arrogant, behavior that goes with
certain kinds of power. It has characterized individuals of various races

in Asia, Africa, and the Caribbean, as well as in the predominantly white areas of the world. It is a function of a position and power rather than of color as such.

The black or white experience is, of course, only one factor in the total environment of the individual, but it affects in some degree almost all other experiences. We have already noted the dilemma of the middle-class Negro who is torn between his identification with less privileged people who share his black experience, and his identification with the values and goals of middle-class whites with whom he shares other kinds of experiences. The black and white poor also have much in common in their disadvantaged positions though their competition for jobs and status often obscures this fact.

2. They Are Not All Alike

Although it has become the fashion to talk about our "racist society" as if it were monolithic and for blacks to lump all whites together —as whites have long put all blacks in the same category—these positions represent obvious oversimplifications. The way in which the structure of a society helps create and maintain attitudes will be treated in a later section. Here two points need to be documented: one, that whites do vary in their attitudes today as they have in the past, and two, that even with the same attitudes, people of different social classes and with different experiences will express their attitudes in different ways. And, of course, both attitudes and overt behavior will vary with time, place, and circumstance. These facts may seem self-evident, but they are often ignored, and our failure to take them into account blurs our understanding of race relations and hinders any effective dealing with the problems inherent in our present situation.

Most people think of the primary differences in the attitudes of whites as being related to whether they are from the North or the South. However the terms northerner and southerner can at best be only loosely defined, and in many ways they represent states of mind rather than geographical residence. In general, northerners, until recent times demonstrated otherwise, usually thought of themselves as more liberal than people in the South, whereas southerners frequently regarded the North as hypocritical, and insisted that it was really the southerners who were the Negroes' friends. Allowing for large elements of self-delusion in each point of view, there is also an element of truth in each.

When Negroes increased in numbers, moved into previously white neighborhoods, or became competitors for jobs, whites in the North tended to react much as their southern counterparts had under similar circumstances. Northern people not so directly affected were likely to remain in ignorance of the Negro's actual position in the North, and of course, the situation has changed greatly in recent years as enormous numbers of black migrants from the South have poured into the cities. In most cases the more privileged and affluent whites retreated to the suburbs leaving the central cities as islands of impoverished blacks surrounded by an ever expanding and generally white suburbia.

Autobiographical accounts of Negroes will aid greatly in understanding how whites behave and why Negroes feel as they do about whites. The stories of Claude Brown, Sammy Davis, Jr., and James Baldwin in Harlem, Malcolm X in Michigan, Wisconsin, and later in Harlem, and Dick Gregory in St. Louis and Chicago give vivid day-to-day pictures of what it has meant to be black in a northern white world. Richard Wright's *Black Boy* and Carl Rowan's *South of Freedom* document the Southern picture. Perhaps the best sociological analysis of a Northern city is the one made by Horace Cayton and St. Clair Drake of Chicago in the 1930s and published as *Black Metropolis*. The mass movement of Negroes into northern cities in the decades following served only to exacerbate the problems and increase the tensions that Cayton and Drake describe.

In general northerners have not objected to the Negro so long as they were not affected directly by his presence. Southerners, on the other hand, feel threatened when Negroes "get out of their place" anywhere. The "Southern way of life" was dependent on all Negroes being subordinate to all whites. This attitude shows up clearly in the fact that in the deep South any white who treated any Negro as an equal was subject to isolation and even to reprisals. He had betrayed his fellow whites.

There are, of course, many different kinds of southerners, white and black. There is at one extreme the genuine white liberal concerned with human welfare regardless of race, and at the other extreme the crude and ruthless exploiter. In between there are a variety of points of view, most of which can be described as in some degree paternalistic.

There is a sense in which many white people, especially in the deep South, have felt that they still "owned" the Negroes. This feeling was unconsciously revealed in the defensive arguments insisting that the Negroes themselves were content if only "outsiders" would leave them alone. The various levels of sophistication showed up in the choice of terms. Whether they were "our niggers," "our darkies," "our Nigras," or "our colored folks," there was this unconscious possessive term. The blacks were an essential element in "our way of life," but only as they remained docile, obedient, deferent, and content with "their place." So long as the proper patterns were symbolically maintained, a considerable measure of freedom was possible. And so long as the system was not threatened, many white persons could be, and were, as kind, fair, and generous as the system allowed.

Many older Negroes, having grown up in the system, accepted it and some even profited by it, though at the expense of self-respect and identity as persons in their own right. The secret of success—and certainly of safety—if you were black, was to attach yourself in a dependent relationship to the "best white folks," that is, those who combined the maximum status and power with the maximum degree of fairness and generosity. Where Negroes could not vote, had no political power, and no economic security, one needed a patron who did have these things. Once such a relationship was established, especially if it had persisted over several generations, the white patron could be counted on to get medical help for you, tide you over an economic crisis, and get your son out of jail or off the chain gang.

These roles of dominance and subordination reinforce and, in a sense, create each other. Whites could think and act as whites only if there were other people who thought and acted as blacks. The deference to white people was not only a survival technique to blacks, learned early and passed on from parent to child; there was also a circular reinforcement of the pattern. "Good" Negroes showed proper respect, deference, and obedience to white people. In turn, "good" white people were paternalistic and protective of "their" Negroes. Many white persons were flattered and gratified by this kind of dependence and homage and it was perhaps inevitable that the incongruity and degradation of these roles should become apparent to Negroes long before most white people were aware of them.

There are differences in the kinds and degrees of prejudice, dislike, hatred, and other emotions and attitudes, and these vary with economic, educational, and class differences, as well as with other factors that enter into the particular kinds of experiences that people have had. In both North and South there tends to be greater prejudice on the part of whites whose lack of education and skill put them in competition with Negroes for jobs. Some of the most prejudiced white groups have been immigrants or others who started at the bottom and whose precariously held gains appear to be threatened by any advance among Negroes.

There are also differences in the way prejudiced attitudes are expressed. If a person is sadistic, crude, and cruel, his prejudice may erupt in the kind of violence against blacks recorded in other sections of this book, documented in the daily press and in the accounts which Negroes give of their experiences at the hands of such persons. However, throughout the country there are men and women of more education and more refined habits who are prejudiced but who express their feelings in less crude and openly offensive ways. Such persons sometimes leave it to the less refined members of the community to hold the Negro down. They do not participate in violent activities but they stand by consenting, and the cruder members of the community sense the permissive attitude. The bombing of churches and schools, the harassment of Negroes, and the murders of Negroes and white civil rights workers, like earlier lynchings, usually occurred in those communities where there was lacking a strong sense of justice and a respect for persons on the part of the community as a whole.

Southern white people who saw the 1954 Supreme Court decision as a threat to their way of life were, of course, correct. Wanting to preserve one's accustomed way of life is, except for the oppressed and the disadvantaged, an almost universal human pattern and is not limited to any race or people. People generally welcome change they regard as beneficial to themselves while at the same time they may resist change that interferes with their cherished values or accustomed privileges. There is therefore nothing unusual in the desire of the white people of the South, or anywhere else, to preserve their way of life. The wrong comes when such a way of life automatically shuts out part of the community from its benefits.

The sins of white Americans and especially of white southerners have been fully documented in these pages. They range from brutal harassment, physical violence, and even murder, to the more refined but equally destructive defiance of the law by people in high places, and the fainthearted tolerance of people who don't want to get involved in unpopular causes. But in spite of the blanket label of "racist" and the militant black youth's designation of "Whitey" as the cause of all evil, most Negroes know that whites, like any other group of human beings, vary in their attitudes and in the way in which these attitudes are expressed. Many older Negroes, especially those in the South, know from experience that there are many whites who have worked tirelessly and courageously for years for the betterment of the lot of black people. There are whites who have suffered social ostracism; there are college professors and editors who have lost their jobs; there are ministers who have been forced out of their pulpits; and there are some whites who have given their lives in the cause of human freedom.

3. Learning to Be White

As we noted earlier, in the past black parents were under the necessity of teaching their children how to be black in order that they might survive in a world dominated by whites. Not everybody is aware that, although the teaching may have been less direct, white children were no less clearly being taught how to be white. All the techniques of subordination described earlier as means of keeping the Negro "in his place" also served to make the white person aware of his own place of dominance.

The segregation patterns that characterized American society in the North as well as the South, served as built-in devices to teach black children to be black and white children to be white. Residential segregation practically guaranteed that the only black people the average white child saw would be domestic servants or unskilled laborers. Middle- and upper-class children in the South were familiar with Negroes as cooks, maids, yard men, and day laborers. Even in the North, middle class Negroes who were teachers, doctors, lawyers, ministers or businessmen were rarely visible to the white child. In most areas of the country the segregated schools and churches prevented any normal association by which white and black children could come to think of one another simply as human beings. Even in northern cities the residential patterns, sometimes helped on by some gerrymandering of school districts, made schools segregated in fact if not in law.

Until the 1960s almost all other institutions were to some degree segregated, off limits, or inaccessible to much of the Negro community. The learning to be white was helped along by practically everything children read or saw. Schoolbooks were based on white middle-class norms. Attention has already been called to the way in which geography books, histories, school readers, and other materials either ignored the black man or portrayed him only in a subordinate role. It was only in the 1960s that these patterns began to be changed, and black people began to show up in advertisements and to appear as normal members of the community in other ways. The end result of these patterns was predictable. Nobody had to tell the white child that he was white or that being white gave him certain privileges and prerogatives.

Although all white children learned to some degree the generalized pattern of being white there were many variations. An essential factor in the way in which people develop the perceptions and learn the roles deemed appropriate to them is the social structure of the particular society in which they live. The relation of race attitudes to social structure is apparent in stratified societies in which people of different races occupy different positions. In societies in which stratification is based on economic, educational or social attainments, role differentiation based on physical difference may be minor or even entirely absent. In studies made for the United States Office of Education in 1939–1941 it was clearly documented that the racial attitudes of white Americans were correlated with such factors as the cotton economy, the proportion of Negroes in the population, and the degree of urbanization and industrialization. Although many of these structural patterns have changed, attitudes may persist long after such structural changes have taken place.

In the United States, and particularly in the South, the child's behavior is molded by his class position in a biracial society. In one city of the upper South, when school desegregation was instituted, some schools in the more privileged residential sections were unaffected because no Negroes lived anywhere in the area. When faculty desegregation was ordered, a competent black teacher was assigned to a first grade class in one of these all white schools. She had no problem at all with the children. One child when asked about school said yes, he liked it but he guessed the teacher must be sick because she sent the maid to teach them. He didn't object at all to being taught by "the maid." It was just beyond his experience to encounter a black woman in any other role. At home "the maid" had helped him in and out of his snowsuit, had supervised his play, comforted him when he was hurt, told him stories, and often granted or refused permission to engage in certain activities. These were, after all, tasks that he was accustomed to seeing his mother perform also. It is only later that by the subtle pressures of his culture he will come to see "the maid" and other black people as being of an inferior order. Even then he may dichotomize, placing the Negroes with whom he is familiar in one category and in an entirely different category the others whom he may fear or dislike.

Given all these circumstances, the attitudes commonly described as prejudiced are almost inevitable. What we grow up with and what is taken for granted in our culture usually come to be thought of not only as right but as natural. Unless and until alternatives are presented, the average person tends to take the accepted routines as a matter of course. At present all patterns are being questioned, but when most of today's adults were growing up no such alternatives were offered them. They learned to be black or white in the same way that they learned their sex roles and the other accepted ways of the culture. Until various alternatives were in the air, as it were, little Hopis grew up to be big Hopis, little Dobuans went the way of their fathers, and so did most Americans, middle-class, lower-class, black or white, follow in the footsteps of their parents in the way the culture defined as right and proper.

4. Rights and Double Rights

At no point has "thinking white" been more in evidence than in the response of many individuals and communities to the question of civil rights. Many persons are confused about the differences in desegregation and integration, about what is public and what is private, and about those things that are properly regulated by law and those that are a matter of private conscience and personal choice. Thus many white persons are surprised to realize that what they were claiming as their "rights" were really double rights, that is, the right to do as they wished but also the right to regulate the behavior of others.

There can be no question that under our constitution all citizens are supposedly guaranteed equal rights, some but not all of which are spelled out. The problems arise in the area of interpretation. Because a great deal of discrimination against Negroes was written into state and local ordinances, and in some cases into state constitutions, these patterns came to be taken for granted as being not only legal but right and proper. Even many federal agencies operated by patterns that were clearly discriminatory.

The basic inequality of most of these practices was tied in with segregation, that is, the maintenance of schools and a variety of other facilities that, though public in character, were operated on a segregated basis. Throughout the South these requirements were written into law and in many other areas the same results were achieved by various extra legal devices and arrangements. Segregation was also practiced by many agencies and organizations that thought of themselves as private, such as churches, privately run schools, hotels, restaurants, parks, playgrounds, and transportation facilities. In some areas there were laws forbidding the use of the same facilities by whites and Negroes. In many northern areas residential patterns served as effective segregation devices.

A racially segregated facility is one in which the members of only one race are admitted. Desegregation requires that such barriers be removed and the facility be open to all on equal terms. A facility is integrated when it is actually used jointly and freely by both races. There is then a sense in which a facility may be desegregated without being really integrated, that is, it may be technically open to all, but in practice not so used. Various devices were used to prevent school desegregation, and as a consequence the courts gradually moved to the point of requiring actual integration even if it required the transportation of school children from one area to another.

Many white southerners complained with some justice that integration in the sense of achieving racial balance in schools was required of southern communities while northern communities, fully as segregated in fact, were left undisturbed. They found it difficult to see why segregation by law (*de jure*) was more discriminatory than segregation in fact (*de facto*) regardless of the way in which it had been brought about. Much of the segregation in both North and South grew out of residential patterns, though northern as well as southern communities were sometimes guilty of gerrymandering school districts to preserve the racial composition of schools.

Although Negro as well as white parents sometimes objected to the busing of children to achieve racial balance as required by some court orders, Negroes found it hard to take seriously the outraged white protests about the sanctity of neighborhood schools. Too many of them remembered how for years black children had been forced to walk several miles to a black school when a perfectly good "neighborhood" school was just around the corner but open only to white children. In some small southern communities where there was no high school for Negroes, the black high school pupils were forced to go thirty or forty miles by bus to the nearest Negro high school, although the white high school was only a ten minutes walk from their homes. Moreover, some white parents sent their children long distances by bus where they enrolled them in private schools set up for the purpose of avoiding integrated public schools.

Most people have accepted the fact that those things that are supported by taxes should be open to the public on equal terms. Everybody, of course, pays taxes in one way or another. Apart from sales taxes and income taxes all property taxes are paid in part by the public because the owners of rental property, shops, theaters, and other such facilities pay property taxes that are reflected in the prices they charge for goods and services. However, many white people do not seem to realize that the public in general also helps pay for all tax exempt properties and activities, sometimes doubly so. Any organization or activity that is exempt from local or state property taxes thereby increases the rate of taxation on non-exempt property within that tax area. Moreover, if gifts to the agency or organization are deductible from federal or state income taxes this will be reflected in an increase in the tax rate. Therefore all private schools, churches, foundations, and other organizations that claim tax exemption in any form are to that extent publicly supported and the public has a legitimate interest in their activities. They can claim to be "private" only if they forego not only direct tax support but also tax exemption in any form. This question came to the forefront when private schools were established to avoid having white children attend desegregated schools.

In the past it has usually been accepted by the community that churches, schools, and various social agencies were useful to the community in general and therefore no questions were raised even though certain organizations were open only to men, or to women, or to people who subscribed to certain beliefs. They were ruled discriminatory only if they excluded people for reasons other than those that furnished the basis of exemption. More recently, however such tax exemption has been called into question by persons who objected to their involuntary tax support of religious institutions or to those that were open only to men or to women. The legal question here is not clear, but in the light of the Supreme Court ruling that exclusion on the basis of race is discriminatory, tax exemption for the support of racially segregated institutions would seem to be clearly out of harmony with the original ruling.

A third category of facilities in which the public has a stake is that of organizations and businesses franchised or licensed to serve the public. Many hotels, restaurants, and other business concerns at one time insisted that they should be free to serve or not serve whomever they pleased. The courts, however, have ruled that they do not have the right to refuse service on the basis of race. Presumably they do have the right to set other standards so long as they apply equally to all persons. For the general welfare there are regulations regarding licenses and franchises that involve zoning laws, sanitary codes, employment practices, and so on. The basis of these regulations is that any business that advertises itself as ready to serve the public is no longer wholly private.

There are admittedly areas that are not so clear. This fact was pointed up in the controversy over the public accommodations act that would exempt "Mrs. Murphy's boarding house" on the basis that the facility was a part of one's personal residence and therefore involved the right of privacy within one's home.

However the question of double rights was clearly involved in the rental or sale of houses on the open market. The people who asked, "Why can't a man sell his house to whomever he pleases?" overlooked two things. In the first place he could sell it to anyone he pleased so long as he did not advertise it for sale or put it on the open market. In the second place his question must be balanced by another: "Why can't a man buy any house that is offered for sale if he has the money to pay for it?" The right to own and control property is meaningless without the right to buy property. The right to spend one's money where one pleases, including the right to spend it for any house or land offered for sale, is fundamental to any concept of "property rights" in a free society.

There is always a fine and delicate balance between the rights of one individual or group and those of another, well expressed in the old saying that the freedom of one man's fist ends where the other man's nose begins. Modern urban living makes the line between one person's rights and those of another a thin and variable one that may have nothing to do with race. How does one judge between one man's right to keep his hi-fi set on all night and another man's right to get some sleep? The man who lets his dog bark all night, his furnace smoke, or his garbage pile up is engaging in activity on his own property but the effect extends beyond his property line. We all tend to think in terms of freedom where we are involved and in terms of restraints where other people are involved. When we cry "there ought to be a law," it is usually a law that will restrain or coerce the other fellow, not one that will place limits on our own freedom.

There are, however, areas of life that cannot properly be regulated by law and that must be left to the individual's conscience and sense of social responsibility. People still have the right to choose their friends and the persons with whom they will interact socially. A bona fide private club that claims no tax exemption and is not franchised to serve the public presumably has the legal right to limit its membership in any way it pleases, just as an individual has the right to make out his own guest list for a private party or to accept or reject any invitation he receives. He gets into the problem of double rights only when he tries to control the choices other people make.

There are, however, certain organizations and activities that fall somewhere between those that are clearly public and those that can be considered private. Many of these cannot properly be regulated by law and yet their racially restrictive policies may have serious social consequences. Fortunately some of the more important of these organizations have yielded to the pressure of public opinion or to a sense of responsibility on the part of their members. Within recent years most of the national professional organizations and many state and local ones have recognized the incongruity of basing their memberships on other than professional competence. Teachers and nurses associations, medical societies, bar associations, and ministers associations that were once racially segregated or racially exclusive are now generally open to any qualified member of the profession involved.

However, one of the serious handicaps still faced by Negroes is the lack of opportunity for give and take with business and professional men in the larger community. A great deal of the know-how and many business and professional opportunities come in the association of the weekly meetings of the so called men's service clubs, and in the informal get togethers in private clubs. The assumed business value of such informal contacts and associations is attested in the common acceptance of these activities as legitimate business expense. As these organizations are voluntary and are not tax supported, tax exempt, or franchised to serve the public, they presumably have the legal right to limit their membership in any way they wish. However, many white men are increasingly uncomfortable at the racial exclusiveness and feel that, regardless of the legal right, they cannot morally justify their own participation in organizations that place such obvious restrictions on the free interchange with a large and already disadvantaged segment of the business community.

It is true, of course, that the great majority of white business and professional men do not belong to such groups and most such groups do not include women. Racial exclusiveness, however, has wider consequences in that it involves the exclusion of an entire group that is already shut off in other ways from free interaction with the larger community.

5. Double Vision

Not only do we judge by a double standard and claim double rights, we actually see people and events differently. Whether we are black or white our perceptions of people of other races is apt to differ from our perception of people of our own race. To some extent this involves class perception also. We use a special kind of glasses when we perceive our own kind of people. What we are here calling double vision is important to an understanding of our racial attitudes but it may be helpful to look first at some of the ways we use this double vision when race is not involved.

Note was taken earlier of the fact that the privileged person is likely to look at the behavior of the poor through glasses that are different from the ones he uses to view the behavior of other privileged persons, and we clearly use double vision when viewing white collar and ordinary crime. Such double vision is also involved in what is commonly labeled the generation gap. What the young are calling hypocrisy on the part of their elders is this double vision, but the fact is that both the young and their elders tend to use it. Many youths defend their use of drugs as being less harmful than their elders' use of alcohol, tobacco, diet pills, pep pills, and tranquilizers. The point here is not whether the two patterns are actually comparable but the fact that youths use their rose colored glasses for youth activities while their elders do the same for adult activities.

Until the revolt against "the Establishment" by both black and white youth in the late 1960s, the behavior of middle-class white youth was generally viewed with extreme indulgence. This tolerant attitude was revealed in the newspaper reports of fraternity doings, panty raids, and general hell raising. In the spring of 1963 UPI reported that two thousand Princeton students had gone on a rampage for no apparent reason. They burned the benches at bus stops, set fire to the tracks of a commuter shuttle train, ripped down a seven foot high wrought iron fence, tossed cherry bombs, and committed various acts of vandalism. Afterwards, according to the dispatch, "they walked back to their dormitories and presumably went to sleep." Although university officials promised severe disciplinary measures, the governor of the state reportedly said, "It's spring and the sap begins to run."

In the spring of 1966 white college students at Ft. Lauderdale looted bakery and cold drink trucks and fruit stands, shattered hundreds of bottles in the streets, bashed in the tops of cars, tried to overturn a bus and threatened the passengers. The press report referred to the students as "youngsters," "collegians," and "kids." The following year, a similar report was headlined, "Pooped Collegians Head Home After Beach Ball," and in the body of the report the melee was referred to as "the annual collegiate rites of spring."

In 1968, according to an Associated Press dispatch, several hundred college students charged almost fifty thousand dollars worth of long distance telephone calls to a phony credit card. The students apparently saw the whole thing as a good joke and some of them were indignant at the telephone company's efforts to collect from the ones making the calls. No legal action was taken.

It is not hard to imagine what the reaction of the public would have been had these rampages been carried out by black youth or ghetto dwellers. One may be permitted to wonder, too, how it all looked to two lower-class youths who were jailed for the unarmed theft of a carton of cigarettes, or seven black youths—all younger than many of the "collegians"—who were given long prison sentences for setting fire to a ramshackle Ku Klux Klan hangout.

In the late 1960s the gap between middle-class conventional adults and the turned on members of the younger generation widened. Youth began complaining with considerable justification that their long hair, beards, and unconventional dress subjected them to harassment even when their behavior was perfectly proper by conventional standards. Policemen and taxi drivers in particular were said to show special antagonism toward the unconventionally dressed youth. There were also numerous cases in which public school authorities demanded hair cuts and more conventional dress as the price of staying in school.

Actually, adults were seeing conventionally dressed youth through one set of glasses and the unconventionally dressed through another set. The unconventional costume does undoubtedly reflect certain attitudes on the part of the wearer, but there is nothing inherently moral or immoral in any particular kind of dress. Skirts that revealed the ankle were once considered immodest in this country, and in some oriental cultures it is still regarded as indecent for a woman to wear a dress that shows her neck. Long hair, beards, lace-trimmed, ruffled shirts—and wigs —at various times in history have been a part of the accepted dress of gentlemen.

This double vision, of course, operates in the field of race relations, particularly as white persons interpret the behavior of black and white by different sets of standards. What is more important, however, is the fact the people don't deliberately set up a double standard—they actually "see" the behavior as different. We have already noted the difference in the definition of "a good man" and "a good Negro," and the different ways in which energy, ambition, and aggressiveness are defined for black and white. In this era of black self-consciousness, a good deal of the "new" behavior of black people has caused only minor reaction in the white community at least in part because white people simply don't hear anything about it.

The advent of a black Santa Claus was generally unnoticed. However, some white people were disturbed and even shocked when they discovered that some Negroes were taking seriously a black priest's insistence that Christ was actually a black man and that the priest used a portrait of a black Christ in his church services. White people apparently saw nothing shocking or even incongruous when some years ago a white artist painted Christ as a blond. This particular portrait achieved considerable popularity.

Nobody, of course, knows what Jesus of Nazareth looked like. He was unquestionably a Palestinian Jew, and there is every probability that he looked much like other Jewish peasants of the area. He almost certainly was not the immaculately groomed and artistically dressed individual usually portrayed, and the likelihood of his being either blond or black is extremely remote. There is, of course, every reason, as Daniel Fleming suggested years ago, that in painting Christ each artist should "paint with his own brush." This has long been done with the pictures of the Madonna and the Christ Child which artists in various parts of the world have painted with the coloring and features characteristic of their own people. There is doubtless a psychological value in the identification this makes possible, and it emphasizes the universality of a great spiritual leader who has become indigenous to many lands. There can be a question as to whether it is entirely honest to lead the unsophisticated to believe that a particular artist's representation is an actual physical likeness. However, the point of importance here is the double vision that leads white persons to react negatively to a black Christ while accepting with equanimity, and even approval, an equally improbable blond one.

Perhaps it is appropriate here to recall the penchant of human beings to create their gods in their own image. As far back as the sixth century b.c. the Greek philosopher Xenophanes pointed out that the Ethiopians pictured their gods with snub noses and black hair whereas the Thracians portrayed theirs with grey eyes and red hair. Furthermore, he said, if animals could create works of art, undoubtedly horses would draw pictures of gods like horses, and oxen would make theirs like oxen. In the 1920s Christopher Morley wrote a gentle spoof on the subject in

which he pictured the anger of a society of dogs when one of their number suggested that it was just possible that God might be a biped. More
recently women have gotten into the act. When the first Sputnik was
orbited, women students in theological schools gleefully passed around
the story that Sputnik had snared an angel who was interviewed by leading theologians. On being asked the question, "What is God really like?"
the angel replied, "Well, of course, you know that SHE is black."

6. The Poor and the Not So Poor

An important but seldom recognized factor in race relations and
the polarization of black and white grows out of the fact that a large
segment of the population carries a disproportionate share of the burden
of the poor and, in a sense, of the country as a whole. Although some
Negroes would be included in this group, attention here is given only
to the whites involved because the special problems of the blacks are
treated elsewhere, and it is the white experience with which we are
concerned in this chapter.

The persons we here call the not-so-poor fall roughly into several
categories. Some of them could be called lower middle-class, which would
include many cab drivers, policemen, waitresses, the lower paid sales
and clerical workers, and many of those considered in the blue collar
category. A second group would include people of middle-class status
and aspiration, often in white collar or lower level professional jobs, but
with 1970 incomes of less than $10,000 a year. A third category would
include salaried workers who have achieved a certain status but who are
finding it difficult to maintain because of rising costs and increased demands. It would also include some self-employed persons of limited
incomes.

All of these people will have in common aspirations to maintain
their present standards or to move into higher ones, and most of them
will find their incomes increasingly inadequate to meet the demands
made upon them. They are likely to see "welfare chiselers" and the people who "won't work" as being factors in their heavy tax burdens. Because of the segregation patterns built into our social structure, the
lower income white person is likely to have had little contact with more
affluent Negroes or even with those in their own economic category.
They may therefore have an exaggerated idea of the proportion of the
poor who are black, and they may especially resent the blacks who, they
feel, are now getting undue favors and attention at the expense of the
white worker.

We have already documented the fact that the majority of people on welfare are neither "chiselers," nor black, but so long as they are believed to be, they will furnish a convenient scapegoat for people who feel overburdened. Moreover, there seems to be no question but that the people we are here calling the not-so-poor carry more than their share of the load. These persons are often referred to as "the ordinary taxpayer" or more graphically "the little man who is always there." This is not to say that the more affluent do not also have their problems, but the affluent are fewer in number, they can afford a more paternalistic attitude, and they are in a better position to look out for themselves. The primary focus of this book is on those things that affect race relations, and the frustrations, resentments, and scapegoats of the not-so-poor white are therefore of immediate concern.

The excessive tax burden of the not-so-poor takes many forms. Although federal income tax rates are supposed to be progressive, in practice the little man usually pays a higher proportion of his income in taxes than does his more affluent neighbor. The biggest difference lies in the various exemptions and deductions available to persons whose incomes are from sources other than wages and salaries. During the late 1960s much publicity was given to the fact that many persons in high income brackets, including some millionaires, paid no federal income tax at all and few wealthy people paid the published rate. There was also general publicity regarding the payment to individuals and corporations of hundreds of thousands of dollars—in a few cases more than a million dollars—in crop subsidies or for keeping land out of production, oil depletion allowances, cost plus contracts, hobby farms used to establish tax losses, and a variety of other forms of special privilege.

The little man has none of these tax advantages. The wealthy individual not only has more "loopholes"—euphemistically labeled "tax shelters"—open to him but he is also in a position to get expert help in finding such shelters. Even if he were not in a position to have the services of a tax expert, there are tax services available by subscription, as well as numerous booklets one of which was frankly labeled "Tax Breaks That Lead to Executive Wealth." Most of these tax avoidance schemes were written into the law and therefore legal though clearly favoring certain categories of people in higher income brackets. Few of them would be of any use to the little man even if he knew of their existence. His employer withholds the amount due the government and that is it.

The not-so-poor whites as well as their black counterparts generally carry more than their share of the state and local tax burdens as well. Many states and local communities impose sales taxes with no exclusion for necessities, and such taxes weigh most heavily on those whose incomes are limited. A home may represent the not-so-poor's major savings, but in most communities there is no homestead exemption and the tax rate is the same for the modest one bedroom home as for the mansion. In many communities the car license fees and special "stickers" are the same for the jalopy the lowest paid worker needs to get to his job and for the Cadillac of the city's most affluent citizen.

The not-so-poor are further penalized when they try to save. The man who can save only a few hundred dollars has found himself limited to Series E or H bonds, or to a savings account in a bank or savings and loan association which are limited by law to relatively low interest rates. The man with more to invest can buy certificates of deposit or Treasury Notes that pay much higher rates. When proposals were made to issue six percent savings bonds and to lower the minimum amount of Treasury bills there was an immediate cry that letting the small investors get in on the higher rates would lure them away from the savings and loan associations and thus reduce mortgage money available to the home buyer. The same objection was raised to a proposal by American Telephone and Telegraph Co. to issue "savings bonds" to family savers. There seemed to be little awareness of the incongruity in artificially restricting the amount of interest the small investor could receive on his savings while leaving the higher interest rates open to the more affluent. The *Wall Street Journal* did have an editorial entitled "Pity the Small Savers" in which the editor remarked that "it's more than a little sad that among those chosen for punishment are the small savers."

The working poor and the not-so-poor seem to be asked to carry more than their share of the burden of slowing inflation in other ways. People in government circles admit that anti-inflationary measures would increase the number of jobless, and there was even talk of "acceptable" levels of unemployment, though everybody knew that the greatest burden would fall on the people at the bottom of the ladder. Moreover, it is hard for the little man to understand why increasing social security payments and personal income tax exemptions—both admittedly long overdue—are dangerously inflationary when, as some of the more sensitive members of Congress bluntly pointed out, a number of high government officials had had their salaries doubled, and Congressmen had enjoyed their second salary increase in a year. The latest congressional increase had amounted to almost as much per month as the proposed— and defeated—personal income exemption for a year, and more per month than the average yearly individual social security payment.

Although social security in its present form undoubtedly has been a boon to the low salaried worker, a disproportionate burden has fallen on the not-so-poor. Many elderly persons were brought under social security although they had contributed for a very short time, and since anyone was "covered" who earned as little as fifty dollars every three months the contributions of these lowest paid, often part time, workers bore no relation to the minimum payments which they would receive on retirement. It would seem obvious that this kind of protection of the poor should have been chargeable to the taxpayer in general, not just to wage earners, but such was not the system. The real burden, however, lay in the fact that the wage base and the rate were the same for the man who made $7800 a year (the top rate in 1970) as for the man who made $78,000 or more. The burden was also the same on the little business man whose highest paid employee got $7800 as on the big corporation whose highest paid employee might receive several hundred thousand a year.

Theoretically, the $7800 man and his $78,000 counterpart would get the same amount on retirement, but the little man would discover that there were two more strikes against him. The man with the larger income who could invest in stocks, bonds, or real estate during his working years, could, on retirement, receive any amount of income from these investments and still collect his full tax-exempt social security. But the $7800 a year man who had been able to save little couldn't possibly live on his social security payments. Because he was usually subject to compulsory retirement at sixty-five, he often engaged in some form of self-employment after retirement. However, if he earned more than $1680 (in 1970) he would be penalized by having part of his social security withheld. Moreover, if his net income from self-employment was as much as $400 a year he had to pay almost ten percent of it as a social security tax. The fact that he might have already paid the maximum social security tax every year for thirty years and now had an income below the poverty level would make no difference. In the meantime his more affluent friend was not only drawing full social security and paying no social security tax (only "earned" income being subject to social security taxes), but his investment income was getting the more favorable capital gains rate on his federal income tax.

When these unequal burdens were added to the discriminations, cited earlier, in law enforcement, the greater vulnerability to the draft of the less affluent, and the general feeling of powerlessness on the part of the people involved, it is easy to see why there should be frustration and resentment. It is not so obvious why the resentment should be directed against the people lower in the social and economic scale rather than against the more affluent and privileged or the inequities of the system itself.

Partly this is a matter of an upwardly mobile society in which people find it easy to envy rather than resent the ones who seem to have it made. Poverty and affluence are, of course, relative terms. We live in a world of rising expectations. The United States in particular is a world of television in which the goods and gadgets of the more affluent life are constantly displayed in all their spectacular allurement as the kind of things you "owe to yourself." In city after city full page newspaper ads picture the ease of buying whatever you want through the use of a credit card and such cards are sometimes sent unsolicited. The whole society is geared to the idea that everybody is entitled to the better job, the better pay, the bigger house, the latest model car, the boat, and the swimming pool. In such an upwardly mobile society people tend to identify with the man who is a step above them.

Moreover, the majority of the not-so-poor do not really know how to analyze the basis of their problems. Some of them do know that they are carrying more than their share of the burden—publications as varied as *Life, Time, Forbes,* and the *Wall Street Journal* repeatedly have pointed out the inequities of our tax system, and the way in which the small-salaried worker carries an undue share of the burden of the poor and of social costs in general. But many of them do not really know what the problems are or how to protest the inequities. All of the name-less fears, stresses, and strains tend to merge into an overall frustration that needs a scapegoat. Thus many people turn against anything that seems a threat to life as it was, as nostalgia pictures it, or as they have dreamed it would be.

The strong reaction of many of the not-so-poor against hippie dress and campus disorder is in part a formless anger against young people who seem to be throwing away what many of the less privileged dreamed of but were never able to attain. But most of all they are likely to see the poor, the people they think of as the "welfare chiselers," and espe-cially the black poor, as being a major cause of their high taxes and other problems.

The ramifications of all of this in terms of human relations in gen-eral, and of race relations in particular, is obvious. This book has spelled out in detail the inequities and injustices inflicted upon the poor, and upon the blacks, whether poor or not. Hundreds of books and articles have portrayed their plight. But the not-so-poor white has had little attention and less sympathy. Mainly he has been berated for his racist behavior. Compared with the burdens borne by the poor and the blacks he may seem well off. From their clearly disadvantaged position Negroes tend to see all whites as privileged. The harassed not-so-poor white, on the other hand, may feel that black people are now getting all the breaks. The black person, of course, knows all too well that these special situations are not the usual run of things, and considering all the dis-abilities put upon Negroes in the past, he may feel that a little com-pensatory favor and even "reparations" are long past due.

What both the white and the black may overlook is that the dis-advantaged or overburdened person feels the hurt as an individual, and it is small comfort to the burdened white person that whites as a whole are more privileged than Negroes as a whole, just as it is small comfort to the jobless and hungry Negro that some blacks are getting more than they used to. Each can put himself in the place of the toad in the furrow who feels the prick of the harrow and who is in no mood to be appeased by somebody out in the road telling him that "his people," whether white or black, are better off than some other group.

However mistaken the not-so-poor may be about th   rce of their burdens it has become increasingly clear that they do   legitimate grievances and that the recognition of this fact and t'   rection of some of the inequalities from which they suffer will ave important consequences in their racial attitudes. At least something is gained when people can analyze the causes of their own frustrations, and when either the more or the less privileged can see the stresses under which the people caught in the middle sometimes operate.

Moreover there is a practical factor involved. If the blacks are to get justice and equality in this country it must come through the democratic process. If democracy goes under, the alternative is totalitarianism —and given the ingredients in our total population, a totalitarian government would be rightist rather than leftist. Under such circumstances the people who would suffer first and most would be the most vulnerable minority. Thus however much the militant blacks may say that they don't care what Whitey thinks, they are ultimately at the mercy of the white majority—and the majority of that majority are the working poor and the not-so-poor whites.

Astute students of social problems have pointed out that social programs for the benefit of any minority stand little chance of success if a large portion of the majority feels that the programs are carried out at their expense and with no regard for their welfare. Thus a practical reason, as well as fairness, indicates that justice is really indivisible and must not be obtained for one group at the expense of another. The fact that the blacks and the poor are most discriminated against should not blind us to the fact that the not-so-poor are being asked to carry an undue share of the social burden. The deep frustrations and anger of the poor, the blacks, and the not-so-poor must all be considered together. These facts make the removal of all injustice, inequality, and special privilege one of the nation's most urgent necessities.

7. Prejudice, Guilt, and Responsibility

A few years ago sociologists, psychologists, and psychiatrists were writing on the nature of prejudice, the kinds of persons most likely to be prejudiced, and the various forms in which prejudice is expressed.

Today the fashion is to label America and all white Americans as racist. As the black separatist movement developed, the terms "black racism" and "racism in reverse" came into use. Whatever the terminology used, there are certain common human tendencies that can be summed up as the we-they syndrome, that is the tendency to categorize people and to attach labels to entire groups regardless of the various individual characteristics of the persons composing the groups. This pattern of lumping people together, and using different standards and values for the we and they groups, is the essence of the problem regardless of the label we attach to the behavior.

When one group in the we-they syndrome is much more powerful than the other, as in the white-black pattern in the United States, the results can be devastating not only for the subordinate group but for the dominant group which tends to develop arrogance, insensitivity, and other qualities that are incongruous in a society supposedly based on a Judeo-Christian, democratic tradition. Too much and too little power are equally corrupting.

Much of this book has been given to the documentation of the results of overt forms of white prejudice. But there is a more subtle form of prejudice that shows up as sentimentality, which may be directed toward the poor and the underdog in general as well as toward the Negro. The sentimentalist will generally attribute complete, if suppressed, nobility to the underdog and assume that if external pressures and discrimination were removed the oppressed ones would all emerge as knights in shining armor. This attitude is not unlike the sentimentalists' ideological forebears' conception of the "noble savage." The savages had far better lives than that attributed to them by the early explorers, colonizers, merchants, and missionaries but they weren't all that noble. And today, the blacks and the poor, white or black, are not the inferior, shiftless, no-use-in-helping lot they are often made out to be, but neither are they all just waiting for the removal of their special disabilities to emerge as noble, energetic, industrious, and responsible paragons of virtue.

Today the people to the far right tend toward overt prejudice and accuse the sentimentalists of being bleeding hearts and knee-jerk liberals. The latter accuse the former of being fascist and racist. To the one the Negro can do no right; to the other he can do no wrong. Neither position credits the Negro with being simply human, good, bad, and indifferent, sometimes right, sometimes wrong, and often a little of both. The good guys and the bad guys come in all colors and from all races, and they are found in all strata of all societies. Underdogs in general are neither more nor less capable of virtues and vices than other people, though their underprivileged position may affect their particular value system and the way in which their feelings are expressed. To lump all Negroes together as uniquely noble is as much a denial of their humanity as it is to lump them all together as inferior. Respect for human beings involves the recognition of individual differences and the judging of each individual on the basis of his personal qualities, with full allowance for unusual handicaps or unusual opportunities.

Persons who try to rid themselves of overt prejudice often swing over to sentimentality. On the other hand, the sentimentalist may become disillusioned because of his unreal expectations and may swing over to overt prejudice. In some ways sentimentality is more damaging than overt prejudice in that it is a more subtle form of contempt. The sentimentalist is deceived about himself and his own motives, whereas the overtly prejudiced individual is at least honest in his convictions.

A relatively new factor in race relations has come to the fore in recent years, that is, an overwhelming feeling of guilt on the part of some white persons. Admittedly, there is ample room for shame about some aspects of our history, and there can be no question that exploitation of the weak by the strong has continued in some degree to the present. Such injustices are fully documented throughout this book.

However, this orgy of guilt has led to all kinds of nonproductive and even destructive behavior, ranging from the sentimental glorification of everything black to the granting of demands that under more rational circumstances would be considered outrageous. Some of the yielding to the more extreme demands of black students fall into this category. Most Negroes have been quick to see through the essential falsity of these guilt-ridden actions, and some of them have not hesitated to exploit the situation by laying the blame for all their problems at the door of white racism, by "non-negotiable" demands for special consideration, preferential treatment, and the payment of "reparations" for past injustice. One can hardly blame them for enjoying Whitey's discomfort on becoming aware of the misdeeds of his forebears. But to hold all whites equally guilty, to blame on the living the sins of past generations, or to absolve blacks themselves of all responsibility, is to distort both truth and history.

Persons who have been personally involved in the exploitation of their fellow humans through unawareness or overt action, whether they are black or white, have reason to feel guilt and are in need not only of repentance but of making restitution. But wallowing in guilt is not a productive emotion even when the guilt is personal. To indulge in an orgy of guilt about events that happened before one was born and in which he could not possibly have had any part is even less productive. Nor does a white person, merely because he is white, need feel a sense of guilt about the reprehensible behavior of other people who happen to have the same color of skin. We have pointed out elsewhere that people are responsible when they stand by consenting or make no effort to prevent or correct injustices. But to feel collective guilt about the behavior of white people in other times and places—as apart from guilt about having profited by such behavior—is as much "racism" as attributing the behavior of all Negroes to their racial identity.

Both C. Eric Lincoln and Frantz Fanon have pointed out that the man who feels guilty for evil he did not do is sick and in need of therapy, but if a man has no sense of guilt for the evil he does do, he is even more sick and a menace to society as well.

What we need, of course, is to replace prejudice, whether overt or sentimental, as well as guilt, with a sense of responsibility. Guilt leads people to do the things that help their own feelings, that is, to assuage the guilt. Responsibility leads people to do what they can to change conditions regardless of who brought them about or when.

There is no question that discrimination and injustice is built into our present social structure, and that the situation has been greatly exacerbated for blacks, not only because of their past history but also because of their physical differences and the pattern of segregation that has held them back as a group and has prevented the kind of individual escape from oppression that was open to the individual members of other groups. But collective guilt for the past is another matter. Most people who are defined as Negroes today had whites among their ancestors, and many whites had ancestors who had no part in exploiting anybody because they themselves were on the bottom of the pile. The great majority of white Americans never owned slaves—though a few black people did—and many of the poor whites of the South not only did not profit by slavery but were themselves victims of the slave system.

What each man can be held responsible for—and this is true whatever his color—is the way he has used, and continues to use, what he has in a responsible way. If the fact that his ancestors exploited others means that he inherited money or got a better start in life, he needs to feel responsible in proportion to his opportunity. Many Negroes today have a better education and economic opportunity than some whites, and the fact that their ancestors were exploited by some white men does not excuse them from social responsibility which, in terms of opportunity, may be greater than that of some poor whites whose ancestors were also exploited and who may still be suffering the consequences. A pretty fair rule is one that equates rights with duties, privilege with obligation, and freedom with responsibility, and these are individual, not racial, matters.

Although individuals cannot be held responsible for actions taken before they were born, institutions and organizations do bear a continuing and collective responsibility and in this all citizens share even though we do not share the guilt. One of the greatest wrongs done to Negroes in the past and which still puts the greatest handicap upon them, lay in the restrictions on their education. Local, county, state, and federal governments all were involved. As was pointed out in an earlier chapter, Negro children and youth were denied equal educational opportunity with the white youth in their own communities, and this continued from the earliest grades through the entire system of higher education. This discrimination still exists so that many present day Negro youth are still suffering a double handicap, one that comes from the cumulative effect that limited the opportunities of their parents, plus the current discrimination which affects them directly.

The fact that some of the demands for "reparations" have been made by self-appointed and irresponsible groups should not blind us to the collective responsibility of institutions and organizations for remedial and compensatory action that would help right some of the long-standing wrongs and speed the time when full equality of opportunity becomes a reality. The greatest discrimination in education, and therefore the greatest responsibility, rests upon governments at all levels from local school boards to the Congress and various federal agencies. Although, in general, remedial and compensatory measures should apply to the disadvantaged regardless of race, a special case can be made for the predominantly black colleges which, as was noted earlier, still provide the higher education opportunity for fully half the black students in the United States. One of the most useful, most appropriate, and most relevant of all remedial and compensatory measures would be the immediate and drastic upgrading of the financial support and whatever other assistance is needed to aid both the institutions themselves and the underprivileged students who make up a large part of their enrollments.

Other remedial and compensatory measures might well involve adult education programs, including such things as nutrition and child care, literacy education, job training, teacher training, day care and Headstart programs, the provision of health care for school children, and numerous other measures. Certainly there should be an immediate elimination of the discrimination still practiced in the financing and equipment of inner city schools as compared with those in the wealthier suburbs. The underprivileged child has even greater need for schools with superior equipment and facilities than his advantaged neighbor.

Private colleges and universities that have been guilty of racial exclusiveness or merely of unawareness may well have an obligation to offer special help in the way of scholarships, remedial pre-admission programs, or flexible time schedules for black youth who have been handicapped by poor schools and general poverty. But to recruit blacks who for any reason are unable to do acceptable work without making special provisions to overcome their handicaps amounts to a cruel hoax. In such cases the institutions will be faced with a choice of alternatives any one of which will be damaging to the students concerned, to the black image, and to the institution itself. If inadequately prepared students are admitted without remedial provisions they will have to be flunked out in droves, given grades they did not earn in regular courses, or put into hastily set up black studies programs made easy enough for any incompetent to pass. No self-respecting person would want such a degree, and no self-respecting institution should grant one. Such a procedure would have the further effect of putting under suspicion the honestly earned degrees of the numerous competent black students who need no special favors.

There is no general agreement as to either the role or the responsibility of the church. There are both good and bad elements in the record. On the credit side, it can be said that most white denominations have made greater efforts than is usually realized. For a long period following the freeing of the slaves, the only education for Negroes beyond the elementary grades was provided by the churches and even today two-thirds of the private, predominantly Negro colleges are church supported. In almost every city of any size in the South there are church-sponsored community centers offering a variety of programs to aid the Negro poor. During the long period when public facilities were closed to Negroes, these agencies often offered the only recreational program for black children throughout an entire city. Until relatively recent times the Christian churches were the only American groups that showed any interest in Africa. And however paternalistic the missionary enterprise may have been it does have three things to its credit. It was Christian missionaries who reduced most of the African languages to writing; until relatively recent times almost all schools in many areas of Africa were provided by missionaries; and practically all African leaders in these areas today owe their early education, and often their college training also, to the activity of the Christian church.

On the other side, it must be said that at the local church level many white congregations operate as exclusive private clubs which feel no particular concern or responsibility for blacks or for the poor, black or white. Churches in general are as segregated as the rest of the community, and people who call themselves Christians justify their prejudice by the claims that "God made us different." What an individual does about his own conscience and his racial attitudes are of course a private matter. But there is one point at which the church as an institution must give an account of itself. As was pointed out earlier, any organization that is tax exempt or that accepts tax exempt contributions is to that extent tax supported and therefore has a public obligation.

In the past, labor unions were notoriously discriminatory and, until the beginning of fair employment legislation in the 1930s, so were most business concerns. As collective entities with ongoing life, they can be thought of as having a collective responsibility.

As will be noted in the concluding chapter, the removal of discrimination and injustice is a shared responsibility involving all members of the society. And as has been fully set forth throughout this book, we are responsible not only for our individual treatment of other individuals but also for our participation in these institutional arrangements of the society that foster or perpetuate injustice and discrimination.

13

The
Human Use
of Human Beings

In the earlier chapters of this book I tried not so much to "tell it like it is," for no person can do that, but to report the facts as they appear to people with different backgrounds, experiences, and points of view. I tried as far as possible to keep my own value judgments subordinated. Without apology, this final chapter is dedicated to certain ideas and values based on the conviction that the primary business of any society is to promote the "human use of human beings."

1. What Does It Mean to Be Human?

There are certain characteristics of the human condition—things that all human beings have in common and have had since the beginning of time. Although the young today complain of a world they never made, this is an essential element in human life. No one ever had any choice in his race, his sex, his parents, his own physical and mental equipment, or the time and place of his birth. It follows that no one deserves either credit or blame for the past achievements or failures of his ancestors, his race, or his country. The fact that one is born with particular potentialities, of particular parents, at a particular time and place are things for which one may feel gratitude or regret, but not things for which one may be held responsible.

Regardless of one's religious orientation or beliefs there is a basis not only for justice but for compassion and concern in the simple facts of the human condition. We are all born helpless and remain so for a longer period than any other animal. We are dependent on the care of our fellow humans not only in infancy but often in old age and in periods of illness, accident, or disaster throughout life. People who have been in earthquakes, tornadoes, hurricanes, floods, or heavy snowstorms may be dramatically reminded that their survival depends on the mercy, compassion, and concern of their fellow human beings. We all must die and we are dependent on others for the disposal of our bodies and of our affairs after death.

But apart from these dramatic experiences, our interdependence is a daily affair. No person in the modern Western world can survive by his own efforts or meet his most elementary needs by the use of his bare hands. There are no self-made men. All material things are valuable in relation to their use by human beings, and the value of any piece of property is related to the presence or absence of people. The finest hotel, the most completely stocked department store, or the richest oil well are of no value if there are no people wanting a place to stay, no customers to buy the goods, or no market for the oil. Our human interdependence is vividly expressed in the question, "Of what use would be one telephone?"

Because a basic condition of human survival is the presence of other people, man can live only in association with other men. Thus, being human always involves being human in a social context. To be human once meant to be involved with only a small group of people known to you—your relatives and your neighbors. The obligation did not always extend to enemies or even to strangers. Today, our interdependence is such that to be human means to be involved with the more than three billion other people with whom we share the planet.

Societies, too, have their necessary conditions of existence. Every society, if it is to survive, must control to some degree the activities of its members. There is no society, however simple, in which one is wholly free to do his own thing. The very fact of living in the same community with others imposes certain restraints on personal freedom even when there are no formal laws. The larger the group and the more closely associated its members, the greater the degree of control required. When people in this country lived on the frontier, out of sight of their neighbors' chimney smoke, they could have a large degree of personal freedom. When the country became more thickly settled people learned, as had the ancient Israelites, that it was no longer possible to allow each man to do what was right in his own eyes. For the protection of all there had to be rules and persons designated to enforce them. In all societies the acceptance of a degree of control over aggressive, sexual, and acquisitive activities is a condition of membership in the society. And all societies have some means of coercing those who refuse to be bound by the rules or who by their conduct infringe on the rights of others.

With the development of urban life, formal restraints became necessary, and, with writing, laws were formulated and codified. There is no question that governments can and do become oppressive, that laws are sometimes unjust, that persons in authority are sometimes arbitrary and corrupt, and that the people assigned to enforce the law may be harsh and even brutal. But the notion that people anywhere can live without some social controls and some means of enforcing them is naive and childish.

Our interdependence is inherent in the human condition, and the well-being of people is dependent on an effective balance between rights and duties, freedom and responsibility, privilege and obligation. Doing one's own thing without regard to its effect on other people, demanding rights without accepting corresponding duties, insisting on freedom of speech for oneself without granting the same freedom to others, attempting the destruction of existing authority without regard to the resulting chaos—all of this shows a lack of awareness of what Loren Eiseley calls "The wonder and the terror of the human predicament: man is totally dependent on society."

But the society must do more than simply restrict the freedom of some for the common good. It must be done in such a way that the members of the society feel is just, and the success ultimately depends on the internalization of the values that make for the necessary restraints. In their book on *The Criminal, the Judge and the Public,* Alexander and Staub point out the necessity of restrictions upon man's instinctual impulses if he is to live in a society with other men. But self-restriction must be rewarded by recognition, respect, and a degree of individual liberty. When these are not forthcoming, if the individual is treated unjustly, he perceives this as a betrayal. And when such injustice is meted out to members of special groups, there may be a sense of group betrayal and group rebellion. This sense of group betrayal is a basic element in the unrest of black people today.

One of the major problems in our society today is the polarization of those who see the problem as law and order to be brought about by stricter controls and those who see the problem as individual freedom and justice. The dilemma is a false one. No society can exist without a degree of law and order, but in the earlier discussion of law it was pointed out that excessive reliance on external controls without due regard for justice is the surest way to increased disorder.

Thus, one of the prime concerns of a free society must be the development of the individual's responsibility for himself and to others. This is a circular matter. The internalization of such controls on the part of individuals is necessary to a just and free society, but only in a society where both justice and freedom are honored can such individuals develop. We are born with human potential but becoming fully human involves the acceptance of some degree of social control, and we are most maturely human when these controls are internalized and thus self-enforcing.

Edward M. Bruner puts the idea in scientific terms when he says that if all the aggressive, sexual, and acquisitive needs of an individual were immediately and completely gratified, then that individual would never become fully human. We develop ego strength, self-awareness, and a sense of reality as a consequence of external controls and inhibitions. Some degree of frustration is necessary for survival to maturity. The philosopher puts it in more dramatic form: "The wild asses and the hyenas have self-expression in full measure. They remain asses and hyenas. Man, through self-discipline, achieves some measure of the divine." That is, he realizes to some degree his human potential.

2. The Human Peril

No one today can be ignorant of the fact that the human species is in peril. Living has always involved risk, but in the modern world there are certain never before true conditions that add to man's peril. Poverty, hunger, and want have always been the lot of many men, but today the effect of such deprivation is accentuated by the affluence with which it is in contrast. Crime, violence, and injustice are as old as man, but today they have reached proportions that threaten the very existence of ordered social life. Wars are seemingly as old as man's history, but in the days of hand-to-hand combat or even with the relatively limited weapons of a century ago they mainly involved the men in battle. Today the destructiveness of war weapons is beyond ordinary comprehensions, and whole populations are involved in the holocaust.

Another aspect of the human peril lies in the fact that modern communication has brought together peoples of enormous diversity. The human species is made up of people of different races who speak several thousand different languages, practice different religions, have diverse culture patterns, and different tribal or national loyalties. Prejudice against the outsider, the foreigner, or the stranger is nothing new, but in the modern world an intense nationalism and a prejudice against people of other ideologies and other races have become cancerous growths affecting people everywhere. We have difficulty in achieving consensus even within nations, yet we must share with billions of people of great diversity a planet that has shrunk to room size proportions.

Accentuating the human peril is the rapidity with which change is taking place. In the Old Stone Age measurable change took place over hundreds of thousands of years. At the time of the agricultural revolution it could be measured in thousands of years. By the time of the Industrial Revolution history could be written by centuries, but now that we have reached the nuclear or space age, greater changes take place in a decade than in centuries preceding. Such an accelerated rate of change creates a whole series of new problems. Man's recorded knowledge doubles in the space of a few years. Keeping up with the developments even in one's own field becomes a major undertaking so that life becomes fragmented, and people in one field may know little about even related areas of knowledge. The rate of change is uneven and affects people differently so there is less consensus and greater stress between groups. The rapidity of change is a major factor in the generation gap. As Margaret Mead points out, this is the first time in history when the specific experiences of the elders were of little help to their children. As a consequence youth is prone to consider the ideas of any older person as completely outdated and irrelevant.

Offering both peril and hope is the fact that radio and television, aided by satellite relays, and the increased mobility made possible by rapid transit have made all the world aware of possibilities once undreamed of. Isolated peoples who were once unaware of life outside their immediate communities and who accepted their deprivations as the normal lot of man are now filled with new ideas, new dreams, and new aspirations. They are aware of the wide gap between the rich and the poor, and they are now vocal and rebellious. There is hope in their awakening, but there is peril in the fact that their aspirations are not matched by available resources and the means of fulfillment.

There are other problems that did not emerge on any wide scale until the modern era. Of perilous significance is the threat of overpopulation. There have always been overcrowded areas, but population was kept in check by unplanned forces. High death rates from disease, famine, and pestilence were beyond the control of man and so could be tolerated as fate or the will of God. Moreover there were new lands not fully occupied to which men could migrate. Today our increased knowledge in the field of health and medicine, added to other technological developments, has created a birth-death imbalance. With many diseases conquered, with acute starvation virtually eliminated, and with no open lands to which overflow populations can go, mankind is threatened with more people than the planet can support.

Adding to the threat of overpopulation, and in part caused by it, is the pollution and destruction of the earth's resources. Offshore oil wells and the leakage from huge oil tankers have ruined beaches and destroyed marine life. Mines have been gashed into the earth leaving large areas of wasteland. Lakes and streams and offshore waters have been polluted by industrial wastes, killing fish and making the water unfit for human use. Forests have been destroyed and trees cut ruthlessly to make highways and parking lots. Pesticides have upset the balance of nature resulting in the destruction of plant and animal life and the endangering of the human species. And air pollution has reached the point of a serious and perhaps irreversible threat to life and health.

A completely new factor is man's global interdependence. Throughout human history there have been plagues, famines, wars, and various other disasters, but they affected only limited areas of the globe at any one time. Nations rose and fell but there were always other people in other places who could carry on. Today, in a most literal sense, we are all involved in mankind, and what happens in any part of the world has immediate repercussions throughout the globe. For the first time in history the human voice can not only be heard around the world but to and from outer space. No part of the world is in time-distance more than a few hours from any other part and an astronaut or an unmanned satellite can circle the globe in a matter of minutes.

Exacerbating all the other threats is the fact that for the first time in human history, man has at his disposal destructive power that could literally render the earth uninhabitable. Moreover, this power is now available to more and more nations with the always awesome possibility that some irresponsible or maniacal individual in a place of power could trigger a nuclear holocaust.

This peril was perhaps most bluntly and explicitly stated in a book entitled *Step to Man*, published in 1966. The author, Dr. John R. Platt, a biophysicist, points to the likelihood that within the next ten to twenty years man will have only a fifty-fifty chance of survival on this planet. This is true, he says, because the underprivileged, the dispossessed, the disadvantaged, the exploited, and the ignorant form a perpetual seed bed for would-be dictators who might well take over nuclear power and destroy us all. It is the wisdom and effort of this present generation that will make this permanent decision for us whether we live or die. We can no longer afford poverty, ignorance, prejudice, and neglect, not so much because they are a sign of wickedness as because they are a sign of incompetence. If we are to survive at all, he continues, it can be only by working out new attitudes of mutual support and tolerance between races, nations, and classes. Thus what man should do out of love and compassion for his fellow human beings, he is now under the necessity of doing as his one hope of survival.

Because full comprehension of the potential of a nuclear holocaust is more than the human mind can tolerate for long, most of us push aside any real awareness of the human peril. This is probably necessary to one's sanity, but the submerged awareness may have more to do with our general malaise and unrest than we realize. Moreover, our greatest danger may be something far less spectacular than nuclear war. As we have noted, human beings can live only in societies, and societies, whether large or small, are held together by a shared system of sentiments on the part of their members. Unless there is a reasonable degree of consensus about basic values, the society will be torn by dissension and its energies used up in the process of keeping a sufficient degree of order for meeting the basic needs of its members. On the other hand, the most serious disorder can arise out of failure to change social patterns as other conditions change.

Much of the turmoil of the 1960s grew out of the fact that not only in the United States but in much of the rest of the world there was a breakdown in consensus. Not only did nations have radically different maps of reality but within nations there were sharp differences between old and young, between privileged and deprived, between black and white, between those who gave priority to law and order and the status quo and those who saw the real issue as justice. And, of course, our global interdependence makes some degree of world consensus necessary. Yet we and the other major nations spend billions on an arms race that in the long run cannot protect us from one another, and we still do almost nothing to find ways of meeting our common perils.

3. The Past as Prologue

It is common today to think of the past as irrelevant. Everything is different, so the argument goes, and what people thought, believed, or did in the past has no meaning for today. We are told that modern life is a whole new ball game. And so it is. Nevertheless, the fundamental problems confronting human beings are essentially more complex versions of those that confronted people in the past. We still belong to the same species as our prehistoric and more recent forebears, and our problems are basically those that are inherent in the human condition. Moreover, to say that modern man can learn nothing from the past is to deny his humanity. One of the major differences in man and other animals is that man has the ability to think, to conceptualize, to create, and to use symbols. Thus human beings are able to look backward and to anticipate the future. Man alone can say, "This once happened, and so . . . ", or "That may happen, and so. . . ." He has the capacity to reason, to plan, to look before and after, to learn not only from his own experiences but from the experiences of other men in other times and places. He has been called a time-binding animal.

Those who see no relevance in the past are prone to condemn Western civilization as something wholly evil. They point to modern man's plundering of the earth, his materialistic values, his worship of success, his preoccupation with brutal wars, his prejudice, and his general inhumanity to man, as marking the total failure of modern civilization, particularly that part of it labeled Western. So disenchanted are many of today's revolutionaries that they are committed to tearing the whole thing down without much thought of the consequences to the human species, or any clear idea as to what they would put in its place.

But those who would destroy "the Establishment," close the universities, and do away with representative government without regard to the resulting chaos, reveal their ignorance of the nature of man and the means of life. The size and interdependence of the world's populations are such that a breakdown in orderly government resulting in a serious reduction in the producing, processing, and marketing of food and the transportation of essential goods and services, would doom literally millions of people to misery and ultimately to famine, pestilence, and death. Before the days of modern technology, famine, plagues, and epidemics periodically decimated many populations throughout the world.

It is the disciplined training provided by universities and governments that produce agricultural experts, engineers, and scientists of all kinds, who can build bridges that do not collapse, devise means of flood control, produce better crops, and breed better animals by which the world can be fed. It is through scientific discipline that men have learned how to conquer malaria, yellow fever, smallpox, polio, sleeping sickness, and numerous other scourges that once took their toll of human life. To downgrade or destroy the institutions and the rigorous scientific training that made these accomplishments possible is to ignore the fact that only civilized man, committed to self-discipline and the pursuit of often seemingly irrelevant knowledge, could have done it.

Youth tend to look at the state of the world as they found it and to blame all its problems on the failure of their elders. But earlier generations inherited their share of problems many of which they did a good deal about. There are people living today who can remember when child labor and the twelve hour factory day were common, when domestic servants worked twelve or fourteen hours for a daily wage well below what they now get for an hour, when the annual lynching toll in the United States numbered in the hundreds, when there were whole counties with no high schools for Negroes, when in the entire United States there were fewer Negroes with doctoral degrees than there now are in the city of Nashville. Conditions in the rest of the world were much worse and the more privileged nations did little about helping the less fortunate. Arnold Toynbee has suggested that at some future time the twentieth century may be remembered as the first age since the dawn of civilization in which people dared to think that the benefits of civilization might be made available to the whole human race.

Not only are the destroyers ignorant of the consequences of destruction, they are also ignorant of man's debt to the past. Modern civilization is badly out of balance and man's inhumanity to man is more glaringly apparent than ever before, but with all its failures, civilization has brought untold benefits and it has the potential for many more. Civilization has been called a gift from the past to the present. It is getting something for nothing, that is, a man born into a civilized society has at his disposal all kinds of things which are the result of the efforts of countless other human beings whom he has never met. Modern man is an obligated man, one who owes a debt to the past that can be paid only to the future.

Thus we are not only bound within a network of obligations to our fellow humans of today but to those who preceded us and those who will come after. Anthropologists have long pointed out the cumulative nature of culture and the way in which modern civilization rests on the discoveries and inventions made by peoples of other races and nations in other times and places. The people to whom we are indebted form a chain from the present back through the centuries to the earliest prehuman who fashioned a stone tool, to the unknowns who domesticated plants and animals and fabricated metals, to the geniuses who invented the wheel, and to the people of many races and many lands who gave us the calendar, a numbering system, writing, the alphabet, paper, printing, the compass, the foundation of our medical knowledge, and our religious and philosophical systems. We often think that as Americans we have given to the rest of the world, but none of the basic discoveries and inventions listed above were of Western man's making.

The Euro-Americans are in fact the greatest takers of history, for we literally stand on the collective shoulders of mankind.

Those who would destroy are also prone to glamorize other systems with little regard for the realities. There are numerous things wrong with Western civilization in general, and with the United States in particular, and much of this book has been given to the documentation of these facts. But there is probably nowhere else in the world, and certainly nowhere in any totalitarian country, in which there is as much freedom to speak one's mind, to criticize, and even to denounce the government and those who constitute "the Establishment" as in the United States.

Moreover the notion that men outside the boundaries of the influence of Western civilization lived in a sort of primitive utopia is naive in the extreme. Anthropologists would be the first to say that the so-called primitive peoples had meaning and significance in their lives that has often been destroyed by Western impact. But few anthropologists would attribute to such people the idyllic life of the "noble savage." And the people themselves are generally quite vocal about their own choice in the matter. They are usually emphatic in their rejection of any control by outsiders, but schools, medical services, and the goods and gadgets produced by the West are eagerly welcomed in most areas of the world.

Man's long history has brought us to the present. It cannot be undone, and we ignore it at our peril. John Donne's prophetic words of every man's involvement in mankind have come to full fruition in man's interdependence and in his conquest of the physical world. We cannot undo it nor erase its effect.

All of this is not to minimize modern man's problems—the threat is real and urgent beyond our imagining. But these problems do not grow out of the fact of technology or of the conquest of the physical world. Technology is neither good nor bad in itself—like fire, water, electricity, or nuclear energy, the value depends on the use made of it. In a sense, our present problems are the result of our success in meeting other problems. Overpopulation and many other conditions are indirectly at least the result of our elimination of disease, floods, famine, infanticide, slavery, and human sacrifice. Where western man went wrong was in his failure to give comparable attention to the human element involved. As a consequence we are suffering an exaggerated and global form of what the sociologists have called social, or cultural, lag—an imbalance growing out of the fact that changes in one aspect of life often outrun other changes needed to keep the system on an even keel.

This imbalance is found in every aspect of our life. Our educational system from kindergarten to university creaks along, laden with outdated ideas and practices. The handling of the very old, the young, the sick, the retarded, the mentally ill, the delinquent, the criminal, and the unemployed are hopelessly outdated. Our educational, penal, and welfare systems are geared to the conditions of a century ago. We have changed from a rural to an urban economy, but our patterns are still geared to horse and buggy days. We have ignorance, poverty, and hunger at home and abroad, while spending enough on war and defense programs to feed and educate most of the world. Our race relations patterns are equally outmoded. Certainly progress has been made, but in comparison with technological changes it is miniscule. The technological changes have widened the gap between the rich and poor regardless of race. And perhaps most insane of all, we have carried into the nuclear age a practice of settling disputes by methods that ceased to be sensible when battles were no longer a matter of hand to hand combat involving personal skill and bravery.

This imbalance has come about because the time, attention, talent, and money of the western world has for generations been given mainly to technological development. As a consequence the whole world has been brought into a vast intercommunicating and interdependent unit. We have dangled before men's eyes goods and gadgets once undreamed of by kings and emperors. We have taken the lead in developing such awesome and expensive powers of destruction as to threaten life on the planet. To a lesser degree we have developed the biological sciences so as to save and prolong life to the point of overpopulating the globe. With it all we have done relatively nothing about the problems of how men are to live together in such a world.

Like so many other things, this imbalance is cumulative and is still being augmented. It is not merely that we spend ever increasing amounts on technological inventions but that our whole society is geared up to fostering technical changes that inevitably affect our social structure and all our ways of living and working. We have, Platt reminds us, many organizations searching all the time for new inventions and combinations of them to solve technical problems. The research and development teams of our industrial and government laboratories do nothing else. But we have no corresponding organizations that spend all their time searching for new inventions and new combinations for the solution of social problems. The main reason that our solution of social problems lags so far behind our technology is that we have not organized the deliberate search for ways of dealing with social change. Yet social inventions are just as possible as technological ones and can be searched for and found in the same way.

4. Our Species Identity

Not only are we tied to men in the past and to those who are to come after us, but we are, whether we realize it or not, tied to the rest of the human species. In earlier days a people's identity was necessarily with those who occupied the same or contiguous territories. Even after the period of exploration and conquest, with many peoples moving into new territories, men were separated by enormous distances and the slowness of communication, by the barriers of language, and the strangeness of alien customs.

This former time-space separation has now been annihilated by our technological advancement. The future of man is one. His differences in race, language, religion, and culture are minor compared to the shared characteristics that separate him from the rest of the animal world. His escape from his own planet into outer space brings him face to face with the fact of the identity of the human species. George Gaylord Simpson emphasizes the perils of our failing to realize and accept such identity. Man is responsible to himself and for himself, he writes. "Himself" here means the whole human species, not only the individual, and certainly not just those of a certain color of hair or cast of features. He concludes that unless most of us do live maturely and rationally "the future of mankind is dim indeed—if there is any future."

Our global interdependence and common destiny make many of modern man's preoccupations seem suicidal. The billions of dollars spent in preparations for warring on other members of the human species, the plundering of the planet, the allowing of conditions that practically guarantee poverty and crime, our racial, religious, national, and class prejudices can be labeled nothing short of incredible stupidity. The destructive power at man's disposal lays upon him the necessity to enlarge the we-group to include the whole of the human species. This does not require the complete elimination of the identity of constituent groups. Modern nations represent essentially the enlargement of the in-groups that once consisted of the extended family, the band, horde, clan, or tribe. But we we are under the necessity of finding ways by which men will recognize our common humanity and our interdependence, perhaps much as states within a nation are willing to yield certain powers and prerogatives in recognition of the value of national unity.

Of particular concern in this volume is the all too common denial of full species identity to persons of other races, a denial often based on the assumption that people of a different physical type are genetically inferior and therefore a threat to the welfare of mankind. S. L. Washburn points out that such attitudes are based on a profound misunderstanding of culture, of learning, and of the biology of the human species. All kinds of performance, he says, whether social, athletic, or intellectual, are built on both genetic and environmental elements, and the level of such performance can be increased by improving the environmental situation so that every genetic constitution may be developed to its full capacity. Any kind of social discrimination against groups of people, whether they are races, castes, or classes, reduces the achievements of our species. Human biology finds its realization in a culturally determined way of life, and the infinite variety of genetic combinations can express themselves efficiently only in a free and open society.

An acceptance of the fact of our species identity and the interdependence of the human family does not preclude the recognition of genetic differences and diversity in human potentialities. There is no question but that the necessities of mankind call for the maximum use of the human potential. There are those who think the way to maximize such potential is by rigid stratification and by the limitation of social mobility so that the assumed superiority of an elite class or race is protected. Theodoseus Dobzhansky points out the fallacy of this judgment. Rigid race, caste, or class lines far from protecting "quality" have just the opposite effect. He insists that genetic diversity is man's most precious resource. All races and classes include persons of great contrast in ability. The degree to which special aptitudes are realized depends in large measure on the freedom of social mobility which a society provides for all of its members. Rigid race, caste, or class lines limit or preclude such mobility. Therefore the one way to assure the maximum use of superior individuals is in a fully open society in which every individual has the opportunity for the fullest development of which he is capable. This does not produce a classless society but one in which mobility is related to personal interest, ability, and motivation, rather than to a predetermined position in a given group.

The world has need of elites in the sense of people of special ability and training. But there is no reason to assume that such elites can come only from certain races or classes or from certain nations. Social upheavals at various periods of history have demonstrated again and again that plenty of talent lay dormant in the underprivileged classes and that new elites can be recruited from below. And in a fluid world, biological as well as sociological fitness often depends upon flexibility rather than rigidity of behavior and upon creativity and educability rather than adherence to old ways.

The United States, as a multiracial society, has both the opportunity and the obligation to set the example of the recognition of our species' identity. We have had the ideal but not the practice of genuine equality of opportunity. We should not be led astray by the assumption that equality implies sameness. It rather requires the provision for each of its members of opportunity for the fullest development of his own potential. In his book *Excellence*, John Gardner writes that it is possible to have excellence in education and at the same time to educate everybody to the level of his ability. In his words the central problem to which we must find the answer is how to "provide opportunities and rewards for individuals of every degree of ability so that individuals at every level will realize their full potentialities, perform at their best, and have no resentment toward any other level."

It should be noted that Mr. Gardner is referring to individual, not racial, potentialities. As we have fully documented elsewhere, all our evidence points to the fact that categorizing people by race or class and failing to provide for the fulfilment of human potentialities is a waste of human resources that no society can afford and that robs our species of talent needed for survival.

To be human today means a recognition of our dependence on other human beings. As someone has put it, we are obligated to pay our dues as members of the human race. The human condition places upon each man the obligation to carry his own load to the best of his ability and to take his turn in helping those who are unable to make it alone. Since we were all at one time young and helpless and may at any time find ourselves dependent on others through illness, accident, misfortune, or age, we are all obligated to protect the weak and the helpless. The fact that none of us asked to be born nor could choose our parents or the time and circumstances of our birth, places upon all of us who have survived a peculiar obligation to the world's children.

We think the exposure of unwanted infants by the ancient Greeks and Romans a barbarous practice, and many people are shocked at societies of the recent past that practiced infanticide. But is it either more sane or more civilized to allow infants to be born and then be condemned by circumstances over which they have no control, to grow up under conditions that practically guarantee that they will live in poverty, misery, and want? It has become increasingly clear that a society has both the right and the duty to protect itself from the excessive fecundity of its irresponsible members. Yet it should be equally clear that when a society allows a human being to come to birth, it has an obligation to give that individual a chance to achieve his human potential. To paraphrase Carl Sandburg, to be human means to recognize that there is only one child, and that child's name is all children. Once a child is born, he has the right to say, "I am here. I am a member of the Family."

And an enlightened society must recognize and act upon that claim.

5. The Human Potential

Although mankind today faces perils never before confronting the human species all at once, he also has at his disposal resources and potentialities never before known to man. Many of the conditions earlier described as perils are also opportunities. Although our technological imbalance is the source of one of mankind's greatest threats, technology itself has made possible the greatest boon ever known to man. For the first time in human history mankind has the power to make possible the human use of all human beings. As we have noted, all the early civilizations were built on the backs of unfree labor. When man's major or only source of energy was the human animal, some men had to toil like beasts to make the good life possible for others. It was not merely that some might live in luxury at the expense of others, though that sometimes resulted. But if some men were to have freedom and leisure to think, to plan, to create, to write, to paint, or to invent, other men had to toil. When we see the pyramids of Egypt, the civilization of Greece and Rome, the achievements of the Maya and the Inca, or the scholars gathered at Timbuctu, we forget that beneath the cultural flowering were masses of toiling slaves whose lives too often were nasty, brutish, and short.

Our technology has not fully eliminated such brutish toil, not even in the West, but we now know that it is unnecessary. There is nothing wrong with physical labor within reason, but for the first time in history we could shift enough of the loads from the backs of men to enable them to live like human beings rather than as beasts of burden. This is mankind's most far reaching potential and, although it calls for many readjustments and rearrangements, it is within man's reach if he chooses to make the effort.

The use of technology makes possible a second potential that we have hardly conceived of, much less exploited. Because of our failure to give adequate attention to the human element, our unplanned technological advances have resulted in major imbalances and the leaving of great masses of the unskilled without work to do. But the potential is there. Even in the midst of critical unemployment there are unlimited things that need to be done. There are neglected children, untaught and undirected youth, adults in need of education and reeducation, and the sick, the elderly, and the mentally ill in need of care and attention. There are hospitals and nursing homes that are understaffed and playgrounds that are unequipped and unsupervised. There is land that needs to be reclaimed, streams that need to be cleared of debris, slum housing that needs to be replaced, ugly spots that could be made beautiful, flowers and trees that need to be planted and tended. There are poems and stories that need to be written and pictures that need to be painted. There are plans that need to be made, creative ideas that need to be developed, and research that needs pursuing.

Of course we do not now know how to get all these things done, to train and match people to jobs, and to put all human beings to human uses. But for the first time in history it could be done if we were willing to give it the same attention, time, money, and effort that we have put into our technological achievements. The billions of dollars and the man hours that modern nations put into the preparation for fighting others of their own species could go a long way toward making a truly human life possible for people everywhere.

Our global intercommunication and interdependence have created perils, but they are equally full of promise. For the first time in history, men can communicate across the former barriers of language and distance. The heads of state can be in instant communication with one another, and a knowledge of the rest of the world is now available to all. Even the awesome power to destroy could be turned to peaceful uses. And there is already evidence that the mounting waste that is the by-product of technology could be recycled and made usable in a variety of ways. All these things await the creative imagination and the will of man.

Another potential lies in the fact of man's educability. We now know that the human potential is not a matter of genetic endowment alone but of such endowment in interaction with the environment. We cannot change the genetic potential, but we can maximize the environmental setting so as to make possible the highest development of each individual. Although as yet we have done little about it, we now know that many of the less well endowed—even those classified as mentally retarded—could in many cases be helped to become useful and productive members of society. Furthermore, we know that all human beings have the potential for good as well as evil and that the good can be fostered. We know that man's progress is recorded not in his germ plasm but in his social institutions, and these institutions can be made to help rather than to hinder man's progress.

There is new potential in the fact that although we do not know the answers to all our problems, we do know how answers can be had. All of our vaunted technology is the result of man's search for answers to problems. Such research is cumulative, and the commonplaces of today—our telephones, radios, and televisions, as well as our jet planes, orbiting satellites, and men on the moon—are the results of long years of research, trials and errors. We have the potential for similar progress in handling the problems of living that would enable human beings to share the globe in peace and justice. For the first time we are beginning to know the right questions, and we know how to get the answers. The human potential is there if we will but use it.

Our racial and cultural diversity has been the basis of much of man's inhumanity to man, but such diversity can be used to add to the richness of life for the whole human species. Note was taken earlier of the scientists' judgment that such diversity should be regarded as one of man's precious resources. We now know that prejudice and discrimination are part of our learned behavior and are therefore neither natural nor inevitable accompaniments of differences. Human beings are as capable of cooperation as of conflict, and there is no genetic hindrance to the enlargement of our interest and concern to include the whole of our species.

This larger identification presents enormous problems, but it also opens up new horizons. We can learn from, enjoy, and be enriched by the contributions of the various peoples whose diverse experiments in living open up new and different avenues for the fulfilment of human personality. These experiments in living were sometimes successful and sometimes doomed to failure, but they all represent man's efforts to deal with those problems inherent in the human condition. Now that the peoples of the world are so completely interdependent, that we daily face specific situations unknown to us before, that the fate not of just one nation but that of the whole human race is at stake, these experiments of different peoples in different times and places open up endless possibilities and alternative ways of coping with the problems that men everywhere have faced.

For the first time in the history of the world, man has the recorded wisdom of the ages at his disposal if he chooses to use it. All peoples have had their saints, their sages, their philosophers, their prophets, and their seers, but for centuries many of the people were unknown outside their own countries. Today the wisdom literature of the world is available in translation so that the many-faceted experiences of man throughout the ages are ours for the asking.

Moreover, the so-called primitive societies of today have their share of accumulated wisdom about the ways of the human animal. There are hundreds of studies of such societies made by anthropologists, most of them buried in scholarly monographs. One example will illustrate the sort of wisdom embodied in the experiences of others. Westerners are only now becoming aware that natural resources are not unlimited and that the planet is being ruthlessly plundered. But the ancient Israelites said it a long time ago as "The earth is the Lord's," and many other pre-industrial cultures have known it, too. They believed that to allow any individual to misuse and destroy what man cannot make or replace is sacrilege.

Most peoples have had some idea of property rights—in many societies you could own a tree, a crop, anything you made, even a song, a magic formula, or the childbearing capacity of a woman. But you could not "own" land in the sense of doing what you pleased with it, regardless of the common good. Land might appear to be owned and might be handed down in a family for generations, but only if it were used. When you ceased to use it, it could be given to someone else. Many peoples in their ignorance of proper soil conservation might not use it wisely, but they recognized that the natural resources of the earth were not, and could not be, man-made and therefore were a tribal possession, held in trust for future generations.

Our pollution, destruction, and private monopoly of land, lakes, rivers, forests, and beaches show how much we have to learn. Some of the African peoples could have taught us that for men to destroy for selfish ends what they cannot replace is antisocial behavior of the most irresponsible sort.

Two recent developments which many people think of as threats actually represent enormous potentials for good. These are the coming alive, as it were, of the young and the blacks. Youth has too often been apathetic and conforming, and both apathy and conformity are dangerous in a world of change. The need is not to suppress youth but to harness this tremendous potential in the service of the human species. It is nonsense to say that maturity has nothing to offer today. Experience is not outmoded, and no society can start over from scratch, much less can an interdependent world. On the other hand, youth are not only the future, they embody qualities that are peculiarly their own. Never before, perhaps, has mankind needed so much the combined resources and the special gifts of youth and age. Yet adults have wasted priceless time and energy in trying to maintain outmoded and trivial patterns, while youth have spent equally priceless time and energy in senseless destruction and negative activities. But the potential of their combined strengths is enormous.

Equally important is the potential that lies in the coming alive of the blacks. No reader of the earlier pages of this book can be unaware of the tremendous cost to the nation of treating a tenth of its people as inferior and subordinate creatures, thus denying them the opportunity for the full realization of their gifts and powers. The fact that Negroes have had the unique experience of being black in a white world makes of them a distinctive resource in a multiracial nation that must live in increasing interaction with a multiracial world.

It is not surprising that many black youth should overcompensate for the repressions that black people have long endured or that both black and white youth should demand miracles and be unaware of either obstacles or dangers. In the larger perspective, these are minor matters. Time moves inexorably forward, and the old men who have clung to power beyond their span of competence must ultimately pass on even if they are not forcibly replaced by an aroused electorate. All too soon the impatient youth of today, black and white, will find that they have become "the Establishment," and that it is on their shoulders that decisions and responsibility will rest. It is they who will soon be answering to another generation about what they did and did not do.

This is as it should be and, though at a slower pace, the way it has always been. Our danger is not in the brashness of youth which, in the very nature of things, must pass. Our danger is that this youthful enthusiasm and idealism may spend itself in senseless and irretrievable destruction or that it may retreat into disillusion and apathy. The road ahead cannot be easy, and it will call for bold dreams as well as prosaic day to day toil. We can be thankful that those who have been a part of our wasted resources—chief among them being the poor, the young, and the black—are coming alive to their own potentialities.

6. Inventing The Future

As stated in the Introduction, the concern of this book is not with improving race relations within the old framework of a dominant white majority and a subordinate black minority. To be sure, there must be a direct attack on racial prejudice and injustice, and there must be a revamping of those institutions with built-in racial discrimination. These direct approaches must have a high priority for a number of reasons. They are matters of simple justice and involve the righting of an ancient wrong. Other major problems such as poverty and crime are interwoven with racial injustice. There are, moreover, certain practical considerations. We live in a world two-thirds of which is made up of people of the darker races, and our position as a nation is compromised until we set our own racial house in order. Furthermore, we need the full utilization of our human resources. A nation that fails to use the full potential of a tenth of its population is engaging in the most wanton extravagance.

However, it is easy to lay all the blame for the black man's problems on racists and racism and thus to obscure the more fundamental problems of which race discrimination is only one manifestation. It has been the thesis of this book that our basic problem is that of the human use of all human beings and that our race problems must be seen within that context. Any movement for the betterment of black Americans must be one that includes the pursuit of justice and equality for all Americans, whatever their race or color. Therefore, inventing the future here means a concern with the problems of the black-white confrontation, but always as a part of the broader problem of promoting the human use of human beings. The two cannot be separated, and both must always be kept in mind.

The activities of a revolutionary minority are a misguided response to the more fundamental problem of our values and our priorities. This whole book has been a recital of our incredible failure to put human beings to human uses. There is no need to repeat again the list of conditions we have complacently allowed to exist. The ghetto uprisings and the activities of the revolutionaries are the almost inevitable consequence of the apathy, indifference, ignorance, greed, and distorted values of what has been called the establishment, but which really includes all of us.

Our choice is not between the present sorry state of the world and an instant utopia. We do not even have the choice of maintaining the status quo. We can continue to allow things to drift with only makeshift patches here and there, with one of two possibilities almost certain. One possibility is the nuclear holocaust of which almost every scientist in the country has warned us. The more likely danger may be that mankind will simply destroy all possibility of life through polluting and wasting the natural resources, through an increasingly disastrous arms race, through continuing to permit poverty and want in the midst of affluence, through prejudice, discrimination, and injustice, all of it leading to such disorder that the means of production and distribution break down with resulting famine, pestilence, and death. It is no exaggeration to say that the human race seems bent on collective suicide, with a toss-up as to whether we shall end with the bang or the whimper.

In his *An American Dilemma* written in 1944, Gunnar Myrdal says that if we act while there is still time history can be made. It is not necessary to sit still and accept whatever comes as mere destiny. In the years that have elapsed since that statement was made, we have accepted a lot of things as mere destiny, and many of the alternatives that were open to us then are now closed. The number of our options is steadily decreasing and the difficulties increasing. Civilizations have come and gone in the past and ours has no guarantee of immunity. What is worse, the modern world is indivisible, and the fate of any part of it is likely to be the fate of all.

Obviously the United States cannot solve the problems of the world alone, but it is one of the few countries still free enough to allow for the experimentation and the creativity necessary to find answers. And it is the only nation with the natural and human resources, the technical expertise, and the financial ability to take the lead. Such a lead will call for the complete reordering of priorities. The gap between our technological development and our outdated and inadequate human relations patterns is wide and deep. We are still giving our major time, attention, and money to highways, supersonic jet planes, adventures in outer space, and preparations for war, while all the problems documented throughout this book receive only the leftover crumbs of our national budget and the half hearted attention of people in the lower echelons.

This book is no blueprint for action, but it points to certain directions in which we can move and certain kinds of things that we can do. We are still obsessed with a belief in magic and still operating on the good-guy, bad-guy syndrome. There are many people who demand that we ban the bomb, get out of Vietnam, stop the manufacture of war materials, abolish the ROTC, and integrate the schools, as if these were all magical means to instant solutions of complex problems that have been years, and sometimes centuries, in the making. Our first step is to accept the fact that there are no magic wands and try to understand how we arrived at the state we are in, then go on to the long, slow, painful, but urgent and demanding, business of trying to make this planet a fit place for human beings.

Speaking specifically of the racial aspect of our problems, the National Advisory Commission on Civil Disorders made clear the magnitude of the changes that are necessary. The Commission was not made up of black radicals, militant youth, or even academic liberals, but of people described as representatives of the "moderate and responsible establishment." Yet its members came to the conclusion that only a commitment to national action on an unprecedented scale can shape a future compatible with the historic ideals of American society. They called it a task that beggars any other planned social evolution known to human history and saw as a major need the generating of a new will to do the job, including the will to "tax ourselves to the extent necessary to meet the vital needs of the nation." Moreover, there are many things that need to be done at the community level that can be done by volunteer services and giving. Needless to say, the obligation rests upon black and white alike.

Not only must we drastically reorder our priorities, but we must work on many problems at once. The problems are so involved and so interrelated that to handle them piecemeal is to be defeated before we start. This book in a sense is a plea for what has come to be called a systems approach. Rather than looking at the innumerable problems as separate and unrelated entities, we need to see the whole, to be clear as to objectives, and then see how we may go about realizing them. We must think in new ways and envision structural as well as behavioral changes.

We already know that there is a relation between poverty and health, between education and unemployment, between housing patterns and delinquency, between our outmoded penal systems and crime, and that as a matter of fact all these and numerous other systems are interrelated. There is certainly a connection running through the problems of ignorance, too many children, poverty, mental retardation, and delinquency. Attempts to improve the schools can bring only limited results so long as the children come from impoverished surroundings, suffer from malnutrition, if not actual hunger, and are the victims of defective vision and numerous health problems. There is little to be gained in desegregating schools if—as in the summer of 1970—more than thirty percent of black youth wander the streets, unable to get jobs, with nowhere to go and nothing to do.

The problems are thus infinitely complex and interrelated. No quick, easy, cheap, or final solutions are possible. We must make progress quickly and rapidly, but if we expect to finish the job quickly and get back to our usual concerns, we will certainly be disappointed. The answer is not more education, more money, more jobs, or more and better housing for the disadvantaged, but all of these things and much more. It involves our relations with the rest of the world and our rethinking of whole areas of life. Most of all perhaps, it involves our willingness to pay the price.

Basically, there are three ways in which changes can be made, that is, by helping people change their attitudes, by changing the individual's behavior, and by changing institutions. Inventing the future will require all three. We cannot change the way other people think and feel, but we can sometimes help people wish to change themselves. To say that people cannot be changed by law is a half truth. The law can require that people behave in certain ways and refrain from other kinds of behavior, and in many cases the changed behavior results in changed attitudes. Because racial bias is built into most of our institutions, the changing of the structure of such institutions is important. All of these procedures are most effective when they operate together. Some years ago a cartoonist showed a member of an audience saying to the speaker, "But how are you going to have this brave, new world with the same old people in it?" The answer, of course, is that you aren't. There is always an interdependence of persons and social institutions. Individuals help to create institutions, but the institutions in turn help to make people what they are.

There are macro and micro jobs to be done, or, if one may borrow from the fashion world, maxi, midi, and mini, and all are important.

There are jobs that can be done only by the federal government, others for the state and local communities. There are jobs for foundations and huge industries, for national organizations, for civic groups, for universities, for churches, for service groups, and for agencies, clubs, and fraternities of all kinds and sizes. There are jobs for professionally trained people and for ordinary individuals. There are jobs that can be done by the aged, the handicapped, by youth, and even by children. In fact, the jobs that need to be done are so multitudinous and so varied that only the hopelessly ill, the mentally incompetent, and infants should be excluded. Anyone who has read the earlier chapters of this book can recognize dozens of places in which situations could have been changed by some individual or organization that really wished to help.

Our individual responsibility falls into two major categories: what we can do to make our own contributions through individual and group activity at the local level, and our participation in the total society through the democratic process. Most people think of service in terms of some great thing, whereas every human being of any age or condition every day of his life has the power to increase the amount of misery and injustice in the world, or to add to the world's well-being. One of the very serious signs of the malaise of our times is the diminished amount of trust, and it follows that anyone who can help restore a sense of trust is making a contribution. Moreover, any specific act is likely to be multiplied in its effect as other people respond to and pass on in their own relationships the kind of behavior they have encountered.

It would be naive and childish to say that modern problems can be solved by simple, individual acts of decency and concern. But they are one aspect of a systems approach that calls also for a great many basic structural changes in our social institutions and in the society as a whole. One of the major structural faults in the society is generally referred to as institutional racism. There can be no question that drastic measures on the part of various institutions and organizations will be necessary even to fully recognize, much less correct, evils of such long standing. But this is not an either-or proposition, and the individual who embodies in his own behavior a respect for all human beings makes life more bearable for the people he encounters, at the same time that he helps promote the structural changes. It is worth noting that the prejudices, cruelty, injustice, greed, unawareness, and disrespect for law that are documented throughout this book are for the most part attitudes and actions of individuals who think of themselves as good citizens.

In every community there are pressing needs that call for attention and help. Almost any church, social agency, or community organization can point out endless jobs waiting to be done, and there are numerous community enterprises where responsible and dependable volunteers can be used. One of the most neglected of our individual responsibilities is that of being informed. Many of the people who complain and protest about conditions have never bothered to find out what the real issues are. Equally important for intelligent service is to understand how people become the way they are and how changes can be brought about. Many of the people who are active in public affairs show an almost complete lack of understanding of human behavior and of the forces that influence public opinion.

Any person who is really concerned with the future must take seriously his responsibility as a citizen. It is astonishing the number of otherwise responsible people who think that if they vote on election day they have fulfilled the obligations of citizenship. What is worse is the number of people who do not vote at all. One reliable study reported that sixty-five percent of eligible voters do not vote regularly and over half of them could not name their senators and congressmen. Only fourteen out of a hundred were able to identify anything their congressman had done, good or bad, and only four out of a hundred could identify any policy their congressman stood for. Yet these are the people who complain about "the system." A democratic form of government is the most rewarding, but it is also the most demanding. No other form of government holds so much promise for the human use of human beings, but it will work only when enough people are willing to pay the price of personal involvement. One's citizenship responsibility must be thought of as something requiring the kind of regular attention we give to our homes and our cars. We have the responsibility not only of choosing local, state, and national officials but of reminding them of their obligations. Hardly a week goes by without the report of some scandal involving either gross inefficiency or corruption on the part of some elected officials at some level of government. Such persons are able to get and keep their jobs because enough people choose to keep them there and because other people are not sufficiently concerned to work for their replacement.

In every community there are some business concerns that engage in illegal, unethical, or antisocial practices but who would be sensitive to public approval or disapproval. Many of the injustices to the poor and the blacks documented in these pages could have been corrected or avoided had there been in the community even a small number of concerned individuals. Even a single person can often exert some influence, and if he multiplies his efforts by enlisting others, the impact can be considerable. Negroes themselves have been able to bring about the elimination of discriminatory employment practices by withholding their trade from the offenders.

People with professional competence have still greater obligations. If we are to invent a bearable future for mankind there must be a serious search for the answers to our basic problems. We must not only take seriously the search for what we do not now know, but we must coordinate, disseminate, and utilize the knowledge we already have. Anthropologists, sociologists, psychologists, political scientists, and other specialists each have knowledge and insights unknown to or unused by their colleagues in other fields. A pooling and coordination of such knowledge and insights would demonstrate that we already have a great deal more knowledge and ordinary know-how than we have assumed. Such knowledge filters down even more slowly to the general public, and until it does reach the general public, it is unlikely to be used very extensively or to influence public policy.

We must somehow get an educational system from nursery school through graduate school that is geared up to fitting people to live in a world that is not yet born. True relevance is not the immediate but the basic. The really relevant thing in education—as apart from job training —is not what to do about a specific problem. It is to learn how to learn, how to analyze and go about solving any problem, how to draw on the accumulated knowledge of the past and present to discover all the possible alternatives, and to develop new insights. The surest road to a dead end existence is to teach people to adjust to the world as it is, for if any one thing is certain it is that the world tomorrow will be different from what it is today.

The kind of world in which we are living is so complex and is changing with such speed that any relevant education must emphasize creativity, flexibility, and responsibility: creativity, because we must be constantly finding new ways to meet both old and new problems; flexibility, because we must be constantly ready to adjust to changing situations; and responsibility, because the peoples of the world are so inextricably bound together that no man can live to himself or do his own thing without regard to his fellow human beings with whom he shares our ever-shrinking planet.

We must be willing to allow for and to learn from mistakes in the human relations field as we now do in technological enterprises. For every advance in technology there have been hundreds of mistakes and failures, but when something doesn't work the effort is not considered wasted. We find out what went wrong and try something different. In a recent advertisement an electronics company boasted of what it called "a little idea that revolutionized the whole camera business." It looks simple, the company said, but it took "more than 100,000 designs and years of fiddling and testing before we made the first one." Before men reached the moon the space program had had numerous failures that cost billions of dollars and the lives of three men. Yet after a short period of hastily planned and inadequately financed programs of remedial education for deprived children and job training for ghetto youth, otherwise responsible people were ready to pronounce the programs failures and press for their termination.

We should not deceive ourselves that social changes can be made without persistent labor or without turmoil. We are a deeply divided people not only on the race question but in numerous other ways. It is not merely a question of good guys and bad guys, and it involves much more than a generation gap. In a 1970 *Wall Street Journal* article one of the staff writers stated the matter bluntly. There are two radically different views of this country, he said, and it is foolish to suppose that better communication alone is going to reconcile them. On the one hand are those, mostly, but by no means all, young, many of them black, who see the society as racist, militaristic, materialistic, and inhumane. At the far extreme of this group are the revolutionaries who would like to see the whole business destroyed. On the other hand are the others, mostly, but by no means all, middle-aged, middle-class, and white, though not necessarily affluent. America has given them more opportunity than their parents had or even dreamed of having, and they want to keep things as they are or as nostalgia pictures the past. Even those who have not quite made it may see the young protesters as throwing away the things for which many other Americans have striven and which they want for their children.

The points of view of these various groups were documented in earlier chapters. It is important to note that the divisions are not absolute and the people in each group are not all alike. There is a black-white polarization, but many of the whites of the extreme left support the more militant blacks, and many of the more conservative blacks have much in common with middle-class whites. The militant black youth who are mainly poor and who have suffered many deprivations are separated by these facts from the militant white youth who are mainly from privileged families. Conservative whites include not only the middle-class privileged but many of the working poor, old and young, who resent the blacks and who may be enraged to see the more fortunate white youth destroying the very things the less privileged have longed for and could not attain. There are innumerable white youth and a considerable number of black ones who have middle-class attitudes and aspirations. Thus we do not have just a black-white or an old-young polarization. There are many maps of reality represented, and oversimplification of the issues is an unprofitable exercise.

Of course there are many people in between, but those with the extreme points of view have such different maps of reality as almost not to speak the same language. If we are not to be torn apart and destroyed in the process, we must somehow recognize that people who see life from such different points of view may be equally honest and sincere in their beliefs. Actually many persons from all of these groups, as well as those in the middle, really are committed to their own versions of the human use of human beings.

A part of the problem lies in the fact that we are reacting to overt behavior rather than getting down to the premises underlying the behavior and that we are confusing means and ends. If we can get at these two things we may find that we have more unity than we thought and that some degree of communication really is possible. The extremes of anarchy and repression are both essentially means of social control, and both are destructive to democratic values. Given the fact that white persons of middle-class values and aspirations constitute not only the largest single segment of the population, but the major concentration of money and power, any large upsurge in the direction of anarchy will inevitably lead to repression and irretrievable loss of freedom and democracy. In other words, given all the circumstances, violence and disruption are inefficient means. There seems to be some evidence that extreme militance on the part of the student rebels may be giving way to a saner and more constructive effort which will have far greater chance of success.

The stakes are too high for us not to find some way to reassert our unity as a people committed to the principles of justice and equality even though these are as yet unrealized ideals. One of the greatest strengths of a democratic form of government is that it does have built-in self-corrective mechanisms not available to any totalitarian system. Can one really imagine that any totalitarian state would tolerate for a moment the kind of criticism and even defiance that are freely voiced by militants in this country? And the problem is not that there are no channels for influencing policy but that we do not have the patience or take the trouble to use them. It is all too evident that Burke was right in saying that the only thing needed for evil to triumph was that good men should do nothing. And Yeats could have been speaking of our own day when he said the best lack all conviction while the worst are full of passionate intensity.

Most of us really know that our choice is between all-out commitment to new ways or the acceptance of the grim fate that the soberest scientists have persistently warned us of. If we are not to sit back and accept whatever comes as mere destiny, good men must set about with passionate intensity to invent the future. The very technological developments that are now leading us toward destruction have also given us the power to make possible the human use of human beings. The one thing that is lacking is enough motivation and will on the part of enough people to set the process in motion. Platt called it "The Step to Man." He agrees that such a goal sounds Utopian. But he also reminds us that the world has grown too dangerous for anything less than Utopia.

Notes, References and Suggested Readings

For full identification of books see the *Selected Bibliography*, pp. 261–272, where books are listed alphabetically by author or editor.

General Background References

Useful background studies are John Hope Franklin's *From Slavery to Freedom* 3rd ed. (1967) and Myrdal's now classic *An American Dilemma* 2 vols. (1944). Other good sources are Ginsberg and Eichner, *The Troublesome Presence* (1964), Quarles, *The Negro in the Making of America* (1967), Bergman, *Chronological History of The Negro in America* (1969), and Frazier, *The Negro in The United States*, rev. ed. (1957). Briefer paperback books include Bennett, *Before The Mayflower* (1966), Bontemps, *100 Years of Negro Freedom* (1961), Franklin and Starr (eds.), *The Negro in Twentieth Century America* (1967), and Lincoln, *The Negro Pilgrimage in America* (1967).

Symposia and documentary histories include Parsons and Clark (eds.), *The Negro American* (1966), *Ebony, The Negro Handbook* (1966), Fishel and Quarles (eds.), *The Negro American* (1967), Osofsky, *The Burden of Race* (1967), Grant (ed.), *Black Protest* (1968), Broderick and Meier (eds.), *Negro Protest Thought in the Twentieth Century* (1965), Aptheker (ed.), *A Documentary History of The Negro People in The United States* 2 vols. (1951), Davis (ed.), *The American Negro Reference Book* (1966), Blaustein and Zangrando (eds.), *Civil Rights and The American Negro* (1968), Meier and Rudwick (eds.), *The Making of Black America* (1969), Isaacs, *The New World of The Negro American* (1963), Friedman, *The Civil Rights Reader* (1968), Meier, *Negro Thought in America* (1963) and Pettigrew, *A Profile of The Negro American* (1964).

The current situation is changing so rapidly that many of the best sources are periodicals. See especially *The New York Times*, the staff written reports of *The Wall Street Journal*, and the journals devoted to social issues such as *Transaction, The Nation, The Annals of The American Academy of Political and Social Sciences*, and *Social Forces*. Periodicals dealing specifically with the problems of race are *The Journal of Negro Education* (Washington), *The Journal of Negro History* (Washington), *Phylon* (Atlanta) and *Ebony* (Chicago). Among the more influential Negro newspapers are *The New York Amsterdam News, The Pittsburgh Courier*, and *The Chicago Defender*. Organizations that regularly publish periodicals, pamphlets and news releases are

The Southern Regional Council (Atlanta), The National Association for The Advancement of Colored People (New York), The National Urban League (New York), The Anti-Defamation League (New York), and The Race Relations Information Center (Nashville).

Books cited for particular chapters are arranged by sections and are identified only by author and date. For fuller information see the *Selected Bibliography*.

Chapter 1. INTRODUCTION: THE WAY THINGS ARE pp. 1–12

1. *Confrontation. Here Comes Tomorrow* (1966, 1967) was edited by Lancaster. For the quotation from the presidential commission see Vol. X, p. xix (1969). Useful books are Lubell (1964), Bennett (1964) and (1965), Silberman (1964), and King (1964).

2. *The Coming of The Blacks.* For the *Ebony* poll see "What's in a Name?" in *Ebony*, 11/67 and 6/68. For the publication dates of the various books mentioned see under author's name in the *Selected Bibliography*. See Bennett (1965), Barbour (ed.) (1968), Hough (1968), Grier and Cobbs (1968), and Lomax (1962). For the early Portuguese patterns see Jobson (1904), pp. 37ff., first published in 1623, and other books listed for Chapter 6, Section 4.

3. *Race and Racism.* For "scientific" racism see *Current Anthropology*, October 1961 and June 1962. Carmichael and Hamilton (1967) make a useful distinction between institutional and individual racism. See also Whitney Young (1969). Prejudice is a better word for many purposes than is racism which allows for no differences. See Allport (1954), Bettelheim and Janowitz (1964), Mack (1970) and the Introduction to Glock and Siegelman (eds.) (1969), and Marx (1967).

4. *What Are "Good" Race Relations?* Moton (1929) made explicit the Negroes' reaction to the common idea of "good" race relations. Modern impatience with the conventional idea shows up in nearly any publication dealing with current black opinion. See Bennett (1964), Grier and Cobbs (1968), Hough (1968) and *Ebony*, 8/70.

Chapter 2. CULTURE AND HUMAN RELATIONS pp. 13–25

1. *The Varieties of Human Groups.* For further elaboration by the author see Brown (1963). For a psychologist's discussion of groups and prejudice see Allport (1954). For the kinds of situations in which particular group patterns tend to develop see Maunier (1949), Nieboer (1910), and Brown (1942).

2. *The Nature of Group Attitudes.* The Herodotus quotations are from the Rawlinson translation (1928), Book I, p. 53, and Book III, pp. 160–161.

3. *Race and Group Relations.* For the U.S. patterns in the 1940s see

Johnson (1943). The verse quoted is from a poem "All Things Bright and Beautiful" by C. F. Alexander in the Oxford Dictionary of Quotations (1955).
4. *Race Relations as An Aspect of Culture.* For the author's elaboration see Brown (1963). For class differences in child training see Davis and Dollard (1940), Davis (1948), Sutherland (1942), and Johnson (1941). For the ways in which children of different cultures are taught acceptable patterns see Mead and Walfenstein (eds.) (1955).
5. *Our Maps of Reality.* For the idea of maps of reality see Huxley (1953). The two Negroes referred to were members of the Nashville City Council.

Chapter 3. RACE AND RACE DIFFERENCES pp. 26–48

For material in this and the following chapter I have relied heavily on those anatomists, biologists, zoologists, paleontologists, and geneticists who have concerned themselves with comparative studies, and on those physical anthropologists in the United States who have pioneered in genetically based population studies. W. E. LeGros Clark and Julian Huxley from England, Ernst Mayr, George Gaylord Simpson, L. C. Dunn, Theodosius Dobzhansky and Bentley Glass in the United States fall within the first group. Among the physical anthropologists who have been most helpful are S. L. Washburn, W. C. Boyd, Stanley Garn, William Howells, F. Clark Howell, Frank Livingstone, Gabriel Lasker, J. N. Spuhler, and Ashley Montagu. Among the psychologists Otto Klineberg has been particularly helpful. The student is referred to the current issues of the *American Anthropologist*, the *American Journal of Physical Anthropology, Current Anthropology, Science, The Scientific American,* and *Human Organization.*

Students should check libraries, book stores, and journals for newer publications and revisions of books by the authors listed. Among the current books on physical anthropology are Montagu (1960), Hulse (1963), Lasker (1961), Brace and Montagu (1965), and Howells (1967). For useful material on race see McKern (ed.) (1966) with articles by Washburn, Dobzhansky, Mayr, Clark, Boyd, Stern, and Klineberg. See also Jennings and Hoebel (eds.) (1966), Tax (ed.) (1962) and (1964), Garn (ed.) (1960), Montagu (ed.) (1964), Mead and others (eds.) (1968) and Garn (1969).
1. *Race and Public Policy.* Popular purveyors of the doctrine of racial inferiority generally use an outmoded definition of race and thus start with premises that are no longer defensible. See comments under Section 6.
2. *What is a Race?* Most popular discussions of race differences are based on what Dobzhansky calls "a form of typological misjudgment" which

assumes that an individual is a manifestation of a racial type. For the newer approach see Dobzhansky (1962) and in Spuhler (ed.) (1967), and Boyd (1950). See Washburn in Jennings and Hoebel (eds.) (1966), and in McKern (ed.) (1966). Mayr (1970) calls the replacement of typological thinking by population thinking "perhaps the greatest conceptual revolution that has taken place in biology."

3. *How Races Came to Be.* Most of the authorities cited for this chapter are in agreement on the basic ideas of the formation of races although they may differ on particulars. See Washburn in *The Scientific American* (1960) and in McKern (ed.) (1966). Coon takes a position different from most of his fellow scientists (1962) and (1965). For criticism of Coon's position see Dobzhansky in Spuhler (ed.) (1967) and Montagu (1964).

4. *Are Race Differences Significant?* Washburn in Mandelbaum and others (eds.) (1963) says that at least 75 percent of the racial studies made in the last sixty years were a complete waste of time because they were based on pre-genetic typology in which people sharing certain physical traits such as skin color are treated as a unit. Livingstone discusses the sickle cell trait in Garn (ed.) (1960). For other useful material see Boyd in *Science* 6/7/63, Dobzhansky (1962) and in McKern (ed.) (1966) and Spuhler (ed.) 1967. Simpson (1951) p. 173 says that "progress is impossible without change and change is impossible without variation. We can therefore expect neither biological nor social progress unless we tolerate human differences both in physical type and in social ideas." For Washburn's statement see Jennings and Hoebel (eds.) (1966).

5. *The Battle of The I.Q.* See Dobzhansky (1962) in Spuhler (ed.) (1967), and in McKern (ed.) (1966). Mayr (1970) says the two great truths of population zoology are (1) no two individuals are alike, and (2) both environment and genetic endowment make a contribution to nearly every trait. For the 1923 and 1930 statements by Brigham see Klineberg in McKern (ed.) (1966). For the complete text of Brigham's statement repudiating his earlier report see *Psychological Review*, Vol. 37 No. 2, 1930.

6. *Why Don't They Find Out?* This question is most often raised by persons who have no claim to competence in the field. Occasionally some psychologist insists on such studies as did Dr. Arthur Jensen in the *Harvard Educational Review*, Winter 1969. A number of psychologists and geneticists replied to Dr. Jensen in the next issue of the *Review*.

As indicated earlier the studies purporting to show racial differences in "intelligence" are generally worthless. They are based on an out-moded typological concept of race; they assume that "intelligence" is a "trait"; and they generally ignore the fact that the phenotype is the result of the continuous interaction of the genotype with the environment from the moment of conception to death. These points are amply documented in the references already cited in Washburn, Boyd, Dobzhansky, Mayr, Montagu, and Klineberg.

Chapter 4. THE MYTHOLOGY OF RACE pp. 47–60

The sources used for Chapter 3 are equally relevant to this chapter. Montagu (1964) discusses most of the myths mentioned.

1. *Myths of Blood.* For various blood myths see Montagu (1964), pp. 280ff. An appendix lists the various state laws regarding interracial marriage.

2. *Myths of Race Differences.* For various myths about Negro and white differences see Montagu (1964), pp. 98, 100, 291. The statement by LeGros Clark is quoted in Montagu (1964), p. 298. Studies of the closure of the sutures of the skull were made by T. Wingate Todd in the 1920's. See Montagu (1964), p. 299. See also Dobzhansky in Spuhler (ed.) (1967), pp. 1ff.

3. *Myths of Race Mixture.* Montagu (1964) gives a full chapter to the questions treated in this section. See also Washburn in Mandelbaum and others (1963). Dobzhansky (1962) and Boyd in Tax (ed.) (1962). For biblical references see Tilson (1958). See Huxley and Haddon (1936), pp. 229ff. for their statement.

4. *The Black Baby Myth.* The incidents reported in this section were personally investigated by the author. For possible characteristics of the offspring of mulatto parents see Glass (1943), pp. 172ff. Dunn and Dobzhansky (1946), p. 47, point out that a child can inherit each kind of gene from only two, never all four, of its grandparents. Boyd (1950), pp. 57–58, says that there is a "distinct though small chance" that not a single one of your chromosomes came from a particular grandparent. See also Snyder (1941).

5. *The Function of Myth.* For the way myth has functioned to justify the treatment of Negroes see Herskovits (1941), pp. 292ff. See also Brown (1963), pp. 126ff., and Montagu (1964). For Baldwin's statement see Goldwin (ed.) (1963), p. 88. See Clark (1965), p. 75, for his statement.

Chapter 5. THE BLACK IMAGE pp. 61–77

Much of the material on which this and the following chapter are based was researched during an extended period in the British Museum and Oxford University Libraries in England and in the Library of Congress and the Oriental Institute in the United States. An examination of recent research in the field confirms the author's conclusion based on the earlier studies. Many of the older sources are omitted for want of space but these references will be found in the author's earlier publications (1942), (1949) and (1957).

1. *The Myth of the Negro Past.* The most comprehensive treatment of this subject is Herskovits (1941). The most readable of the recent studies are those of Bovill and Davidson cited in the appropriate places. For the period when Africa was more advanced than most of Europe see Bohannan (1964).

2. *Slavery, Race and Color.* The primary source for Egypt's early relations with black Africa is the five volume work of Breasted (1906–7). Other older volumes still useful are Budge (1907) and (1928), Breasted (1909), Hall in the *Cambridge Ancient History*, Vol. 1, (1925) and Pittard (1926). Davies and Gardiner (1936) show the Egyptian artists' conceptions of various peoples.

   A pioneering study of Greek attitudes is Beardsley (1929). Westermann (1955) says that antipathy based on color was totally lacking in the Greek world. This conclusion is confirmed by the recent comprehensive study of Snowden (1970), and Baldry (1965). For Rome see Buckland (1908) and Barrow (1928). Sherwin-White (1967) deals with prejudice against the Jews and the northern barbarians who were white. For the source of slaves see Gordon in the *Journal of Roman Studies*, Vol. 14 (1924) and LaPiana in the *Harvard Theological Review* (Oct. 1927). For the spread of Christianity and the role of the early church see Latourette (1937–38). For the Muslim trade in Africa see Bovill (1958) and Davidson and Buah (1966).

3. *The Notion of Racial Inferiority.* The development of the idea of racial inferiority is treated in Brown (1957), Herskovits (1941) and Montagu (1964). The best recent treatments are in Davidson (1961), (1966), and (1969), and in Bohannan (1964). For the relations of Europeans to black Africa see Wyndham (1935) and (1937), Blake (1937), Martin (1927), and Meek and others (1940). The visits of "black gentlemen" to England and the continent are reported in various issues of the *Gentleman's Magazine* and the *Minutes* of the Royal African Company. See also Vol. 2 of Donnan (1930–35). The reference to the little-known island called England is in Davidson and Buah (1966), p. 41.

4. *Reading History Backwards.* See the references for sections 2 and 3 and Davidson (1959) and (1969). For a list of the Arab writers see the Notes and References for Chapter 6, section 3. See Jobson (1623), 1904 edition, pp. 34–77, and 112 for his various comments. See Lane-Poole (1901), pp. 87–89, 145–150 for his comments. See also Davidson (1966) and Davidson and Buah (1966).

5. *Perpetuating the Myth of Inferiority.* In spite of recent efforts to correct the neglect and distortion of Africa and the Negro in histories,

encyclopedias, and textbooks there are still many omissions and much bias. See Kane (1970).

Chapter 6. THE BLACK MAN IN HISTORY pp. 78–94

1. *The Peoples of Africa.* For the major geographical factors see Stamp (1953) and Fitzgerald (1957). Check for possible later editions of these standard works. For the people of Africa see Bohannan (1964), Oliver and Fage (1962), and the Introduction to Ottenberg (1960). For languages see Greenberg (1963). For the variety of social patterns and political systems see Forde (ed.) (1954). Radcliffe-Brown and Forde (ed.) (1950), and Fortes and Evans-Pritchard (eds.) (1940). For recent studies of African religions by an East African see Mbiti (1969) and (1970). For African art see Davidson (1966), Rattray (1927), and Fagg in Ottenberg (1960). There are of course numerous anthropological monographs dealing with specific peoples but most of these are too specialized for the general reader.

2. *The Negro in the Ancient World.* See the references cited for Chapter 5. For the black rulers of Egypt see Breasted (1906–7) and (1909) and Budge (1907) and (1928). Champollion's description is reported in Pittard (1926). See also Davies and Gardiner (1936). The Herodotus quotations are from the translation by Rawlinson (1928) VII, 379 and 111, 153. For Negroes in Greece and Rome see the references for Chapter 5. For the people of Meröe and Egypt's other neighbors see Davidson (1966) and Shinnie (1967).

3. *Black and White in The Middle Ages.* The best available sources are Bovill (1958) and the various volumes of Basil Davidson. Melvin Knight (1926) is still useful. For the quotation given see p. 99. For the crusades and the relation of Christians and Muslims see Latourette (1937–38). A picture of the Catalan map is found as a frontispiece in Bovill (1958). Among the most interesting of the Arab writings are those of Leo Africanus c. 1526, translated by John Pory (1896), Ibn Battuta 1325–1354, translated by Gibbs (1929), and Es Sadi translated into French by Houdas (1900). See also the Voyages of Cadamosta c. 1455 translated by Crone (1937). Charles Monteil (1932) gives much information about Jenne.

4. *The Land of the Fathers.* Many of the slave "factors" who served the great trading companies on the west coast of Africa left diaries, records and documents that, while often biased in interpretation, contain much valuable information. Among the first hand accounts consulted by the author are those of William Bosman, agent general of the British royal navy (1678), John Atkins, Surgeon General of the British royal navy (1735), C. B. Wadstrom, Swedish scientist (1787), William Snelgrove (1734) and Thomas Phillips (1693), both ship cap-

tains. Practically all of this material is inaccessible to the general reader but extensive extracts will be found in Donnan (1930–35). Some accounts are found in Hakluyt which is available in many libraries in the nine volume Everyman's edition (1907). One of the richest sources on the Portuguese beginnings in West Africa is the account of Azurara (c. 1450) the official chronicler of Prince Henry. It was translated into English by Beasley and Prestage (1896–1899).

For the peoples of the West Coast see, for the Ashanti, Rattray (1923), (1927) and (1929). The historical references given are from Claridge (1915). For the Dahomeans see Herskovits (1938) and Herisse (1911). The historical material cited is from Forbes (1851). For general treatments of West Africa see Davidson and Buah (1966), and Fage (1968).

5. *Negroes in American Life.* For the story of Estevan see Winship (1896) and Winsor (1889). Tracing the story of Job ben Solomon began in the Library of Congress with a small book by Thomas Bluett (1734). The rest of the story was pieced together from various *Minutes* of the Royal African Company, the *Gentleman's Magazine* and Frances Moore (1738). Moore was a factor for the Royal African Company and was made responsible for getting Job back home. For Langston Hughes' Poem see Hughes (1959). Baldwin's comment is in Goldwin (ed.) (1963). For the contributions of individual Negroes and the development of Negro enterprises see Quarles (1967), Bardolph (1961), Redding (1958), Butcher (1956), Locke (1925), Hughes and Bontemps (eds.) (1949), Margolies (1968) and LeRoi Jones (1963).

Chapter 7. THE WAY WE CAME pp. 95–113

1. *The Relevance of History.* Most of the books listed as general background studies will be useful for this chapter. See also Chapter 5, section 4. Lincoln (1967) has a chronology of events important to Negroes from 1492 to 1966.

2. *The Black Thread.* For accounts of the slave trade and the situation in the colonies see the background books listed earlier. See also Davis (1966) and Donnan (1930–35). For differences in the U.S. and Brazilian patterns see Ramos (1939), Tannenbaum (1947), and Freyre (1946).

3. *Race and Sectional Patterns.* The best discussion of the differences in the Northern trading colonies, the middle farming colonies, and the plantation south is in DuBois (1896). See also Nieboer (1910), Maunier (1949) and Stampp (1956). For the New England trade see Greene (1942). For northern and western attitudes see Berwanger (1967) and Litwack (1961). For the statements of Douglass and Du Bois see DuBois (1935), pp. 6–8 and 56–57.

4. *The Black Man's Burden.* For the slave revolts and "self emancipations" see Aptheker (1943). For a statement of his own experience and the attitudes of slaves toward their masters see Douglass (1855) pp. 42, 118, 129, 161, 177. See DuBois (1935) p. 9 for his statement about the slaves and pp. 702ff. for what slavery did to men's minds. For the Negroes' conduct during the war see Quarles (1953) and for the reaction to the coming of freedom see Washington (1900) and DuBois (1935).

5. *After Freedom.* For the South after the war see Myrdal (1944), vol. 1 pp. 226ff., Franklin (1961) and (1967), Bennett (1967), and DuBois (1935). For the development of the sharecropper system see Raper and Reid (1941), Logan (1954) and Woodward (1966). See also Baker (1908).

6. *From Sharecropper to Ghetto.* See the books listed for section 5. Also Couch (ed.) (1934), and Brown (1942). How the Negro fared in the North is reported in Drake and Cayton (1945), and Warner and others (1941). For the middle states see Frazier (1940).

7. *1954 and After.* For the various executive orders see Blaustein and Zangrando (eds.) (1968). For the Southern Manifesto see the *Congressional Record* for March 12, 1956. For other writings see Broderick and Meier (eds.) (1965), and Meier and Rudwick (1966), Clift and others (eds.) (1962), and Ginsberg (1956). The Durham statement was edited by P. B. Young and issued by the Southern Conference on Race Relations (1942). The statement quoted from Logan (1944) is on p. 71. The 1954 statement of Negro educators was issued as a press release as was the 1957 statement of June 10–11.

Chapter 8. RACE, CLASS, AND POVERTY pp. 114–129

As deprivation is cumulative, background studies are important to an understanding of today's problems. See general studies listed and especially Myrdal (1944), Raper and Reid (1941), Brown (1942), and Vance (1945). All of these books have extensive bibliographies on the Southern regions in the 1930's and 1940's when many of today's leaders were growing up.

For current poverty see Ferman and others (eds.) (1965) and (1968), Seligman (1968), Caplovits (1963), and Green (1967). Inexpensive paperbacks include Gordon (1965), Budd (ed.) (1967), Elman (1968), Harrington (1963), Larner and Howe (eds.) (1968), and May (1964).

1. *What Does It Mean to Be Poor?* For the Tufts Medical Center Report see the *New York Times* 5/19/68. For the survey of malnutrition among the poor see *Science News* 2/15/69. For the grinding poverty in many areas of the world see Ward (1962), Fanon (1968), Redding (1954), and Rowan (1956).

2. *Who Are the Poor?* For the various categories of the poor see Harrington (1963), Seligman (1968), Elman (1968), Budd (ed.) (1967), and Ferman and others (eds.) (1965).
3. *The Cycle of Poverty.* See Oscar Lewis (1966). For the story of "Willie Mae," the *Nashville Tennessean* 7/16/67. For the estimate for children affected by lead poisoning see a UPI report for 10/12/69. The visual defects were reported by the *Nashville Tennessean* 2/16/67. Various studies have documented the fact that most of the poor do not desire large families. See Ferman and others (eds.) (1965).
4. *Race as a Factor in Poverty.* For 1971 figures see "Job Outlook Poor for Black Youth" in *New York Times* 5/30/71. For the relative earnings of blacks and whites of comparable education see Ferman and others (eds.) (1965), and Seligman (1968). For discrimination in housing see Javits (1962). For unemployment and underemployment of Negroes see Ferman and others (eds.) (1968), and Marshall and Briggs (1967).
5. *Poverty and the Affluent Society.* According to a *Wall Street Journal* report for 6/16/69 cotton payments alone were expected to total $826 million in 1969, and an AP dispatch of 9/5/70 estimated that U.S. Government subsidies of business, farms and other undertakings would total more than $9 billion. Harrington (1963), p. 158, says "the poor get less out of the welfare state than any group in America." For the punitive attitude toward the poor see the *Wall Street Journal* 11/30/67, Budd (ed.) (1967), and Meissner (ed.) (1966). The account of urban renewal is a summary of a signed article by Tom Gillem in the *Nashville Tennessean* 3/1/70. For differences in school expenditures in inner city and suburban schools see Conant (1961).

Chapter 9. RACE, CRIME AND THE LAW pp. 130–145
   For various aspects of the crime problem see Cressey and Ward (eds.) (1969), the reports resulting from the studies of the National Commission on the Cause and Prevention of Violence (1969), and the reports of the President's Commission on Law Enforcement and The Administration of Justice (1967).
1. *The Problem of Lawlessness.* For the general problems of lawlessness see the daily papers and almost any responsible periodical. Articles in *Forbes* and the *Wall Street Journal* are particularly concerned with white-collar and organized crime and with unequal treatment in law enforcement.
2. *Ordinary Crime.* The inequities in the treatment of criminals are fully documented in the various reports cited above. For the statement that most crimes of violence are committed by people known to the victims see *Science* 4/25/69. Robert M. Cripes in the *New York Times*

10/6/68 says the chance of being killed in a car accident is more than four times greater than the chance of being murdered and the Allstate Insurance Company in the *Atlantic* 5/70 claims that drunk drivers kill more people than the combined deaths of Americans in Vietnam and those murdered at home. For difference in white and Negro arrests see Cressey and Ward (eds.) (1969).

3. *White Collar Crime.* See Geis (ed.) (1968). Ramsey Clark (1970) says bank embezzlements cost ten times as much as bank robberies. See the *Wall Street Journal* 2/17/70 for business crime and 2/5/70 for the extent of employee theft. See also articles in *Forbes* 11/15/67 on shoplifting and "Bull Market in Thievery" 12/15/68.

4. *Organized Crime.* The statement referred to was made by Nicholas Katzenbach, Chairman of the President's Commission on Law Enforcement and the Administration of Justice. The final statement in the section is from the *Annals*, May 1963. See an interview with Robert M. Morgenthau in the *New York Times Magazine* 2/15/70 and the collection of *Wall Street Journal* articles edited by Gartner (1968–1971).

5. *The Unequal Protection of the Law.* See Bruce Jackson in the *Atlantic* for January 1966. For the youth required to work out his fine and the reports following see the *Nashville Tennessean* 10/19/68 and subsequent issues. The Ku Klux Klan incident was reported in *Time* 7/11/69. For other such injustices see Friedman (ed.) (1965). In an article in the *Harvard Law Review*, November 1956, attention was called to the fact that following the 1954 Supreme Court decision 50 groups of whites organized for the purpose of maintaining school segregation in defiance of the law. Membership ran into hundreds of thousands and included prominent business, professional and political leaders.

6. *The Black Man as Victim.* The U.S. Civil Rights Commission counted more than 2500 lynchings between 1882 and 1959 with not one resulting in a white man's conviction (*Time* 10/4/68). For the death of the man accused of stealing the automobile tire see Beisel (1955). For similar cases see Mendelson (1962), and Lomax (1962).

7. *Violence as a Form of Protest.* While there has been a strong negative reaction to the violence of Negroes the violence of whites is often ignored. See the various reports on Violence in America (1969). Hartung (1965) makes some useful points on the role of self-conception.

8. *Law and the System of Values.* Alexander and Staub (1956) point up facts still useful today. For the harassment of Negroes see Friedman (ed.) (1965). Judge Wright's article in the *New York Times Magazine* 3/9/69 is useful. The quotation from Anatole France is taken from

the Judge's article. The Learned Hand quotation is found in the Preface to Trebach (1964).

Chapter 10. THE BLACK EXPERIENCE pp. 146–164

1. *The Blight of the Color Line.* For the experience of black children and youth see in the order listed DuBois (1903), Cullen (1925), Mickey Booth in the *Nashville Tennessean Magazine* 7/6/69 and 7/13/69, Malcolm X (1966), and Sammy Davis (1965).

2. *Separate and Unequal. The National Survey of the Higher Education of Negroes* (1942–43) fully documents these inequities. See especially Brown, vol. 1, (1942). The report of Negroes in northern and southern colleges is in vol. 2. For the situation in the 1960's see McGrath (1965). For the family background of black students see Zinn in *Harpers* 5/66. For the favoring of prestigious, mainly white, universities see the National Science Foundation report on *Federal Support to Universities and Colleges* (1967), and Egerton (1971).

3. *Economic and Cultural Deprivation.* Books written in the 1930's and 1940's give a picture of the conditions which confronted Negroes who are middle aged today. See Brown (1942), Raper and Reid (1941) and Johnson (1943). For the report of recent employment in northern cities see the *U.S. Investor* 11/13/67. For cultural limitations see Mendelson (1962). The statement from President Kennedy is in Fishel and Quarles (eds.) (1967).

4. *Techniques of Subordination.* See Doyle (1937), the autobiographical accounts of Negroes, and the studies made by the U.S. Office of Education, The American Council on Education, and by Myrdal and his staff. Violence as a technique of subordination has long been employed by whites. In 1955 and 1956 the Southern Regional Council recorded more than 100 incidents of violence, intimidation and reprisal in opposition to the 1954 court decision. See Lubell (1964).

5. *The Middle Class Dilemma.* Frazier (1962) first published in 1957, is the most comprehensive study of the Negro "striver." For the various comments listed see Washington (1900), pp. 122–24 and (1909), Sammy Davis (1965), p. 387, Lomax (1962), p. 20ff., Rowan (1954), and Lincoln (1968). The quotation from Redding is in Glock and Siegelman (eds.) (1969), pp. 9–16. The Black Muslims are treated in Essien-Udom (1962), Malcolm X (1966), and Lincoln (1961).

6. *The Mark of Oppression.* See Clark (1965), Kardiner and Ovesey (1951), and Frazier (1962), pp. 18–19, and (1957), (1966). For the West Indian patterns see Williams (1942), p. 64, and James quoted in Williams (1942), and Fanon (1967). For the attitudes toward hair and color see Chapter 7. For the accounts given see Malcolm X (1966),

pp. 2–4, Clark (1965), p. 64, and Mrs. Innis in *Life* 8/9/68. Servan-Schreiber's statement was made in an interview with an editor of *Forbes* 11/15/68, based on his book (1968).

Chapter 11. WHY THE BLACKS WON'T WAIT pp. 165–191

1. *The Black Revolution.* For the actual coming of the revolution see King (1964), especially pp. 15–26, and the special issue of *Ebony*, August 1969. Fanon's books (1967) and (1968) have been popular with black youth. See Rowan (1954), p. 252, for his comments. See Bennett (1964), p. 32ff. for his characteristics of life styles.

2. *What Do They Want?* For Baldwin's comments see Goldwin (ed.) (1963). See also Rowan (1954) and Bennett in the special issues of *Ebony* for August 1969 and August 1970. The "taking over" was advocated in an article by Vincent Harding in *Ebony* 8/69 and 9/69. For the others quoted see Young and Wilkins in *Ebony* August 1970, Mboya in the *New York Times Magazine* 7/13/69, Wright (1954), and Redding (1954), and in Glock and Siegelman (eds.) (1969). See also Rustin in *Ebony* 8/69, Lomax (1962), and Hughes (1940). The varying points of view of today's blacks and his own ideas were summed up by the editor in a special issue of *Ebony* 8/70.

3. *The Revolt Against Authority.* See "The Reform of the University" in *Law and Order Reconsidered* (1969). For student rebellions in Canada see the Canadian *Financial Post* for 8/23/69 which estimated the computer damages at 2.5 million. For London School of Economics see *Science* 6/20/69, for Japan see *Science News* 5/3/69, and for France, *Science* 6/13/69.

4. *The Now Generation.* Among the books on the generation gap widely read and both favorably and unfavorably reviewed see Mead (1970), Toffler (1970), Reich (1970), Roszak (1968), Feuer (1969), and Toole (1971). In a release for June 21, 1970 the United Press Education editor reported that thousands of qualified students were turned away from state universities because of lack of room or inadequate facilities. The protest of classes on Good Friday occurred at Tennessee Technical University, reported in the *Nashville Tennessean* 4/4/69. Etzioni's report on the Columbia confrontation was in the *New York Times Magazine* 9/15/68. For the contrast in black and white students see *Ebony* 8/67 and the *New York Times* 11/8/70.

5. *The Search for Identity.* For Comer's statement see Barbour (ed.) (1968) pp. 72ff. For the comments of Lorenzo Turner see Poinsett's discussion in *Ebony* 12/68. For slavery among the Muslims of the Sudan see Meek and others (1940) and Skinner (1964). For the Eastern Sudan see Lawrence Fellow's article in the *New York Times* 9/22/68, and current news releases.

6. *The New Blacks and the White Liberals.* The statement of Malcolm X was quoted in an article by Whitney Young in *Ebony* 8/70. For the statement by Young see *Ebony* 8/70. See also Grant (1968), Lomax (1962), and Bennett (1964).

Chapter 12. THE WHITE EXPERIENCE pp. 192–218

1. *Thinking White.* See Baldwin in Goldwin (ed.) (1963), and Chapters 5 and 6 in *The Politics of Protest* (1969). Fanon (1967), p. 202, says the problem is that "of Negroes exploited, enslaved, despised by a colonialist, capitalist society that is only accidentally white." Eric Williams (1944) makes a similar comment.

2. *They Are Not All Alike.* To see the behavior of white people through the eyes of Negroes see Brown (1965), Davis (1965), Baldwin (1963), Cleaver (1968), Gregory (1964), Malcolm X (1966), Wright (1945), Rowan (1954), Thompson (1946), Waters (1951), and Hansbury (1969). For a northern city see Drake and Cayton (1945). For the South see Cash (1941) and McGill (1963). See also Silberman (1964) and Ellison (1966).

3. *Learning to Be White.* For the way children learn their race, class, and family roles see the *Notes and References* for Chapter 2, section 4. The incident of the child who thought the black teacher was "the maid" was given the author in a personal communication. See Clark (1963).

4. *Rights and Double Rights.* For church members who take their double rights as a matter of course see "Prejudice and The Churches" in Glock and Siegelman (eds.) (1969). See also "White Attitudes Toward the Negro" in Parsons and Clark (eds.) (1966).

5. *Double Vision.* The reports of the activities of middle class white youth were taken from AP or UPI dispatches for Princeton, UPI 5/8/63, Fort Lauderdale, UPI 3/25/66 and 3/27/67. The telephone binge, AP 5/23/68. Accounts of the "Black Christ" have appeared in *Ebony* and in various other publications. James H. Cone (1970) insists that both God and Jesus must be black and that white men must come to "hate their whiteness." The translations of Xenophanes vary. I have used Freeman (1948). For the dog story see Christopher Morley (1924).

6. *The Poor and the Not-So-Poor.* See "Government and the Forgotten Man" in *Law and Order Reconsidered* (1969). For the increase in salaries of congressmen and high government officials see Fulton in the *Nashville Tennessean* 2/5/70. See the *Wall Street Journal* 2/16/72, 10/13/70, 10/14/70, and 4/4/69 for the quotation regarding the small saver, the ATT savings bond proposal, and an article on "Taxes and the Rich."

7. *Prejudice, Guilt and Responsibility.* See the *Notes and References* for Chapter 1 Section 3. For Eric Lincoln's statement see his review of *Black Rage* in Psychiatry and Social Science Review 3/69.

Chapter 13. THE HUMAN USE OF HUMAN BEINGS   pp. 219–245
1. *What Does It Mean to Be Human?* The title for the chapter is from Wiener (1950) revised edition (1954). See Loren Eiseley (1946) for his comment. Bruner's statement is in Tax (ed.) 1964 p. 74.
2. *The Human Peril.* For a modern analysis of the effect of rapid change see Toffler (1970). See Margaret Mead (1970) and her comments in *Science* 4/11/69. Platt (1966), p. 192ff. says men are playing nuclear roulette.
3. *The Past as Prologue.* For further elaboration of our debt to the past see Brown (1963), p. 136ff., Howells (1967) and (1954).
4. *Our Species Identity.* Both Simpson's and Washburn's comments will be found in Jennings and Hoebel (eds.) (1966). For Dobzhansky's comments see *Science* 7/13/62. See Gardner (1961). Carl Sandburg's comments will be found in Edward Steichen (1955).
5. *The Human Potential.* See Dobzhansky (1962), Platt (1966), p. 133, and Huxley (1953), pp. 162ff.
6. *Inventing the Future.* For the report of The National Advisory Commission on Civil Disorders see the Bantam edition edited by Wicker (1968), p. 203ff. The unemployment of black youth was reported by the Bureau of Labor Statistics in a UPI news release for 8/17/70. The condition had not improved in 1971. The figures on the number of people who do not vote was reported by James Reston in a *New York Times* news release 6/25/70. The advertisement referred to was General Telephone and Electronics in *Life* 8/22/69. For a report on the cost of early space failures see a *New York Times* news release for 8/14/66. The *Wall Street Journal* article was by John Pierson 6/19/70. See Platt (1966) for his remarks on Utopia.

Selected Bibliography

Included here are the chief sources used by the author, books mentioned but not fully identified elsewhere, and books suggested for further reading. For comment see the *Notes and References*. Many of the older and less accessible sources are not listed here but may be found in the author's earlier publications. The dates given are for the edition consulted by the author. When a reprint of a much earlier publication is used the original date is given in parenthesis. To find whether books listed are available in paperbacks the student should consult *Paperbound Books in Print* to be found in most libraries and bookstores.

ALEXANDER, FRANZ AND HUGO STAUB, *The Criminal, The Judge and The Public*. (rev. ed.) New York: Free Press, 1956.

ALLPORT, GORDON W., *The Nature of Prejudice*, Boston: Beacon Press, 1954.

APTHEKER, HERBERT, *American Negro Slave Revolts*, New York: Columbia University Press, 1943.

APTHEKER, HERBERT, ed. *A Documentary History of the Negro People in the United States*. 2 vols. New York: Citadel, 1951.

AZURARA, GOMES EANNES DE, *The Chronicle of the Discovery and Conquest of Guinea* (c. 1450). Translated and edited by C. Raymond Beazley and Edgar Prestage. 2 vols. London: Hakluyt Society, 1896–1899.

BAKER, RAY STANNARD, *Following The Color Line*. New York: Doubleday, 1908.

BALDRY, H. C., *The Unity of Mankind in Greek Thought*. Cambridge: Cambridge University Press, 1965.

BALDWIN, JAMES, *The Fire Next Time*. New York: Dial Press, 1963.

BARBOUR, FLOYD B., ed., *The Black Power Revolt*. Boston: Porter Sargent, 1968.

BARDOLPH, RICHARD, *The Negro Vanguard*. New York: Holt, Rinehart, & Winston, 1961.

BARROW, R. H., *Slavery in The Roman Empire*. London: Methuen, 1928.

BATTUTA, IBN, *Travels In Asia and Africa—1325–1354*. Translated by H. A. R. Gibb. New York: McBride, 1929.

BEARDSLEY, GRACE HADLEY, *The Negro in Greek and Roman Civilization*. Baltimore: Johns Hopkins, 1929.

BEISEL, ALBERT R., JR., *Control Over Illegal Enforcement of The Criminal Law*. Boston: Boston University Press, 1955.

BENNETT, LERONE, JR., *Before the Mayflower*, Baltimore: Penguin, 1966.

BENNETT, LERONE, JR., *Black Power, U.S.A. The Human Side of Reconstruction, 1867–1877*. Chicago: Johnson, 1967.

BENNETT, LERONE, JR., *Confrontation: Black and White*. Baltimore: Penguin, 1965.

BENNETT, LERONE, JR., *The Negro Mood.* New York: Ballantine, 1964.

BERGMAN, PETER M., *The Chronological History Of The Negro In America.* New York: Harper & Row, 1969.

BERWANGER, EUGENE H., *The Frontier Against Slavery.* Urbana: University of Illinois Press, 1967.

BETTELHEIM, BRUNO AND MORRIS JANOWITZ, *Social Change and Prejudice.* New York: Free Press, 1964.

BLAKE, JOHN W., *European Beginnings in West Africa—1454-1578.* London: Longmans, Green, 1937.

BLAUSTEIN, ALBERT P. AND ROBERT L. ZANGRANDO, eds. *Civil Rights and the American Negro.* New York: Washington Square Press, 1968.

BLUETT, THOMAS, *Some Memoirs of The Life of Job, The Son of Soloman.* London: Printed for Richard Ford, at the Angel in The Poultry, 1734.

BOHANNAN, PAUL, *Africa and Africans.* Garden City, N.Y.: Natural History Press, 1964.

BONTEMPS, ARNA, *100 Years of Negro Freedom.* New York: Dodd, Mead, 1961.

BOVILL,E. W., *The Golden Trade of The Moors.* London: Oxford University Press, 1958.

BOYD, WILLIAM C., *Genetics and the Races of Man.* Boston: Little, Brown, 1950.

BRACE, C. L. AND M. F. ASHLEY MONTAGU, *Man's Evolution—An Introduction to Physical Anthropology.* New York: Macmillan, 1965.

BREASTED, JAMES HENRY, *Ancient Records of Egypt.* 5 vols. Chicago: University of Chicago Press, 1906-7.

BREASTED, JAMES HENRY, *A History Of Egypt.* New York: Scribner's, 1950 (1909).

BRODERICK, FRANCES L. AND AUGUST MEIER, eds., *Negro Protest Thought in the Twentieth Century.* New York: Bobbs-Merrill, 1965.

BROWN, CLAUDE, *Manchild in the Promised Land.* New York: Macmillan, 1965.

BROWN, INA CORINNE, *Race Relations in a Democracy.* New York: Harper & Row, 1949.

BROWN, INA CORINNE, *Socio-Economic Approach to Educational Problems.* Washington, D.C.: Government Printing Office, 1942.

BROWN, INA CORINNE, *The Story of the American Negro.* (2nd rev. ed.) New York: Friendship Press, 1957.

BROWN, INA CORINNE, *Understanding Other Cultures.* Englewood Cliffs, N.J.: Prentice-Hall, 1963.

BUCKLAND, W. W., *The Roman Law of Slavery.* Cambridge: Cambridge University Press, 1908.

BUDD, EDWARD C., ed., *Inequality and Poverty.* New York: Norton, 1967.

BUDGE, E. A. WALLIS, *The Egyptian Sudan.* 2 vols. Philadelphia: Lippincott, 1907.

BUDGE, E. A. WALLIS, *A History Of Ethiopia, Nubia, And Abyssinia.* 2 vols. London: Methuen, 1928.

BUTCHER, MARGARET JUST, *The Negro in American Culture.* New York: Knopf, 1956.

CAPLOVITS, DAVID, *The Poor Pay More.* New York: Free Press, 1963.

CARMICHAEL, STOKELY AND CHARLES V. HAMILTON, *Black Power.* New York: Random House, 1967.

CASH, W. J., *The Mind Of The South.* New York: Knopf, 1941.

CLARIDGE, W. W., *A History of the Gold Coast And Ashanti.* 2 vols. London: John Murray, 1915.

CLARK, KENNETH B., *Dark Ghetto.* New York: Harper & Row, 1965.

CLARK, KENNETH B., *Prejudice and Your Child.* Boston: Beacon Press, 1963.

CLARK, RAMSEY, *Crime in America.* New York: Simon and Schuster, 1970.

CLEAVER, ELDRIDGE, *Soul On Ice.* New York: McGraw-Hill, 1968.

CLIFT, VIRGIL A., and others, eds. *Negro Education in America.* New York: Harper & Row, 1962.

CONANT, JAMES B., *Slums and Suburbs.* New York: McGraw-Hill, 1961.

CONE, JAMES H., *A Black Theology of Liberation.* Philadelphia: Lippincott, 1970.

COON, CARLETON, *The Origin of Races.* New York: Knopf, 1962.

COON, CARLETON AND EDWARD E. HUNT, JR., *The Living Races of Man.* New York: Knopf, 1965.

COUCH, W. T., ed. *Culture in the South.* Chapel Hill, N.C.: The University of North Carolina Press, 1934.

CRESSEY, DONALD R. AND DAVID A. WARD, *Delinquency, Crime, and Social Process.* New York: Harper & Row, 1969.

CRONE, C. R., edited & translated, *The Voyages of Cadamosta (c. 1444–45).* London: The Hakluyt Society, 1937.

CULLEN, COUNTEE, *Color.* New York: Harper & Row, 1925.

DAVIDSON, BASIL, *Africa—History of a Continent.* New York: Macmillan, 1966.

DAVIDSON, BASIL, *The African Genius.* Boston: Little, Brown, 1969.

DAVIDSON, BASIL, *The Lost Cities of Africa.* Boston: Little, Brown, 1959.

DAVIDSON, BASIL, *Black Mother.* Boston: Little, Brown, 1961.

DAVIDSON, BASIL, with F. K. BUAH, *A History of West Africa To The Nineteenth Century.* Garden City, N.Y.: Doubleday, 1966.

DAVIES, NINA M. AND A. H. GARDINER, *Ancient Egyptian Paintings.* 3 vols. Chicago: University of Chicago Press, 1936.

DAVIS, ALLISON, *Social Class Influences Upon Learning.* Cambridge, Mass.: Harvard University Press, 1948.

DAVIS, ALLISON AND JOHN DOLLARD, *Children of Bondage.* Washington, D.C.: American Council on Education, 1940.

DAVIS, DAVID BRION, *The Problem of Slavery in Western Culture.* Ithaca, N.Y.: Cornell University Press, 1966.

DAVIS, JOHN P., ed. *The American Negro Reference Book.* Englewood Cliffs, N.J.: Prentice-Hall, 1966.

DAVIS, SAMMY, JR., AND JANE AND BURT BOYAR, *Yes I Can.* New York: Pocket Books, 1965.

DOBZHANSKY, THEODOSIUS, *Mankind Evolving.* New Haven: Yale University Press, 1962.

DONNAN, ELIZABETH, ed. *Documents Illustrative of the History of the Slave Trade to America.* 4 vols. Washington, D.C.: Carnegie Institution, 1930–1935.

DOUGLASS, FREDERICK, *My Bondage And My Freedom.* New York: Miller, Orton & Mulligan, 1855.

DOYLE, BERTRAM W., *The Etiquette Of Race Relations In The South.* Chicago: University of Chicago Press, 1937.

DRAKE, ST. CLAIR AND H. R. CAYTON, *Black Metropolis.* New York: Harcourt, Brace, Jovanovich, 1945.

DU BOIS, W. E. B., *Black Reconstruction.* New York: Harcourt Brace Jovanovich, 1935.

DU BOIS, W. E. B., *The Souls of Black Folk.* Greenwich, Conn.: Fawcett, 1961 (1903).

DU BOIS, W. E. B., *The Suppression of the African Slave Trade to the United States of America, 1638–1870.* New York: Longmans, 1896.

DUNN, L. C. AND THEODOSIUS DOBZHANSKY, *Heredity, Race and Society.* Baltimore: Penguin, 1946.

EBONY, *The Negro Handbook.* Chicago: Johnson, 1966.

EGERTON, JOHN, *The Black Public Colleges.* Nashville: Race Relations Information Center, 1971.

EISELEY, LOREN, *The Immense Journey.* New York: Random House, 1946.

ELLISON, RALPH, *Shadow and Act.* New York: Random House, 1964.

ELMAN, RICHARD M., *The Poorhouse State.* New York: Dell, 1968.

ERIKSON, ERIK H., *Identity, Youth and Crisis.* New York: Norton, 1967.

ESSIEN-UDOM, E. U., *Black Nationalism.* Chicago: University of Chicago Press, 1962.

FAGE, J. D., *An Introduction to The History of West Africa.* (rev. ed.) Cambridge: Cambridge University Press, 1968.

FANON, FRANTZ, *Black Skin, White Masks.* New York: Grove Press, 1967.

FANON, FRANTZ, *The Wretched of the Earth.* New York: Grove Press, 1968.

FERMAN, LOUIS A., and others, eds., *Negroes and Jobs.* Ann Arbor: University of Michigan Press, 1968.

FERMAN, LOUIS A., and others, eds., *Poverty in America.* Ann Arbor: University of Michigan Press, 1965.

FEUER, LEWIS S., *The Conflict of Generations.* New York: Basic Books, 1969.

FISHEL, LESLIE H., JR., AND BENJAMIN QUARLES, eds., *The Negro American.* New York: Morrow, 1967.

FITZGERALD, WALTER, *Africa, A Social Economic And Political Geography Of Its Major Regions.* (8th ed.) New York: Dutton, 1957.

FORBES, FREDERICK, E., *Dahomey And The Dahomeans.* 2 vols. London: Longmans, 1851.

FORDE, DARYLL, ed. *African Worlds.* New York: Oxford University Press, 1954.

FORTES, M. AND E. E. EVANS-PRITCHARD, eds. *African Political Systems.* New York: Oxford University Press, 1940.

FRANKLIN, JOHN HOPE, *From Slavery to Freedom.* (rev. ed.) New York: Knopf, 1967.

FRANKLIN, JOHN HOPE, *Reconstruction after the Civil War.* Chicago: University of Chicago Press, 1961.

FRANKLIN, JOHN HOPE AND ISIDORE STARR, eds. *The Negro in Twentieth Century America.* New York: Random House, 1967.

FRAZIER, E. FRANKLIN, *Black Bourgeoisie.* New York: Collier Books, 1962.

FRAZIER, E. FRANKLIN, *The Negro Family in the United States.* (rev. & abridged.) Chicago: University of Chicago Press, 1966.

FRAZIER, E. FRANKLIN, *The Negro in the United States.* (rev. ed.) New York: Macmillan, 1957.

FRAZIER, E. FRANKLIN, *Negro Youth at the Crossways.* Washington, D.C.: A.C.E., 1940.

FREEMAN, KATHLEEN, *Ancilla to the Pre-Socratic Philosophers.* Oxford: Blackwell, 1948.

FREYRE, GILBERTO, *The Masters And The Slaves.* New York: Knopf, 1946.

FRIEDMAN, LEON, ed. *The Civil Rights Reader.* New York: Walker, 1968.

FRIEDMAN, LEON, ed. *Southern Justice.* New York: World, 1965.

GARDNER, JOHN W., *Excellence.* New York: Harper & Row, 1961.

GARN, STANLEY, M., *Human Races* (2nd ed.) Springfield, Ill.: Charles C. Thomas, 1960.

GARTNER, MICHAEL, ed. *Crime and Business.* Princeton: Dow Jones, 1968–1971.

GEIS, GILBERT, ed. *White Collar Criminal.* New York: Atherton Press, 1968.

GINZBERG, ELI AND ASSOCIATES, *The Negro Potential.* New York: Columbia University Press, 1956.

GINZBERG, ELI AND ALFRED S. EICHNER, *The Troublesome Presence.* New York: Free Press, 1964.

GLASS, BENTLEY, *Genes and the Man.* New York: Columbia University Press, 1943.

GLOCK, CHARLES Y. AND ELLEN SIEGELMAN, eds. *Prejudice U.S.A.* New York: Praeger, 1969.

GOLDWIN, ROBERT A., ed., *100 Years of Emancipation.* Skokie, Ill.: Rand McNally, 1963.

GORDON, MITCHELL, *Sick Cities.* Baltimore: Penguin, 1965.

GRANT, JOANNE, ed. *Black Protest.* Greenwich, Conn.: Fawcett, 1968.

GREEN, CHRISTOPHER, *Negative Taxes and the Poverty Problem.* Washington: The Brookings Institution, 1967.

GREENBERG, JOSEPH H., *The Languages of Africa.* Bloomington, Ind.: Indiana University Press, 1963.

GREENE, LORENZO J., *The Negro In Colonial New England, 1620–1776.* New York: Columbia University Press, 1942.

GREGORY, DICK with ROBERT LIPSYTE, *Nigger—An Autobiography.* New York: Simon & Schuster, 1964.

GRIER, WILLIAM H., M.D., AND PRINCE M. COBBS, M.D., *Black Rage.* New York: Basic Books, 1968.

GRIFFIN, JOHN HOWARD, *Black Like Me.* New York: New American Library, 1960.

HAKLUYT, RICHARD, *The Principal Navigations, Voyages, Traffiques And Discoveries Of The English Nation.* 9 vols. New York: Dutton, 1907.

HALSELL, GRACE, *Soul Sister.* Greenwich, Conn.: Fawcett, 1970.

HANSBERRY, LORRAINE, *To Be Young, Gifted and Black.* Englewood Cliffs, N.J.: Prentice-Hall, 1969.

HARRINGTON, MICHAEL, *The Other America.* Baltimore: Penguin, 1963.

HARTUNG, FRANK E., *Crime, Law and Society.* Detroit: Wayne State University Press, 1965.

HERISSÉ, A. LE, *L'Ancien Royaume Du Dahomey.* Paris: Emil Larose, 1911.

HERODOTUS, *The History of Herodotus.* Translated by George Rawlinson. New York: Tudor, 1928.

HERSKOVITS, MELVILLE, *Dahomey.* 2 vols. New York: Augustin, 1938.

HERSKOVITS, MELVILLE J., *The Myth of the Negro Past.* New York: Harper & Row, 1941.

HOUGH, JOSEPH C., JR., *Black Power and White Protestants.* New York: Oxford University Press, 1968.

HOWELLS, WILLIAM, *Back of History.* Garden City, N.Y.: Doubleday, 1954.

HOWELLS, WILLIAM, *Mankind in the Making.* (rev. ed.) Garden City, N.Y.: Doubleday, 1967.

HUGHES, LANGSTON, *The Big Sea.* New York: Knopf, 1940.

HUGHES, LANGSTON, *Selected Poems.* New York: Knopf, 1959.

HUGHES, LANGSTON AND ARNA BONTEMPS, eds. *The Poetry of The Negro 1746–1949.* Garden City, N.Y.: Doubleday, 1949.

HULSE, FREDERICK S., *The Human Species.* New York: Random House, 1963.

HUXLEY, JULIAN, *Evolution in Action.* New York: Harper, 1953.

HUXLEY, JULIAN S. AND A. C. HADDON, *We Europeans.* New York: Harper & Row, 1936.

ISAACS, HAROLD R., *The New World of the Negro Americans.* New York: John Day, 1963.

JAVITS, JACOB K., *Discrimination U.S.A.* (rev. ed.) New York: Washington Square Press, 1962.

JENNINGS, JESSE D. AND E. ADAMSON HOEBEL, *Readings in Anthropology.* (2nd ed.), New York: McGraw-Hill, 1966.

JOBSON, RICHARD, *The Golden Trade* (1623). Edited by Charles G. Kingsley. Teignmouth-Devonshire: Speight and Walpole, 1904.

JOHNSON, CHARLES S., *Growing Up in The Black Belt.* Washington, D.C.: A.C.E., 1941.

JOHNSON, CHARLES S., *Patterns of Negro Segregation.* New York: Harper & Row, 1943.

JOHNSON, JAMES WELDON, *Along This Way.* New York: Viking, 1933.

JOHNSON, JAMES WELDON, *Autobiography of an Ex-Colored Man.* New York: Knopf, 1927 (1912).

JOHNSON, JAMES WELDON, *Black Manhattan.* New York: Knopf, 1930.

JOHNSON, JAMES WELDON, *Negro Americans, What Now?* New York: Viking, 1934.

JONES, LEROI, *Blues People.* New York: Morrow, 1963.

JORDAN, WINTHROP D., *White Over Black.* Chapel Hill, N.C.: University of North Carolina Press, 1968.

KANE, MICHAEL B., *Minorities in Textbooks.* Chicago: Quadrangle, 1970.

KARDINER, ABRAM, AND LIONEL OVESEY, *Mark of Oppression.* New York: Norton, 1951.

KING, MARTIN LUTHER, JR., *Why We Can't Wait.* New York: Harper & Row, 1964.

KLINEBERG, OTTO, *Race Differences.* (3rd ed.) New York: Harper & Row, 1935.

KNIGHT, MELVIN M., *Economic History Of Europe.* Boston: Houghton Mifflin, 1926.

LANCASTER, PAUL, ed. *Here Comes Tomorrow!* Princeton: Dow Jones, 1966.

LANE-POOLE, STANLEY, *A History Of Egypt In The Middle Ages.* (2nd ed.) London: Methuen, 1901.

LARNER, JEREMY AND IRVING HOWE, eds. *Poverty: Views from the Left.* New York: Morrow, 1968.

LASKER, GABRIEL W., *The Evolution of Man*. New York: Holt, Rinehart & Winston, 1961.

LATOURETTE, KENNETH SCOTT, *A History Of The Expansion Of Christianity*. 2 vols. New York: Harper & Row, 1937–38.

LEO AFRICANUS, *The History and Description of Africa*. 3 vols. Done into English, 1600 by John Pory. Edited by Robert Brown. London: The Hakluyt Society, 1896.

LEWIS, OSCAR, *La Vida*. New York: Random House, 1966.

LINCOLN, C. ERIC, *Black Muslims in America*. Boston: Beacon Press, 1961.

LINCOLN, C. ERIC, *The Negro Pilgrimage in America*. New York: Bantam, 1967.

LINCOLN, C. ERIC, *Sounds of The Struggle*. New York: Morrow, 1968.

LITWACK, LEON F., *North of Slavery: 1790–1860*, Chicago: University of Chicago Press, 1961.

LOCKE, ALAIN, *The New Negro*. New York: Boni, 1925.

LOGAN, RAYFORD W., *The Negro in American Life and Thought*. New York: Dial, 1954.

LOGAN, RAYFORD W., ed. *What The Negro Wants*. Chapel Hill: University of North Carolina Press, 1944.

LOMAX, LOUIS E., *The Negro Revolt*. New York: The New American Library, 1962.

LUBELL, SAMUEL, *White and Black*: New York: Harper & Row, 1964.

McGILL, RALPH, *The South and the Southerner*. Boston: Atlantic, Little, Brown, 1963.

McGRATH, EARL J., *The Predominantly Negro Colleges and Universities in Transition*. New York: Columbia University Press, 1965.

McKERN, THOMAS W., ed. *Readings in Physical Anthropology*. Englewood Cliffs, N.J.: Prentice-Hall, 1966.

MACK, RAYMOND W., ed. *Prejudice and Race Relations*. Chicago: Quadrangle, 1970.

MALCOLM X, *The Autobiography of Malcolm X*. New York: Grove, 1966.

MANDELBAUM, DAVID G. and others, eds. *The Teaching of Anthropology*. American Anthropological Association, Memoir 94, 1963.

MARGOLIES, EDWARD, *Native Sons*. Philadelphia: Lippincott, 1968.

MARSHALL, F. RAY AND VERNON M. BRIGGS, JR., The Negro and Apprenticeship. Baltimore: Johns Hopkins, 1967.

MARTIN, EVELINE C., *The British West African Settlements, 1750–1821*. London: Longmans, 1927.

MARX, GARY T., *Protest and Prejudice*. New York: Harper & Row, 1967.

MAUNIER, RENE, *The Sociology of Colonies*. 2 vols. London: Routledge & Kegan Paul, 1949.

MAY, EDGAR, *The Wasted Americans*. New York: Harper & Row, 1964.

MAYR, ERNEST, *Populations, Species, and Evolution*. Cambridge, Mass., Harvard University Press, 1970.

MBITI, JOHN S., *African Religions and Philosophy*. New York: Praeger, 1969.

MBITI, JOHN S., *Concepts of God in Africa*. New York: Praeger, 1970.

MEAD, MARGARET, *Culture And Commitment*. Garden City, N.Y.: Natural History Press, 1970.

MEAD, MARGARET and others, eds. *Science and the Concept of Race*. New York: Columbia University Press, 1968.

MEAD, MARGARET AND MARTHA WOLFENSTEIN, eds. *Childhood in Contemporary Cultures*. Chicago: University of Chicago Press, 1955.

MEEK, C. K. and others, *Europe And West Africa*. New York: Oxford University Press, 1940.

MEIER, AUGUST, *Negro Thought in America, 1880–1915*. Ann Arbor: University of Michigan Press, 1963.

MEIER, AUGUST AND ELLIOTT RUDWICK, eds. *The Making of Black America*. 2 vols. New York: Atheneum, 1969.

MEIER, AUGUST AND ELLIOTT M. RUDWICK, *From Plantation to Ghetto*. New York: Hill & Wang, 1966.

MEISSNER, H. H., ed. *Poverty in the Affluent Society*. New York: Harper & Row, 1966.

MENDELSON, WALLACE, *Discrimination*. Englewood Cliffs, N.J.: Prentice-Hall, 1962.

MONTAGU, M. F. ASHLEY, *An Introduction to Physical Anthropology*. (3rd ed.) Springfield, Ill.: Charles C. Thomas, 1960.

MONTAGU, ASHLEY, ed. *The Concept of Race*. New York: Free Press, 1964.

MONTAGU, ASHLEY, *Man's Most Dangerous Myth*. (4th ed.) New York: World Publishing, 1964.

MONTEIL, CHARLES, *Une Cité Soudanaise: Djenné*. Paris: Société D'Éditions Géographique, Maritimes et Coloniales, 1932.

MOORE, FRANCIS, *Travels Into The Inland Parts of Africa*. London: Printed by Edward Cave at St. John's Gate, for the Author, 1738.

MORLEY, CHRISTOPHER, *Where The Blue Begins*. Garden City, N.Y.: Doubleday, 1924.

MOTON, ROBERT RUSSA, *What The Negro Thinks*. Garden City, N.Y.: Doubleday, 1929.

MYRDAL, GUNNAR, *An American Dilemma*. 2 vols. New York: Harper & Row, 1944.

National Commission on the Causes and Prevention of Violence, *Violence in America*, Vols. 1 & 2. *The Politics of Protest*, Vol. 3. *Law and Order Reconsidered*, Vol. 10. Washington, D.C.: G.P.O., 1969.

National Science Foundation, *Federal Support to Universities and Colleges*, Fiscal Years 1963–66. Washington, D.C.: G.P.O., 1967.

National Survey of the Higher Education of Negroes. 4 vols. Washington, D.C.: G.P.O., 1942–43.

NIEBOER, H., J., *Slavery as an Industrial System.* The Hague: Nijhoff, 1910.

OLIVER, ROLAND AND J. D. FAGE, *A Short History of Africa.* Baltimore: Penguin, 1962.

OSOFSKY, GILBERT, ed. *The Burden of Race.* New York: Harper & Row, 1967.

OTTENBERG, SIMON AND PHOEBE, *Cultures and Societies of Africa.* New York: Random House, 1960.

PARSONS, TALCOTT AND KENNETH B. CLARK, eds. *The Negro American.* Boston: Houghton Mifflin, 1966.

PETTIGREW, THOMAS F., *A Profile Of The Negro American.* New York: Van Nostrand Reinhold, 1964.

PITTARD, EUGENE, *Race And History.* New York: Knopf, 1926.

PLATT, JOHN RADER, *The Step to Man.* New York: John Wiley, 1966.

President's Commission on Law Enforcement and the Administration of Justice, *The Challenge of Crime in a Free Society.* Washington, D.C.: G.P.O., 1967.

QUARLES, BENJAMIN, *The Negro in the Civil War.* Boston: Little, Brown, 1953.

QUARLES, BENJAMIN, *The Negro in the Making of America.* New York: Collier, 1967.

RADCLIFFE-BROWN, A. R. AND DARYLL FORDE, *African Systems of Kinship and Marriage.* New York: Oxford University Press, 1950.

RAMOS, ARTHUR, *The Negro In Brazil.* Washington, D.C.: Associated Publishers, 1939.

RAPER, ARTHUR F. AND IRA DE A. REID, *Sharecroppers All.* Chapel Hill, N.C.: University of North Carolina Press, 1941.

RATTRAY, R. S., *The Ashanti.* Oxford: Clarendon Press, 1923.

RATTRAY, R. S., *Ashanti Law and Constitution.* Oxford: Clarendon Press, 1929.

RATTRAY, ROBERT R., *Religion and Art in Ashanti.* Oxford: Clarendon Press, 1927.

REDDING, J. SAUNDERS, *An American in India.* New York: Bobbs-Merrill, 1954.

REDDING, J. SAUNDERS, *Lonesome Road.* New York: Doubleday, 1958.

REICH, CHARLES A., *The Greening of America.* New York: Random House, 1970.

ROSZAK, THEODORE, *The Making of a Counter Culture.* Garden City, N.Y., Doubleday, 1968.

ROWAN, CARL, *The Pitiful and The Proud.* New York: Random House, 1956.

Rowan, Carl T., *South of Freedom*. New York: Knopf, 1954.

Sàdi, Es, *Tarikh Es Soudan*. Translated from the Arabic into French by O. Houdas. Paris: Publications De L'Ecole Des Langues, Orientales Vivantes, 1900.

Seligman, Ben B., *Permanent Poverty*. Chicago: Quadrangle, 1968.

Servan-Schreiber, J.-J., *The American Challenge*. New York: Atheneum, 1968.

Sherwin-White, A. N., *Racial Prejudice in Imperial Rome*. Cambridge: Cambridge University Press, 1967.

Shinnie, Peter L., *Meröe: A Civilization of the Sudan*. New York: Praeger, 1967.

Silberman, Charles E., *Crisis in Black and White*. New York: Random House, 1964.

Simpson, George Gaylord, *The Meaning of Evolution*. (Rev. and abridged ed.) New York: New American Library, 1951.

Skinner, Elliott P., *The Mossi of the Upper Volta*. Stanford: Stanford University Press, 1964.

Snowden, Frank M., *Blacks in Antiquity*. Cambridge, Harvard University Press, 1970.

Snyder, Lawrence, *Medical Genetics*. Durham, N.C.: Duke University Press, 1941.

Spuhler, J. N., ed. *Genetic Diversity and Human Behavior*. New York: Wenner-Gren Foundation, 1967.

Stamp, L. Dudley, *Africa, A Study of Tropical Development*. New York: John Wiley, 1953.

Stampp, Kenneth M., *The Peculiar Institution*, New York: Knopf, 1956.

Steichen, Edward, *The Family of Man*, with Prologue by Carl Sandburg. New York: Maco Magazine Corp. for the Museum of Modern Art, New York, 1955.

Sutherland, Robert L., *Color, Class, And Personality*. Washington, D.C.: American Council on Education, 1942.

Tannenbaum, Frank, *Slave and Citizen*. New York: Knopf, 1947.

Tax, Sol, ed. *Anthropology Today—Selections*. Chicago: University of Chicago Press, 1962.

Tax, Sol, ed. *Evolution After Darwin*, Vol. 1–The Evolution of Life, Vol. 2–The Evolution of Man, Vol. 3–Issues in Evolution. Chicago: University of Chicago Press, 1960.

Tax, Sol, ed. *Horizons of Anthropology*. Chicago: Aldine, 1964.

Thompson, Era Bell, *American Daughter*. Chicago: University of Chicago Press, 1946.

Tilson, Everett, *Segregation and the Bible*. Nashville, Tenn.: Abingdon, 1958.

TOFFLER, ALVIN, *Future Shock*. New York: Random House, 1970.

TOOLE, K. ROSS, *The Time Has Come*. New York: Morrow, 1971.

TREBACH, ARNOLD S., *The Rationing of Justice*. New Brunswick, N.J.: Rutgers University Press, 1964.

VANCE, RUPERT, *All These People*. Chapel Hill, N.C.: University of North Carolina Press, Norton, 1962.

WARD, BARBARA, *The Rich Nations and The Poor Nations*. New York: Norton, 1962.

WARNER, W. LLOYD and others, *Color and Human Nature*. Washington, D.C.: American Council On Education, 1941.

WASHBURN, SHERWOOD L., ed. *Social Life of Early Man*. New York: Wenner-Gren Foundation, 1961.

WASHINGTON, BOOKER T., *The Story Of The Negro*. 2 vols. New York: Doubleday, 1909.

WASHINGTON, BOOKER T., *Up From Slavery*. New York: A. L. Burt Co., 1900.

WATERS, ETHEL with CHARLES SAMUELS, *His Eye is on the Sparrow*. Garden City, N.Y.: Doubleday, 1951.

WESTERMANN, WILLIAM L., *The Slave Systems of Greek and Roman Antiquity*. Philadelphia: The Philosophical Society, 1955.

WICKER, TOM, ed. *Report of the National Advisory Commission on Civil Disorders*. New York: Bantam, 1968.

WIENER, NORBERT, *The Human Use of Human Beings*. (rev. ed.) Boston: Houghton Mifflin, 1954 (1950).

WILLIAMS, ERIC, *Capitalism and Slavery*. Chapel Hill, N.C.: University of North Carolina Press, 1944.

WILLIAMS, ERIC, *The Negro In The Caribbean*. Washington, D.C.: Associates in Negro Folk Education, 1942.

WILSON, JOHN A., *The Culture of Ancient Egypt*. Chicago: University of Chicago Press, 1965.

WINSHIP, GEORGE P., *The Coronado Expedition, 1540–42*. Washington, D.C.: U.S. Bureau of Ethnology, 1896.

WINSOR, JUSTIN, *Narrative and Critical History of America*. Boston: Houghton, 1889.

WOODWARD, C. VANN, *The Strange Career of Jim Crow*. (rev. ed.) New York: Oxford University Press, 1966.

WRIGHT, RICHARD, *Black Boy*. New York: Signet, 1945 (1937).

WRIGHT, RICHARD, *Black Power*. New York: Harper & Row, 1954.

WYNDHAM, H. A., *The Atlantic And Emancipation*. New York: Oxford University Press, 1937.

WYNDHAM, H. A., *The Atlantic And Slavery*. London: Oxford University Press, 1935.

YOUNG, WHITNEY M., JR., *Beyond Racism*. New York: McGraw-Hill, 1969.

Index

Affluent society and poverty, 124–29
Africa, peoples of, 78; languages, 79; religions, 79
African Negroes, 50, 62, 78–80
Afro-Americans, 5–6, 147, 171, 180
Ahmed Baba, 86
Ancient world, 63, 80–83
Arab culture, 34, 84, 185; scholars, 83; slave traders, 66–68
Ashanti, 6, 37, 51, 87–88, 185
Askia the Great, 85
Authority, revolt against, 174–76

Baldwin James, 60, 92, 195
Ben Solomon, Job, 74, 91
Bennett, Lerone, 168
Black baby myth, 54–57
Black experience, 146–64; economic and cultural deprivation in, 152–54; educational deprivation in, 149–52; learning to be black and, 146–49; 197–98; middle-class blacks and 156–60; self-image in, 160–64; subordination in, 154–56
"Black gentlemen," 71–72, 91
Black history, 78–94; African peoples and, 78–80; in America, 89–94; in Ancient World, 80–83; distortion of, 73–76; in Middle Ages, 83–86; in West Africa, 86–89
Black image, 61–77, 160–64; distortion of history and, 73–76; myth of racial inferiority and, 68–73, 76–77; myths of, 61–63; slavery, race, color and, 63–68
Black Manifesto, 24
Black Revolution, 165–68
Black Studies, 185–87
Blacks, coming of, 3–6, 236–37
Blood, myths of, 47–49
Bovill, E. W., 66, 85
Brain size, 50–51
Breasted, James Henry, 81
Breeding populations, race defined by, 30–31, 44
Britain, 69–71
Bruner, Edward, 222
Budge, E. A. Wallis, 82
Bunche, Ralph, 53

Cayton, Horace, 157, 195
Children, rearing of, 20–21
Christian Leadership Conference, 175
Civil rights struggles, 3–4, 112–13, 165–91; black revolution and, 165–68; goals of, 168–74; now generation and, 177–83; search for identity in, 183–87; white liberals in, 187–91
Civil War, 100–104
Civilization, 37, 54, 80, 187, 226–29, 233
Clark, Kenneth, 60, 161, 163–64
Clark, W. E. LeGros, 50
Classes, antagonism between, 16–17; mobility between, 15; perceptions by, 24
Colonization, 14–15
Color line, 55–57, 146–49, 152–54, 164
Coronado, Francisco Vásquez de, 90
Crime, 130–45; Blacks victimized by, 137–39; law enforcement and, 136–37; lawlessness and, 130–31; ordinary, 131–32; organized, 134–36; protest as, 139–43; value systems and, 143–45; white-collar, 133–34
Cullen, Countee, 148
"Cultural backwardness," 51–52, 62
Culture, 13, 19–25, 37; biological development and, 32; deprivation of, 152–54; perceptions of reality and, 22–25; race relations as aspect of, 19–22

Dahomey, 37, 51, 88
Davidson, Basil, 67, 68, 72, 76, 80, 83
Davis, Sammy, Jr., 148, 159, 195
Dobzhansky, Theodosius, 39, 40, 43, 231
Domination, 9, 11, 59–60, 154–56, 193
Double rights, 199–204
Douglass, Frederick, 101, 102, 110, 167
Drake, Sir Frances, 90
DuBois, W. E. B., 5, 101, 102, 110, 147–48
Dunbar, Paul Lawrence, 94, 110

Ebony, 5, 173, 179
Economic conditions of Blacks, 10–11, 152–54
Educability, 39
Education, segregation in, 108–110, 149–52, 166, 200–201
Egypt, 52, 54, 63–64, 73, 75, 80–83, 233
Emancipation, 103–106
Environment and heredity, 38–43, 45
Estevan, 90
Ethnocentrism, 8–9, 16, 63, 193
Etzioni, Amitai, 179

Fair Employment Practice Act (1941), 109
Fanon, Frantz, 162, 167, 174, 215
Frazier, E. Franklin, 157–58, 162, 182
Frost, Robert, 164